The Openings Revealed in Makkah

Book 3

Shuiayb Dr Eric Winkel

1 2 3 4 5

978-1-945083-54-9

Based on the critical edition of the Futūḥāt al-Makkīyah by 'Abd al-'Azīz Sulṭān al-Manṣūb

Translation reprinted with permission of Pir Press, New York

Calligraphy on the title page: 'al-futūḥāt' by Haji Noor Deen Mi Guang Jiang

Oceans Within

This world is a bridge of planks over a great river,
and you are traversing, then departing.

Chapter 33

The boat of the Futūḥāt embarked with new routes opening into many communities, into hearts and homes. The Futūḥāt is not for everyone but is for all who have ears to hear and hearts to see. Haji Noor Deen kindly gifted us a piece of Sini Arabic calligraphy, below. These letters are elegantly moving on the tablet. May we learn from them and observe them, how they beautify our journeys across the lands and seas; and may they be the guides - as Ibn al-ʿArabī says, the letters are the guides of the phrases - into the Vast Earth.

'al-ḥamdulillāh'
All praise belongs to God
Calligraphy courtesy of Haji Noor Deen

Introduction

With Book 3 we are still in the maʿrifah section of this great work, presented with knowings and tastings of what we must recognize (i.e. have maʿrifah of). The structure of these two books - that is, of the icons etched in lights in the first, maʿrifah, portion of the body of the Youth in Book 1 - is centered on Chapter 22. Here, we are introduced to the manzil (alighting place). The manāzil (pl.) will reemerge with the fourth portion of the body of the Youth, the fourth section of *The Openings Revealed in Makkah*. The 114 chapters will correspond to the suwar (sg. sūrah) of the Qurʾān, which Ibn al-ʿArabī wants us to see afresh. Indeed, to this translator these chapters read like maps, with their discoverer pointing out features - verses and topics - along the way. The chapters are concluded with lists of such features, such as (from Chapter 326) 'There is a knowing of the difference between the first thought (impression) and the second', and 'There is a knowing of affiliation - meaning, the affiliation of the branches to the roots - and who joins as a branch without a root, and what God's rule is for him, from a path of kashf.'

The way Ibn al-ʿArabī has us comprehend these alighting places is through ummahāt (where umm is mother; so, mother-lodes). There are nineteen steps, but this is not all; there are four more kinds associated with mother-lodes, and onward; and 'the multiplicity is uncountable'. While the uncountable multiplicity is a counsel to us to see afresh, not reducing complexity to a number, perceiving structure in The Openings is a way to gain insight and understanding. The reader may consider whether or how the nineteen steps described in Chapter 22 can be found in subsequent chapters: the first step involves the Pivots (aqṭāb, sg. quṭb) around whom the universe revolves, and the second step, symbols, arises in Chapter 26.

Ibn al-ʿArabī presents in Chapter 22 a structure which corresponds to the Qurʾān in the following way: first, the Qurʾān is a jamʿ, a collection - we can use the metaphor of an atlas, a collection of maps; second, the suwar of the Qurʾān are not chapters but fenced-in areas, much like the terrain a map encloses; third, in these areas there are signs and verses (āyāt).

Muḥammad ﷺ is the living Qurʾān. The first to recognize this was Khadījah, whom he acknowledged as the first to recognize that he was receiving Divine words, 'when everyone else was denying me'. And there is the story of ʿĀʾishah - Mother of the Faithful, who for decades was the teacher of Islam - related by two nervous seekers of knowledge, tongue-tied, who finally asked, 'What was the character of the Prophet?' They were abashed at her response: 'My sons, have you not read the Qurʾān? Indeed, you have tremendous character (al-qalam 68:4). His character was the Qurʾān.' Hence the epithet of the Qurʾān and of the Prophet is ʿaẓīm (tremendous).

The letters are the guides of the phrases;
the tongues of the guardians testify to this.

By them the celestial bodies circulate in their
whirling orbits in His higher kingdom
in the midst of the muted sleepers and the roused, alert.

I was given to see from the corner of my eye the
names and nouns in their hidden place;
thus they shone, becoming greatly glorious to that glimpse.

The names say, 'If not for the overflowing
abundance of My goodness, there would not
shine radiantly,
upon the Word being uttered, truths of the phrases.'

Name	Letter	Palatino	Zapfino	Number
alif	a	ا	ا	1
bāʾ	b	ب	ب	2
tāʾ	t	ت	ت	400
thāʾ	th	ث	ث	500
jīm	j	ج	ج	3
ḥāʾ	ḥ	ح	ح	8
khāʾ	kh	خ	خ	600
dāl	d	د	د	4
dhāl	dh	ذ	ذ	700
rāʾ	r	ر	ر	200
zāʾ	z	ز	ز	7
sīn	s	س	س	60, 300
shīn	sh	ش	ش	300, 1000
ṣād	ṣ	ص	ص	90, 70
ḍād	ḍ	ض	ض	800, 90
ṭāʾ	ṭ	ط	ط	9
ẓāʾ	ẓ	ظ	ظ	900, 80
ʿayn	ʿ	ع	ع	70
ghayn	gh	غ	غ	1000, 900
fāʾ	f	ف	ف	80
qāf	q	ق	ق	100
kāf	k	ك	ك	20
lām	l	ل	ل	30
mīm	m	م	م	40
nūn	n	ن	ن	50
hāʾ	h	ه	ه	5
wāw	w, u	و	و	6
yāʾ	y, i	ي	ي	10

Chapter 17

The Shift

On ma'rifah of the transfer of cosmic sciences, and fragments of the Divine sciences, the replenishers, the originals

The Shift

Chapter 17

Knowings of existence shift, passing
from one state to another;
but a knowing of the Face: there is no fear of absence.

We confirm and we negate the knowings,
all together,
and we traverse their high mountain
road time after time.

Divine! How can anyone know You who is other
than You?
And (also) Your like, who is abundantly
blessed, or exalted over all?

Divine! How can anyone know You who is other
than You?
And is there another who could be Your like?

Whoever seeks the path, with no indication from
the Divine, has sought the impossible.

Divine! How do they love You, being loving hearts?
What do they hope for - unification and connection?

Divine! How does anyone recognize You
except You?
And is there anything other than You? No, and not no!

Divine! How do they see You - with eyes?
You are not illumined light or shadows.

Divine! I do not see myself, other than You;
and how do I see the impossible, or the astray?

Divine! You are You; and indeed I am I,
in order to seek from Your. Being the gift of being,

Because there is poverty standing established in
me, basic to my existence,
born from Your richness, this is a changing state.

He brought me out to make me appear to hu,
and no one but hu sees me; so I am an āla.

For āla, Lane cites, 'a mirage like water between the sky and the earth

Only the Face of your Lord will continue on al-Raḥmān 55:27

With 'recognize' in this verse, from 'arafa, as in 'I am a treasure, concealed, but I love to be recognized,' Ibn al-'Arabī is speaking of the hu who is 1 in the many.

(in appearance) raising figures seen from a distance, and making them to quiver'. As described in Chapter 72, with the moving ember (also the flip-book and films), all that is seen is the light - the ember is never seen. So Light exalted is visible and creation is invisible. 'We' are the flickering, quivering entities that are moving so quickly (with the New creation) that we are invisible. We are invisible to all but God, and therefore we can see only God.

cf. al-nūr 24:39

Whoever chases the mirage, wanting water,
sees a spring of life there, cool water.

The critical editor 'Abd al-'Azīz Manṣūb notes that the x-ed out word in manuscript Q was al-wujūd (being, what is found) and below the line it is corrected to 'life'.

I am the new existence of which nothing is my like,
and the One whose likeness I am accepts likenesses.

This is one of the most wondrous things!
Look! Perhaps you will see His likeness transforming.

There is not in the cosmos anything but a single,
prime Being,
all too transcendent to be withstood, or handed over.

When the command comes to *Be!*, no entity withstands its becoming, and no entity can maintain (hand over) its being from one moment to the next.

إعلم

Learn, may God assist you, that everything in the world is something changing and shifting from moment to moment; so the world of time period during every time period is shifting, and the world of the breaths during every breath, and the world of tajallī during every tajallī.

tajallī (pl. tajalliyāt): a Divine vision, the brilliant radiance of Being

The motive of this is His word: *Every day He is upon a radiant brilliance.* (al-Raḥmān 55:29).

And this is supported by His word, *We shall finish with (and attend exclusively to) you, you weighty ones.* Human beings find in themselves different kinds of thoughts coming into their hearts while they are moving or still; but every fluctuation happening in the upper or lower world is based on a Divine turning-to-face with a specific

al-Raḥmān 55:31. The weighty ones are the jinn and the humans.

tajallī to this entity ('ayn); thus, your leaning for support on that tajallī will be commensurate with what its truth provides you.

For the terms below: in Lisān al-'arab, 'God mukawwinu the thing in extracting it from non-existence to wujūd.' Thus kawn is something that is new, and newly created. The universe is kawn, and kawnīyah is 'related to the newly created universe'. The plural akwān means 'things newly created'. The plural of ma'rifah is ma'ārif.

Learn that existence-based (kawnīyah) ma'ārif include: knowings derived from existent things (deduced from how they function) where their objects of knowings are themselves existent things; knowings derived from existent things where their objects of knowings are correlates - and the correlates are not themselves existent things; knowings derived from existent things where their objects of knowings are the dhát of the True (e.g. *By the Cherisher of the heavens and the Earth, indeed it is the True, as it is that you are endowed with speech* ⊛ *al-dhāriyāt 51:23*); knowings derived from the True where their objects of knowings are existent things; and knowings derived from correlates where their objects of knowing are existent things. These, all of them, are called existence-based knowings - and they shift and pass with their objects of knowings during their states (from one to another).

Zayd is 'correlated' to his father 'Amr, so Zayd 'son of 'Amr is a correlate.

The format of their shifting is a changing: human beings seek an initial ma'rifah of one of the existent things, or they derive from one of the existent things evidence for that which they seek. When they achieve what they were seeking, there shines on them a face of the True in there in that existent thing, while that face was not actually what they were seeking. These seekers then remain with it and abandon their initial aspirations. The knowledge they were seeking shifts to what that face provided them.

The 'face' of anything is its truth, and its truth is what differentiates it from everything else. Each pulsing fluctuation, each thought coming in, is something new (kawn). The imagery is that of the mirage story cited above.

Among the people this happens to is someone who recognizes this process, and among them are those whose state is this and yet they do not recognize what was shifted away from nor what was shifted to - so that some of the people of the path err and say, 'When you see a man standing in one state for forty days, then know that he is a poseur.'

murā': someone doing something to be seen doing it

How strange! Do the realities let a single thing persist even for two breaths, or two time periods in one state not shifting to another? If so, the Divine would be idled, inactive in its regard!

An illustration: place three coins on a table; move all three together once, and a second time. Now move only two. For the last iteration, *one coin is independent of you. And it is impossible that creation be independent of the Divine, who is the only Independent (al-ghanī).*

This is unimaginable, unless this 'ārif did not know what was meant by shifting-transference, since transference is to similars.

And as Ibn al-'Arabī explains, the New creation occurring every quantum time period (zaman fard) is like the previous creation but never exactly the same.

Everything transfers with the breaths, from one thing to its like. He may have been confused about the form, because the state of the individual above did not change from the first state - as he assumes. It is as one says, 'So-and-so continues to this day to walk around, not sitting.' There is no doubt that 'walking' is a very large number of movements, each movement not exactly the next movement; rather, each moment is like the next. Your knowledge passes with its passing. When someone says, 'His state has not changed' - how many states have actually changed with him!

Section

As for the shifting of Divine knowings, it is the 'loosening' which was argued for by Abū'l-Mu'ālī Imām al-Ḥaramayn and the 'connections' that were argued for by Muḥammad bin 'Umar bin al-Khaṭīb al-Rāzī.

See al-Burhān fī uṣūl al-fiqh by al-Juwaynī Abū al-Mu'ālī, and K. al-Mubāḥath al-mashriqīyah by al-Rāzī. Ibn al-'Arabī discusses the issue later (Chapter 404), when he says that 'the difficulty is removed for this issue - according to us (the people of kashf - revelatory disclosure - and wujūd and Divine dictation) - that knowledge is a correlation between the knower and the known things; and there is then nothing but a dhát of the True, and she is exactly His wujūd - and His Being has no commencement and no ending'. Then, 'there is nothing but the True; and some of it enters into wujūd, and ends, due to its entrance into being; and some of it does not enter into wujūd, so it is not described by termination'.

As for the people of firm footing among the people on our path, they do not speak here of shifting, because the things are (with the True) visible, known; they are entities and states with the forms they come in to and from, when their entities are created - and so on infinitely. Therefore, there does not newly arise a 'connection', as with the school of Ibn al-Khaṭīb, nor a 'loosening', as with the school of Imām al-Ḥaramayn - God be pleased with all of them. The sound intellectual proof provides what we argue for; and this is what the people of God discuss, and we are in agreement with them about it - provided (as it is) from kashf, from a place which is back beyond the limit of the brain. So the whole is confirmed, and each faculty (even the intellect) is provided for accordingly.

The Shift

Chapter 17

When God made the entities to exist, He made them exist for their own sakes, not for Him; and they are in their states in different sites and durations. One thing after another is stripped off the core entities and their states, on to infinity, consecutively and successively.

In the sense of the Independent not needing to have entities created; it is the entities who needed to be found.

This is part of his description of the fixed entities (a'yān al-thābitah) which are the 'thing' cited in, 'Indeed, Our word to a thing, when We desire it, We but say to it Be! and it is' ۞ al-nahl 16:40.

The command in relation to God is 1, just as He said, *Our command is only 1, like the blink of the eye*. Multiplicity is just in the countable numbers. This idea reached me during a sudden moment, and I was not disordered by it. The idea of multiplicity is 1, according to me - nothing becoming unseen or disappearing. And so it is seen by anyone who tastes this.

al-qamar 54:50

The key verse al-Raḥmān 55:29 has the shā'n singular, not plural. The word 'day', as Ibn al-'Arabī will explain elsewhere, includes the 'smallest time quantum' (the zaman fard). So there is only, ever, 1 thing happening. Compare this with atemporal descriptions of physics - for example, in Julian Barbour (1999) The End of Time: The Next Revolution in Physics.

Allegorically, the entities found are like a single individual who has different states. If you are this individual, images are formed for each state you have; every individual is this way. A veil is placed between you and these images. You are given a kashf removing their veils - and you are one of the sum-total of images there. Thus, you perceive the sum-total of what is there in these layering images formed upon a lifting of the veil by means of a single view. The True does not turn the single view away from the layered images in that space of the single view; instead, He removes their veiling and clothes them with their wujūd, and they see themselves with the wujūd they are in forever.

About the perspective of the True in His timeless knowledge, there is no time past or future; rather, the matters - all of them - are known to Him in their strata according to the number of forms they have there.

For example, picture a single, atemporal sketch illustrating the stages (levels) of a plant's life, each layer superimposed one after the other. The images formed one on top of the other make layers, or strata. The Divine view may be of all of the layers as a single whole; the creature's view is this state-layer or that state-layer.

Their strata are not described by finitude or confinement, and they have no limit at which they would halt. This is the way the True perceives the cosmos and the sum-total of the enabled beings, during their state of non-existence and their state of being. A great variety of states occurs to these enabled beings - in their imagination, not in their knowledge. (They can imagine a great variety of states but they cannot know them.) They are provided the benefit of knowledge upon their kashf disclosing what they had not had before, because of a transference they had not had before. Verify this for yourself, as it is an issue quite hidden and obscure, connected to the secret of predestination; only a few of our friends have discovered it.

As for the connection of our knowledge to God, it is in two categories: a maʿrifah of the Divine dhāt, based on vision and seeing in a dream - but it is a vision with no encompassing (because nothing encompasses God); and a maʿrifah that He is a god, based on two matters, or one of the two: the one is gift-based, and the other is examination and using evidence. This is the maʿrifah that is acquired. As for knowledge with regard to His being 'free to choose' - in fact, choice is incompatible with a 'singleness of predestined will'. Its relation to the True, if He is described with it, is instead in regard to what He is able to do, not in regard to what the True does by right. He said, *But the word will come out rightfully by Me*; and He said, *Is the one (for whom) the word of punishment is rightfully his (equal to one who eschews evil?)*; and He said, *The word does not change with Me*. And how exquisitely this verse is completed! *And I do not oppress My creatures.* Here He alerts us to the secret of predestination; and by means of predestination there is the final word belonging to God with regard to His creation. This is the predestination which is appropriate to the Divine Side (and He will act only by what is right, not according to what He could have done). The predestination which refers to the people is, *Had We wanted, We would have brought every soul to her guidance - 'but We did not so wish'. (But the word will come out rightfully by Me)* is a verse-connecting emendation, because the enabled being is receptive to guidance and misguidance; it is our truth. We are a place of dividing - one to the Fire, one to the Garden - and division comes to the enabled being. But in reality God has only a single situation in the enabled being, and that situation is foreknown to God: it is the ultimate state of the enabled being.

al-sajdah
32:13
al-zumar
39:19
qāf 50:29
qāf 50:29

al-sajdah
32:13

⌒

Issue: The intelligible manifestation of the invention, having no template ever seen: how can there really be an invention of something when there never ceases to be a vision before Him of that thing already known? The matter is as we settled it, with regard to God's knowledge of things, in a book titled al-Maʿrifah bi'llāh (Recognizing God).

Below, a 'possessive' is God's x; then, the relation of a father to a son, for example, is abstract, a 'non-thing'.

Issue: The Divine names are relations and possessives referring to an 'ayn wāḥdat (a single entity). If there were no real multiplicity by means of the existence of entities - as someone presumes who does not have knowledge of God (among some of the philosophers) - and if the adjectival attributes were additional entities and He would be God only by means of them, Divinity would be a cause of their effect; then it could only be that they would be a god themselves. But the thing cannot be a cause of itself, or it would not be. God is not a cause of an effect that is not He Himself, because the cause is prior to the effect in the step-level, so that would require the god to depend - given that he is a cause - on additional entities which are the cause for Him; and that is impossible. Then consider that the caused thing does not have two causes, and these additional entities are many, and He would not be God except by means of these many; therefore, it is false that the names and the adjectives could be additional entities on top of His dhát - God is too exalted beyond what the wrong-thinking people say! *He is Elevated, Great.*

e.g. the Divine adjectival names Life, Desiring

al-isrā' 17:43

Issue: The image in the mirror is a jasad barzakhī,

An imaginal body on a bounded null surface, a body which is in the barzakh, the Jabarūt; a body or figure in your dream is a jasad, while the organic body is a jism.

like the figure which the sleeper sees when the dream figure matches the external figure. (The first is a virtual figure; the latter is the figure seen while awake, outside the dream.) It is this way for the person dying and for someone given kashf. (The person dying, or in the grave, sees figures approaching from the imaginal realm - the Jabarūt - and someone whose eyes have been unveiled sees the 'bulk' of the iceberg.) The image form in the mirror is the most veracious thing the barzakh provides of images, if the mirror has a special shape and a particular size. If the mirror is not this way, she is not veracious in everything she reflects; instead, she will be true only for some things.

Learn that as the mirrored shapes (concave, convex) differ, so the virtual images differ. If the viewing perspective were through the reflecting ray toward the reflected images - that is, on the surface of the polished body, as some of them believe - the viewer would perceive them as they are on the polished body. What enlarged their sizes, and what made them small? The answer is: the mirror. As for us, we see in the small polished body the large image form reflected to be actually small. And similarly, we see the large polished body enlarging the image form / in the eye of the viewer, and it may take her out beyond her limit and similarly give the image more width, length, and waviness.

Since the surface dimensions of the flat mirror have no effect on the image size, we should probably take Ibn al-'Arabī's descriptions here to be 'the small-ing' mirror and the 'enlarging' mirror. In Chapter 177,

Ibn al-'Arabī speaks about the waviness of the water (used as a mirror) making the image wavy; in Chapter 350 he speaks of the images becoming turbulent as a result of the turbulence (or wavy deformity) of the polished bodies.

Therefore, it is not the reflecting rays focused on the surface of the mirror that provide that distortion; so it is impossible for us to argue anything but that the polished body is one of the things that convey image forms of the barzakh as virtual images in the seen world. This is why the sight does not connect to them except by means of the senses, because the imagination cannot grasp anything that does not first have a sensory image form, or is something collected together from parts of things that are sensory - the image-making faculty collecting them together into a composite. The image-making faculty provides an image form which does not have any sensory existence at all, but parts of what are collected together are sensory for this viewer - no question.

A unicorn seen in a dream, for example, is something composed of sensory parts, even if the unicorn as a whole is not something the senses see in this world.

Issue: The most complete configuration to appear among the created beings is the human being, according to most people, because the complete human being (insān) was found 'flush against the image' - but not the animus-human being. (This 'animal'-human being has only an animated nature, without the higher functions of the true insān, the complete human being.) The image is what has perfect completeness. But having this image does not make us the 'best', in God's view, because humanity is the most complete in aggregate. If they argue: 'God says, *The creation of the heavens and the Earth is greater than the creation of the people, but most people do not know*; and it is well known that He does not mean "greater" in size but rather greater in signification' - We say to them, 'You are right.' But there is one who argues, 'They are "greater" than humanity in the spiritual regard.' No, the meaning and signification of the heavens and the Earth (with regard to what each one of the two points to concerning the mode of signification isolated from the special arrangement their two bodies have) is greater in the meaning dimension than the mass of the human, not each individual human. This is why there originates from the movements of the heavens and the Earth entities reproduced and created. The human with regard to his physical mass is one of the reproduced beings. This does not originate from the human. The nature of the (four) elements is part of this reproduction. This is why the two are greater than the creation of the human, as the two are to him like two parents; he is part of the 'command that is sent down between heaven and the Earth'. But we have actually been considering the perfectly complete human being (the insān al-kāmil), so we are arguing that he is more complete. As for the question whether he is more excellent according to God, that is up to God - exalted is He, One Alone.

ghāfir 40:57

Indeed, the created being does not know what is in the Heart of the Creator; only someone who is told by Him does.

Issue: The True does not have a fixed identity-attribute except wāḥdat (one, single). It is impossible that there be with Him two, and three, and so on; if there were, His dhát would be composed of two things, or three, or four - and composition involving Him is impossible. Therefore, a fixed attribute that is additional over the wāḥdat is impossible.

Issue: As adjectival attributes are relational and possessives, and the 'relation' is a non-thing, and there is not at all anything but a single dhát, from every perspective - this is why it is possible for the creatures to be objects of Divine kindness at the ultimate end of the affair; and they will not experience an eternal absence of kindness with no end - as indeed there is no one to force Him to be other than mercifully kind. The names (such as the Compeller) and the adjectives (such as the Wrathful) are not entities necessarily having authority over Him with the things; so there is no one to prevent an all-encompassing kindness for everyone. And especially when there is a report that 'My Kindness outstrips My Wrath.' Therefore, when Wrath comes to an end before Kindness *f*, the determining rule becomes hers. It is as we have argued. This is why He said, *If God had so willed, He would have guided the people, all together.* The determining property of this volition (*had He willed*) belongs in this world, based on being tasked.

See earlier sidenote on possessives, this chapter.

al-ra'd 13:31

Thus, those who are guided to fulfill the obligations tasked to them are the people God willed to be guided in this world; for everyone else, in the next world, the determining property will be where My Kindness outstrips My Wrath.

As for the next world, the determining property is connected to His word, *He does as He wishes.* Who is able to prove that He will wish to give only eternal punishment to the people of Fire, and only so? Or to a single one out of the entire universe, so that the rule of the names Punisher and Tester and Avenger and the like would be true? The name Tester, and its like, is relational and possessive; it is not a concrete thing. How could something substantive be under the ruling power of something that is not existent, not concrete? Everything said in His word *If He wishes* and *If it were Our wish* is said on account of this basis, and 'He' (the basic name 'He' of *He does as He wishes*) is universal.

al-baqarah 2:253

al-baqarah 2:20

al-isrā' 17:86

There is no other text at all to refer to which touches on the possibility of eternal punishment such as there exists with us for arguing for eternal happiness; so there remains only the possible, the open, for Him to do as He wishes - and

'anna-hu raḥmānu'd-dunyā wa'l-ākhirat
'Hu is Raḥmān, Supremely Compassionate,
in this world and the next.'

And when you understand what we are hinting at, your resistance will be lessened - and will even disappear altogether.

Issue: Absolute 'He is allowed to' attributed to God is bad manners toward God. The intent of absolute 'He is allowed to' is achieved instead with the word 'possible'. This is more appropriate, as the Law does not mention 'allowed', and the idea does not occur to the intellect - so understand. And this amount is enough, because Divine knowledge is too vast to be penetrated deeply.

al-aḥzāb 33:4 *And God speaks the true, and Hu is the guide to the way.*

وَاللَّهُ يَقُولُ الْحَقَّ وَهُوَ يَهْدِي السَّبِيلَ

Chapter 18

The Mut-aha-jjidin

On ma'rifah of the knowledge of the ones who pray at night (the tahajjud), and what is connected to tahajjud of issues, and its valuation in the step-levels of knowledges, and what comes from it of sciences of being

The Mutahajjidin

Chapter 18

Knowledge of the tahajjud is a
knowledge of the unseen -
nothing sensed or seen, regardless
of what the eye alights on.

Lo, a descent is given to tahajjud, and in
your sleepless eyes there are fenced areas
of the Qur'ān which make forms rise.

If you are called to a night ascent to your Creator,
there will appear to you fenced
areas amidst higher signs.

All of it is an alighting place providing another
alighting place,
when sleeplessness takes over your eyelids.

As long as you do not sleep, this is your condition
during the night,
or until your sight perceives dawn on your horizon.

Vesicles of the musk of blossoms; no wafting scent
do you receive
as long as the day with fresh gentle
breeze does not break.

The kings, even if they are exalted in their ranks,
they share in the same mysteries and night
conversations as the common people do.

إعلم

Learn, may God assist you, that the mutahajjidīn have no special Divine name provided to them by the tahajjud and by their standing up during the night for the tahajjud prayers as there is for the one who simply stands up all night in prayer. The ones standing up all night in prayer have a Divine name that called them to it and moved them to do so. So, in fact, tahajjud is an expression for the person who gets up, sleeps, gets up, sleeps, and gets up again. The one who does not interrupt the night with intimate conversation with one's Cherisher this way is not a mutahajjid doing tahajjud. He *exalted* said, *Part of the night, do tahajjud therein as an extra for you*. And He said, *Your Lord knows that you stand up almost a third of the night, or its half, or its third*.

al-isrā' 17:79; the extra is nāfilah, 'supererogatory prayers'. al-muzzammil 73:20

Such a person (a mutahajjid) has special knowledge from the Side of the True. However, for this state *f*, you will not find of the Divine names any to lean on, and you will not see any closer connection to them than the name Ḥaqq (the True; also, a right due). Therefore, lean on the name Ḥaqq and this name will accept her. Each piece of knowledge coming to the mutahajjid is indeed from the name Ḥaqq, because the Prophet ﷺ said to the one who fasted continuously and stood all night, 'Your self has a right (ḥaqq) over you, and your eyes have a right over you; so fast and eat, and get up and sleep.' He combined for you standing up in prayer at night and sleeping, so as to fulfill the right of the eye to sleep and the right of the self for the Side of God. Rights are not fulfilled except by the name Ḥaqq, and they are fulfilled from him, not from another name - and this is why the mutahajjidūn lean on this name.

Then for the mutahajjid there is another matter not recognized by everyone, and this is where the mutahajjid does not reap the fruits of intimate conversation in tahajjud and achieve its knowledge unless one's prayer at night counts as extra. As for the person whose obligation with regard to the prayers is incompletely filled, it is the obligatory prayers that are being completed by his extra prayer.

nāfilah; cf. above al-isrā' 17:79

At the moment of Accounting, according to a famous ḥadīth, 'extra' (voluntary) prayers may be transferred to complete the obligatory prayers that are defective or incomplete in some way.

If the obligatory prayers are being completed by the extras for the worshiping mutahajjid, with no extras remaining to be counted as extras, then one is actually neither a mutahajjid nor someone with extras. Therefore, such a person does not receive the state of the extras or their knowings, or their tajalliyāt. Thus understand.

The sleep of the mutahajjid is for the right (ḥaqq) of the eyes, and your getting up is for the right of your Lord. What Ḥaqq gives you of knowledge and tajallī in your sleep is a fruit reaped from your having got up; and what is given during your standing - such as energy, strength, and the tajallī of both, and the kinds of knowledge from both - is a fruit reaped from your having slept. It is this way for all the actions of the creature that are obligatory upon it. The interlacing of knowings for the mutahajjidīn is like the interlacing of the braids of hair; the interlacing is one of the kinds of knowledge the beloved souls have when the braid is interlaced. From this interlacing there emerge mysteries of the upper and lower cosmos, and the (Divine) names which point to deeds and tanzīh.

For example, God does, not creation; and God is exalted, that is, transcendent (tanzīh).

It is His word, *The leg is interlaced with a leg* - that is, the situation of this world is joined with the situation of the other world; and there is nothing but this world and the other. It is the praised station (maqām al-maḥmūd), which is the result of tahajjud. He *exalted* said, *Part of the night, do tahajjud therein as an extra for you; and perhaps for you your Lord will send you up to a praised station.* And then 'perhaps' with God is 'obligatory' - that is, He will (cf. Qurṭūbī's Jāmiʿ aḥkām al-Qur'ān: '"Perhaps" with God is "obligatory" in the entire Qur'ān'); and the praised station is the one which comes as a result of praise - that is, to it all of the praise returns.

al-qiyāmah 75:29

al-isrā' 17:79

As for the measure of knowledge of the tahajjud - it is dear in value. And that is, as it does not have a Divine name to lean on, as do the rest of the rites, it must be recognized with regard to the whole; there must, after all, be some matter the person doing the rites is hidden from, and the rites must be hidden from him. So you study what it is and bring your sight toward a removal in kashf of the veil from the Divine names - whether they have entities, or whether they are relational - so that the referent of the rites will be seen: whether the Divine names refer to something concrete or something non-existent. When you look, you see that the names are not concrete entities, but they are rather relations; thus, you see that the consequences are leaning on a non-existent thing.

Thus, the tahajjud says, 'To make my story short, my return is to a non-existent thing.' Then the tahajjud *m* focuses the view on this and sees himself as being born from getting up and sleeping. He sees the sleeping as the return of the soul to her essence,

'Abd al-'Azīz notes that this first word may be mutahajjud.

See al-zumar 39:42, 'God takes to Himself the souls when they die, and the ones that are not to die, during their sleep. He holds the ones fixed for death and sends back the others, until a set time. In that surely is a sign for a people who reflect.'

and something she demands; and he sees the getting up as a right that is due to God from him. As the essence of tahajjud is composed of these two matters, he looks at Ḥaqq with regard to a dhát of Ḥaqq. He receives a flash that concerning Ḥaqq, if He stood alone in His dhát for the sake of His dhát only and not for the sake of the creation, there would be no universe. But when He turns to face the universe, the very being of the universe emerges visibly by that facing-toward. You see that the universe, all of it, receives existence from that facing-toward, with different relations to the Divine names. Thus, the mutahajjud sees one's essence as being built up from the view of Ḥaqq toward one's self asleep from the world - and that is the state of sleep for the sake of the sleeper; and from His view toward the universe - and that is the state of getting up to fulfill the right that Ḥaqq is due. Thus, you know that the reason for the existence of your core being is the most panoramic of reasons, inasmuch as you depend, from one perspective, on the dhát stripped of co-relations to the (Divine) names which the world demands for its existence. You verify for yourself that your wujūd is the greatest wujūd and that your knowledge is the most radiant of knowings; and what you aimed for, you received; and He is your goal. The reason for that was your being shattered and your being poor, needy. When you received what you wished for, you may say about that something proverbial:

Many a night I spent awake,
its dawn not coming until I received what I wished -

From a place I was the most passionate for,
by means of a conversation with a goodly predicate.

And one says about the (Divine) names,

I did not find with the names any 'signifier'
other than the one who was the 'object of the verb'.

Thereafter its truth was given to us -
given that it is an 'object of the
intellect' for the intellect.

We pronounced it with courtesy,
but I believed the matter to be an unknown object.

The value of your knowledge, concerning kinds of knowledge, is the measure of your known; and that is the dhát in the things known. Therefore, connected to knowledge of tahajjud is knowledge of the entirety of names, all of them; and the most entitled of them to tahajjud is the name al-qayyūm (Standing Up, Self-Subsisting), who *is not seized by sleep or slumber* - and this is the creature in the state of intimate conversation. Names are known in cut-

From the āyatu'l-kursī al-baqarah 2:255

out pieces - that is, each name comes to you. What is encompassed in it of the mysteries is known, whether concrete or non-existent, to the extent provided by the truth of that name. And parts of what is connected to this state of knowings are the following: knowledge of the barzakh surface, knowledge of Divine tajallī in image forms, knowledge of the Market of the Garden, and knowledge of the expression and interpretation of the dream. It is not the dream herself from the perspective of the one who saw her; instead, she is from the side of the one she was shown to.

It may be that the one seeing is the one who sees the dream oneself, or someone else may see the dream for you. And the interpreters of the dream are those who have one of the rewards of prophecy, as they know what was meant by that image form in the dream and who is the possessor of that station of prophecy.

Learn that the praised station which belongs to the mutahajjid may be for its possessor a specific prayer - and that is the statement of God to His Prophet ﷺ commanding him to say: *Say: My Lord, let me in through the true entrance* - meaning, for this station, because al-isrāʾ 17:80
it is a halting place specific to Muḥammad, praising (yuḥammidu) God there with praises (maḥāmid) he did not know until he entered that station - *and exit me through the true exit*; that is, when he passes al-isrāʾ 17:80
from there to another one of the stations and the halting places, that there should be grace there with him in his exit from it, just as there was with him in his entrance in upon it. *And grant me from Your Side an aiding authority* - required because there are opponents al-isrāʾ 17:80
there. The possessor of the panoramic station is still someone who is the object of jealous envy; and as the people cannot reach up there, they return to seek some disproving aspect which will be an exaltation of the state they are in, so there will not be related to them any shortcoming with regard to this panoramic station. Therefore, the legitimate possessor of this station seeks aid through the decree that is an authority over the deniers of the panoramic nobility belonging to this step-level. *And say: The true has come and the false has come to* al-isrāʾ 17:81
naught; indeed, the false has come to naught.

And God speaks the true,
and He is the guide to the way. al-aḥzāb 33:4

وَاللَّهُ يَقُولُ الْحَقَّ
وَهُوَ يَهْدِي السَّبِيلَ

Chapter 19

Knowings Decreased/Increased

On the reason for the deficit of knowings and their increases; and His word, Say: Lord, increase me in knowledge; and his word, 'God does not constrain knowledge by removal, removing it from the chests of the knowledgeable ones - but He constrains it by constraining (taking away in death) the knowledgeable ones.'

Knowings Decreased/Increased

Chapter 19

A tajallī of the wujūd of the True
in the orbit of the soul is
a proof for what there is in knowings of decrease.

If someone is hidden from that tajallī by one's self,
is the shining radiance something perceived
by investigation and scrutiny?

If multiplicity appears to knowledge in the self,
then the covering, verified, is
established by the clear text.

The clear text (naṣṣ - Qur'ān or ḥadīth) establishes that the self is covered - the 'hidden' of the preceding couplet - and this may be verified for oneself.

Nothing shines from the Sun of being, and of
her light,
over a world of the spirits at all - except a disk.

The true 'ayn is not bestowed in other than a site
of emergence,
even if the human being is destroyed
by a great aspiration.

There is no doubt in my statement which
I propagate,
and there is no false embellishment or conjecture.

إعلم

Learn, may God assist you, that every living being and everything described with perception has, in fact, in every breath new knowledge with regard to that perception; but the individual perceiving may not be among those who pay attention to what knowledge really is - though it is in fact knowledge. Describing knowings as decreased in regard to the one who knows is when perception experiences (a blockage) interposing between you and many things which you could have perceived - if there had not arisen in you this blockage such as in someone who became blind or deaf or something else.

Because knowings rise or fall depending on what is known, energy is connected to the panoramic knowings, elevated - with which, when the human being is described with them, one's self is increased and one's level is raised. The highest is knowledge of God. The highest path to knowledge of God is knowledge of the tajalliyāt.

Less than that is investigative knowledge. And there is nothing less than investigative knowledge of the Divine; instead, for the general population in creation, there are beliefs, not knowledge.

These knowings are the ones God commanded His Prophet ﷺ to seek increase in. He *exalted* said, *Do not hurry the Qur'ān before completed for you is its revelation. And say: My Lord, increase me in knowledge* - that is, 'Increase of Your word what will increase knowledge in me of You.' He received here increase of knowledge; it was knowledge of the goodness of going slowly with the revelation, with courtesy toward the teacher (Gabriel) who brought it to him on his Lord's behalf. This is why this verse is complemented by His statement, *All faces will be humbled before the Living, the Self-Standing* - that is, made low. And it means knowings of tajallī, and tajallī is the most panoramic path to achieve knowledge - it is tasted knowledge.

ṭā-hā 20:114

ṭā-hā 20:111

Because receipt of tajallī causes lowliness and humility

And learn that for increase and decrease there is another topic we shall also discuss, God willing, and that is that God made for everything - and the human soul is included in the entirety of things - an outward and an inward. It is the perception in the outward of matters called entity ('ayn), and perception in the inward of matters called knowledge; and the True is Outward and Inward. By Him, perception occurs - because it is not in the power of everything other than God for someone to perceive anything by oneself; rather, one perceives it with what God placed in it. The True gives tajallī to everyone to whom He gives tajallī; and from whatever world it may be - such as the unseen world or the seen world - it is in fact from the name Outward. As for the name Inward: part of the truth of this relation is that a tajallī never occurs there in the invisible, ever - neither in this world nor in the next - as the tajallī is an expression for its appearance (becoming visible) to the one to whom that tajallī is given in that site of tajallī. It is the name Outward, because the intelligibility of the relation does not change; even if it does not have a wujūd of 'ayn (i.e. does not have the concrete being, wujūd, of an entity, 'ayn), still it has an intellectual existence - so it is intelligible.

When the True gives a tajallī, either by pure grace or in answer to a request, He gives the tajallī to the outward of the self. Perception occurs in the senses in the image form, which is in the intermediary, image-making barzakh (intermediary world between the spiritual and corporeal world).

The key concept here is tamaththala, as with Gabriel being imaged, and imagined by Mary, as a well-proportioned man during the Annunciation.

It is there increase occurs at the site of tajallī you receive: in the knowledge of legal principles, if one is among the scholars of the Law; or in the knowledge of measures of meaning, if one is a logician; or in the knowledge of poetic meter, if one is a grammarian. It is just in this way for each expert in knowledge, whether it is one of the knowings of existent things or other than knowings of existent things. There occurs for these experts some addition in themselves to their knowledge base which they were working with.

The people of this path (the gnostics) are aware that this increase is in fact from that Divine tajallì to these kinds of experts, because they are unable to deny what is disclosed in kashf to them. People who are not gnostics sense the increase, but they relate this to their own thinking. Others find some increase and do not realize that they have experienced any increase at all. They are, in a parable, *like the donkey carrying volumes of books, not understanding them; evil is the similitude of the nation who deny the signs of God* - and that is this increase and its basis. Really amazing are the ones who relate this to their thinking and do not realize that their thinking and their examination and their investigation of any one of the issues actually came from an increase of knowledge in themselves from that tajallì which we have just mentioned. The observer is occupied with what his view is attached to and the goal he is seeking, so he is veiled from the knowledge of the moment; he is amidst an increase of knowledge, but he does not realize it.

al-jumu'ah 62:5

And when the tajallì also occurs with the name Outward to the inward of the soul, there occurs perception by insight into the world dimension of truths and into meanings abstracted from their substance. They are expressed by 'proof-texts', as the proof-text is that which has no complication or ambiguity from any perspective; but this is only in the dimension of meaning. The companion of meaning has rest from the labor of thinking, and increase occurs to one with the tajallì of Divine knowings, and knowings of the mysteries, and knowings which are inward, and what is connected with the next world. This is specific for the people of our path; this is the reason for the increase.

As for the reason for knowledge's decrease, there are two issues: either there is a fault in the constitution, in the basic configuration, or something spoiled by chance in the faculty which connects to it, and this cannot be mended - just as Khaḍir said about the boy, 'His innate nature is ungrateful,' and this was in the basic configuration; or, the chance fault in the constitution could disappear, if it was in the faculty, through medicine. And if it was in the soul and one was preoccupied with love of being in top positions and following lusts, distracted from acquiring the knowledge by which one is honored and is ultimately happy, then this sickness too may disappear - by means of an attractor of the True from one's heart; and one will return to sound thinking and recognize that this world *f* is only one of many way-stations for the traveler; and that she is a bridge to be crossed; and that human beings, if they do not adorn themselves here with knowledge and generous characteristics and attributes of the higher beings - such as purity, and being transcendent from natural lusts which turn one away from sound observation, and acquiring Divine knowledge - then there is no way to felicity. Let them try for this from the beginning; otherwise, this (lack of adornment) is a means of knowledge being decreased.

I do not mean by 'knowledge in which there is decrease' a deficit in the human being of anything but Divine knowledge - only this. Truth provides that there is then (with Divine knowledge) no decrease at all and that the human being is forever acquiring an increase of knowledge, always, from the perspective of what is being continually provided by one's senses and the alterations of one's states in oneself and in one's incoming thoughts. Human beings are in a place of increasing knowings, but they do not necessarily benefit from them, nor do they benefit from opinion, doubt, examination, ignorance, distraction, and forgetfulness. Each of these and its like will not be simultaneously the knowledge which you may receive (beneficially) from senses and states and incoming thoughts, because of the negative properties of opinion, doubt, examination, ignorance, distraction, and forgetfulness.

As for the decrease in tajallī knowledge and its increase, the human being is in one of two states: the prophets have come out to propagate the message; or the friends have, by the authority of prophetic inheritance - as Abū Yazīd said when he was conferred with the robe of deputy-ship. God said to him, 'Go out to My creation with My attributes so that one who sees you sees Me.' He could not help but obey the command of his Lord, so he turned around to walk away from his Lord - and he fainted. There was a call: 'Return him to Me, My beloved; he cannot bear to be away from Me.' He was annihilated in the True, like Abū 'Iqal al-Maghribī, so He sent him back to the station of annihilation at the Divine Side, in which there were spirits assigned to him to help him, after he had been commanded to go out. Thus, he was sent back to the True, and a robe was made for him of humility, dependence, and brokenness. He recovered his life and saw his Cherisher, and his intimacy increased; and he was eased in carrying the trust lent to him, which he inescapably had to bear.

You have at the moment of your advancing up the stairs of ascent a Divine tajallī commensurate with the stairs of your ascent, because for every person among the people of God there is a stairway specific to you, none other ascending on it. If there were a single ascent on a single stairs, prophecy could be acquired - because each stairs provides a special level to everyone who ascends on it, and the knowledgeable ones could ascend up the stairs of the prophets and obtain prophecy by their ascent. But the matter is not like this, and the Divine vastness would disappear with the repetition of the matter - and we have already established that there is no repetition on the Divine Side.

However, with the numbering of step-degrees in the dimension of meaning, all of them - prophets, friends, faithful, messengers - are equal, no stairway exceeding another stairway by a single step. The first step is al-islām: it is submission. The last step is annihilation in the ascent and persistence in the disembarkation. Between the two steps, first and last, there remain faith, goodness, knowledge, consecration, removal of impurities, independence with regard to creation, dependence on God, humility, dignity, flexibility, strengthening in flexibility; and annihilation if you are outside, and persistence if you have entered inside. For each step, in your exit from one to another, there is a decrease in your inwardness commensurate with an increase in your outwardness - meaning, tajallì knowledge, until you end up at the next step.

If you are outside and you reach the next step, the step itself appears in your outwardness according to your measure, and you are a site of manifestation of its character. Nothing remains in your inwardness of it at all, and the inward tajallìyāt disappear from you all at once. (Every inward aspect has shifted to outward manifestations - everything unrealized is realized, and you are ready for the next step.) If you are invited and called to enter inside - it is the first step appearing in tajallì for you in your inwardness, to the extent there was a decrease in that tajallì in your outwardness - then the step itself appears to your inwardness, and there remains in your outwardness nothing of tajallì at all. The reason for this is that the creature and the Lord stay together in complete wujūd, each one in one's own; so the creature stays a creature and the Lord a lord, despite this increase or decrease. (The ascent is readied by shifting the inward to the outward, and vice versa, to exit and enter; for the creature, all one or the other is unstable - and propels one to another step.)

This is the reason for the increase of tajallì knowledge and its decrease in the outward and the inward. The motive for this is the composition. This is why everything God created and brought out is itself composite, having an outward and an inward. Concerning what you heard about the basic elements: in contrast with composition, they are rather intelligible matters, not concrete things; and everything existent other than God is composite. This was given to us by sound kashf, with no contesting in it. Composition (in the sense of being a composite being) is the necessary factor for pairing dependence with you, because dependence is your essential attribute.

The four classical elements. While air and water, for example, are theoretically simple and basic, they do not exist in a pure, unmixed state.

If you understand, I have clarified for you the way and have prepared for you the stairway: so journey and ascend, and you will see and witness what we have explained to you. As we have described for you the steps of the stairway, there remains no more advice for us to give to you, advice which we had been commanded to offer by Messenger of God ﷺ. Had we described for you the fruits and the results of the ascent but had not illustrated for you the path to the stairway, we would have made you yearn for a great matter without your knowing the path to get there.

By the One in whose hands my soul is; indeed, He is the ascent!

al-aḥzāb 33:4 *And God speaks the true, and hu is the guide to the way.*

وَاللَّهُ يَقُولُ الْحَقَّ وَهُوَ يَهْدِي السَّبِيلَ

Chapter 20

Jesus-Based Knowing

On ma'rifah of knowledge of Jesus, and where it comes from, and to where it goes finally, and how. And whether it is connected to the 'lengthwise' of the world, or its 'widthwise', or both.

Jesus-Based Knowing

Chapter 20

Jesus knowings - the one whose
measure the creation is ignorant of.

By it he revived him whose
grave was the earth.

The breathing-into took the place of the permission
of the One who was
unseen in him, and commanded him.

His Divine site which is in
the unseen is his sacred kin.

Divine site: Here, lāhūt (divine) is contrasted with nāsūt (human). Osman Yahya notes that al-Ḥallāj was the first to use this term.

He is a spirit, an exemplar;
God brings out his inner secret.

Coming from an unseen presence,
his full Moon has been effaced by God.

He became a creation after
he was a spirit, and it nourished him
as a bird feeding its young.

As in kāna yaghurru ʿaliyan bi'l-ʿilm, 'He (the Prophet) used to nourish ʿAlī with knowledge like as the bird feeds its young one' (Lane).

His situation ends in hu;
then he draws near, and He gladdens him.

Whoever is like him,
God has magnified his reward.

'Abd al-'Azīz notes that written below 'magnified' is 'multiplied', and below 'his reward' is 'his goodness'.

إعلم

Learn, may God assist you, that Jesus-knowledge is knowledge of the letters, and for this the breath was provided, and this is the air exiting from the well of the heart, which is the spirit of the life-force. When the air is clipped along its exit path toward the bodily mouth, the sites of its clipping are called letters, and the entities of the letters appear.

When they (the letters) are composed, a sensory life appears in the meaning dimension, and this is the first thing that appears from the Divine Presence to the world; and there is nothing belonging to the entities at the moment of their non-existence with regard to co-relations except audition (hearing *Be!*). The entities are prepared in their substantives, at the moment of their non-existence, in order to receive the Divine command when it comes to them with wujūd. When He desires for them wujūd, He says to them *Be!* and they come into being. They emerge visibly in their entities. The Divine word was the first thing perceived, coming from God in the speech which is appropriate to Him.

So the first word composed was the word kun (*Be!*) and she is composed of three letters: kāf, wāw, and nūn. Each of the letters is three. There arises the 9, whose square root is 3. It is the first of the primes. The one-digit number base ends with the presence of 9 (1-9, then 10-99, then 100-999), based on kun. So by kun the counted and the counting itself emerge.

For example, kāf is composed of kāf alif fā'.

The phrase is fa-ẓahara (there emerges) bi-kun (by the *Be!*) 'aynu (exactly) al-ma'dūd wa al-'adad (the counted and the counting itself). Ibn Manẓūr in Lisān al-'arab has: 'In His exalted word, wa aḥṣā kulla shay'in 'adadan, there are (many) meanings.' Before we consider them, note that ḥaṣat (aḥṣā) is our root concept of calculus, the counting of something by placing small pebbles for each thing counted. Small pebbles are calculi, and ḥaṣat. Ibn Manẓūr: 'The calculation of each thing is ma'dūd-an' - meaning 'counted'. The word is in a passive form, counted. The second meaning is 'connected to the present (tense)' - that is, 'counting'. Then, 'One says, I counted the dirhams with a count, and what was counted, was ma'dūd wa 'adad' - which we now can translate as 'counted and counting'. Returning to the phrase: 'So by kun the counted and the counting itself emerge' - the first number counted historically, which is the kun, is 3, and the first prime number on the counting number line is 3.

And from here a root of composed antecedents is based on 3, even though they are visibly composed of 4: the 1 repeats in the two antecedents, so they are really 3. (For example, in 'All men are mortal; Socrates is a man,' we have four antecedents, one of which is a repetition - men, man.) From the prime, existence comes into being - not from the 1.

The True has informed me that the reason for the life in the forms born procreatively is in fact the Divine Breath - in His word, *Then, when I have fashioned him and blown into him of My Spirit*. It is the al-ḥijr 15:29 breath by which God revives faith and makes it manifest. He ﷺ said, 'A Breath of al-Raḥmān comes to me from Yemen'; so by this breath are made alive a form of faith in the hearts of the faithful and a form of the principles of the Law.

Jesus was given knowledge of this Divine Breath and its relation to him. He used to breathe into the form placed in the grave, or into the form of a bird which he had made from clay, and they stood up alive by Divine permission, suffused by this breath and by that breeze. If the Divine permission had not suffused there, life would not have entered into the form at all. From the Breath of the Supremely Compassionate (al-Raḥmān) came Jesus-knowledge to Jesus, and he made the dead alive with a breath of his عليه السلام, and the bird ended up in the form he blew into. This is the allotment which belongs to every being from God, and thereby you reach Him when the matters, all of them, are suffused into you.

When human beings disengage in their ascent to their Lord and take each event along their path connected to them, there remains in them nothing except this secret (sirr) which is - according to us - from God. They see Him by the sirr only and hear His word by the sirr only, because He is too exalted, too wholly apart to be perceived except in this way. When individuals return from this vision, and their form, which had been decomposed during their ascent, is mounted and made composite, and the world returns to them everything they had taken from it - that is, what was correlated to them (because each world does not overstep its genus) - then the All joins together in this Divine sirr and encompasses them; and by the sirr, the image *f* celebrates Him with His praise, and praises her Lord - as nothing but Him praises Him. If the image praised Him with regard to herself, not with regard to this secret sirr, the Divine surplus would not appear, nor the grace showering this form. And grace is confirmed on His Side over all of the created beings. And it is confirmed: that which is from the created being which belongs to God, such as magnifying Him and praising, is in fact from this Divine sirr; thus, it is in every thing with its spirit, and there is nothing in it. Therefore, the True is the one who praises Himself and celebrates Himself; and whatever there is of Divine good for this form during that praising and celebrating is from the context of grace, not from the context of what is existentially deserved. If it were deemed by the True to be rightfully deserved by that form, it would be only with regard to the fact that He made that incumbent on Himself.

As Ibn al-'Arabī asked in the Address in Book 1, 'If you take the Garden *as a reward for what you did, where is the Divine generosity which you think you understand?"*

Words are based on letters, and letters are based on air, and air is based on the Compassionate Breath (nafas al-Raḥmānī); and by means of the (Divine) names, the āthār

The athar (sg.) is a 'remain, or relic', and a 'sign, mark, or trace; opposed to the 'ayn, or thing itself: a footstep, vestige, or track', and 'an impress, or impression, of anything' (Lane).

emerge visibly in the worlds, and the Jesus-knowledge ends up at them. Then human beings with these words make the Kindly Presence provide them from Her Breath that which stands up alive, which they requested by these words, and the process becomes circular, (around and around) forever.

Learn that the life of spirits is a life essential,

As we saw, the life of spirit, for example, is eternal, while the life of the bodily human being is not - and so the eternal life leaves the human being at death (even while the mineral body remains alive).

and this is why everything full of spirit is alive in its spirit. When the Sāmirī learned this, when he saw Gabriel and knew that his spirit was his very being (and therefore not human and subject to death), and that his life was essential (such that wherever he stepped, the place became alive by the direct connection of this exemplary form), he took from his footprint (athar) a handful - it is His word, about what was reported about him, that he said, *I took a handful from a footprint of the messenger* and threw it on the golden calf. So when he had fashioned the calf and formed it, he threw some of this handful and the calf lowed.

ṭā-hā 20:69

As Jesus ﷺ is a spirit, as God called him; and as he was configured a spirit in the form of a human being stabilized throughout his lifetime - (remember) the configuration of Gabriel in the form of the desert Arab Diḥyah was unstable - he used to give life to the dead by stripping off the breath. Then he supported the revived person with a holy spirit; it is a spirit supported by a spirit clean from any existential impurity. The root of this, all of it, is the ḥayy al-azalī (the eternal Life), the forever (abad) Life itself. It is distinguished by two limits; I mean azal and abad: the being of the world and its newness in Life. This information is connected to the length of the universe, meaning the world spiritual - it is the world of meaning and Command; and to the width of the universe - it is the world of creation and Nature and bodies. It all belongs to God: *Does He not have the creation and the command?* ❁ *Say: The Spirit is from a command of my Lord.* ❁ *Blessed is God, Lord of the worlds.* This was known to Ḥusayn bin al-Manṣūr al-Ḥallāj, God be kind to him.

Jesus, child of Mary, a messenger of God and His word, cast into Mary, and a spirit from Him ❁ *al-nisā' 4:171*

al-a'rāf 7:54
al-isrā' 17:85
al-a'rāf 7:54

When you hear one of the people on our path speaking about the letters, saying, 'The letter of so-and-so, its length is such-and-such feet or inches, and its width is such-and-such' - such as al-Ḥallāj and others - one means by 'length' his activity in the world of the spirits (verticality) and by 'width' his activity in the world of bodies (horizontality). This is the above-mentioned measure by which one distinguishes. It is the technical convention set down by al-Ḥallāj.

The one among the ones who verify for themselves who knows the truth of kun knows higher knowledge; but whoever brings something about by one's effort in existence, this is not part of this knowledge.

As the 9 comes about in the truth of these three letters, there come from them the countable nine orbits; and by the movements of the entire nine orbits and the celestial bodies coursing, this world is made to exist and what is in it - just as it is destroyed by their movements. By the upper movement of these nine, the Garden is made to exist; and with the movement of that upper comes into existence everything in the Garden. And by the second movement - which is adjacent to the upper - the Fire which is there comes into existence, and the Arising, the Resurrection, the Gathering, and the Announcement.

By what we have cited, this world becomes mixed: good fortune mixed with torment. And by what we have cited also, the Garden is good fortune, all of her; and the Fire is torment, all of her. This mixture disappears from her respective people, as the next world configuration does not accept the mixture of the configuration of this world. It is the criterion separating the configuration of this world from the next. However, the configuration of the people of Fire - I mean her people - when the Divine wrath ends for them, there is spread out and attached the Supreme Compassion *f*, which is the winner over Wrath, finally; the ruling authority of hers returns over them. Jahannam's form is still her own form, not changing - if she had then changed, they would have become tormented! So ruling over them, initially, by permission of God and His putting her in charge, is a movement of the orbit second from the upper - by which there emerges some torment in every site capable of receiving torment. In fact, we said 'in every site capable of receiving torment' on account of the one who is in her who does not receive torment.

The duration is finished - it is 1,045 years - and there is a punishing torment against the Fire's family (ahl, people), who are tormented in there with a continuous, unabating torment of 1,023 years. Then al-Raḥmān sends a sleep to them in which they are absent from their senses - and that is His word, *he will not die in her, nor will he revive.* His ﷺ word about the people of the Fire who are her people is that 'they do not die in her nor do they live' - meaning, their condition in these moments in which they are in her but absent from their senses, like the one who faints among the people *ṭā-hā 20:74* of torment in this world from the intensity of anxiety and the intensity of excessive pains. They abide that way for 1,019 years.

Except for the prime number 1019, these numbers are multiples, e.g. of 5.

Then they awaken from their faint, and God has changed their skin into another skin; and they are tormented in the new skin for 1,025 years. Then they faint. They linger in their faint for 1,011 years. Then they awaken and God has changed their skin into another skin, so they will taste the torment again. They experience the pain of torment for 7,000 years; then they faint for 3,000 years; then they awaken and God nourishes them with pleasure and rest, like the one who goes to sleep in discomfort and wakes up. This is part of His 'kind compassion, which outstrips His wrath' and *vastly encompasses everything.* She has with that a property of everlastingness, from the name the Vast by whom He vastly spreads over everything in kindness and in knowledge;

al-a'rāf 7:156

> *'Knowledge' here is the foreknowledge that the end belongs to the Supremely Compassionate, and so He encompasses everything with compassion and the fore-awareness of everyone's fortuitous end.*

so they find no pain, and this remains for them, ever. They take advantage of their situation and say to themselves, 'We were forgotten, so let's not ask for anything, lest attention be called to ourselves. God has told us, *Be you driven into her, and do not speak to Me*' - so they are silent, and they are in the Fire despairingly quiet; but there remains no torment for them except the fear of the torment returning to them.

al-mu'minūn 23:108

This extent of torment is the one which is never-ending for them - it is the psychological (nafsī, self-induced) fear, not sensory. They may not notice it at some moments. Their good fortune is the rest from the sensory torment through what God placed in their hearts - such as that He is full of compassion, vastly encompassing. God says, *Today We have forgotten you as you have forgotten.* Based on this truth, they say, 'We were forgotten' - when they do not feel pains. And similarly, His statement, *They have forgotten God, so He has forgotten them* ❁ *and like that today you will be forgotten* - that is, they were left in Jahannam, as 'forgetting' is 'leaving behind', and with the glottal stop it is 'postponement'.

al-jāthiyah 45:34

al-tawbah 9:67

ṭā-hā 20:126

> *Lisān al-'arab says the meaning of nisyān is tarak; thus, 'forgetting' is 'leaving behind'. And with the glottal stop, there is nasā', 'delay'.*

The allotment of good fortune to people of the Fire is an absence of torment; and their allotment of torment is its anxious anticipation, because there is no security promised to them by means of the reports of God. They are veiled from anticipatory fear in some moments; there is a moment they are veiled from it for 10,000 years and a moment of 11,000 years and a moment of 6,000 years. They do not exit from this measure cited above: there is necessarily this measure of time for them.

If they had faith, they would have had faith in the reports that God's kindness will prevail over His wrath, for example.

When God wants to give them good fortune from His name al-Raḥmān, they look at their condition which they have at the moment, and their exit from what they were in of torment, and they are given good fortune to that measure of looking; thus, one moment this look persists for them for 1,000 years and another moment for 9,000 years and another moment for 5,000 years. So it increases and decreases. Their condition stays this way forever in Jahannam, as they are her people. And this which we have discussed, all of it, is part of Jesus-knowledge inherited from the Muḥammadī station.

And God speaks the true, and hu is the guide to the way. al-aḥzāb 33:4

وَاللَّهُ يَقُولُ الْحَقَّ وَهُوَ يَهْدِي السَّبِيلَ

Chapter 21

Three Knowings

On ma'rifah of the three knowledges of existence, and the interpolation of one of them into another

Three Knowings

Chapter 21

Knowings of inter-penetrations: knowledge
of reflection accompanies it;
knowledge of end results relates it to observation.

They are the proofs, if you verify for yourself
their formats,
an analogue of the proofs in the
feminine with the masculine;

This is Ibn al-'Arabī's theme of kun and human sexuality, in which the kāf is the external, masculine, the nūn is the internal, feminine, and the wāw is the penis which hides when the two join in nikāḥ. Ibn al-'Arabī sees the kun as three letters (even though in Arabic calligraphy it is visible as two only).

Indicating the one who taught that which
was created, gathering it together
in the truth of Be! in the realm of image forms.

The u (of kun, invisible in Arabic calligraphy):
if the n ∫ of kun were not stilled (surd, with
the grammatical stop), He would have made
her appear
in the paradigmatic middle letter (the
'ayn of fa'ala) as something self-standing,
pacing with an appointed stride.

i.e. the imperative *Be!* (kun) becomes kawn(un), a being.

So learn that the being of existence
is in the King's possessions,
and in His turning to face the jawhar
(core) of the human animal.

'Abd al-'Azīz notes that written above the word milk (possessions) is 'both', and in the margin, falak (orbit), pointing to the validity of either of the two words (milk and falak): the being of existence is both a possession of and in the orbit of the King.

إعلم

Learn, may God assist you, that this is the knowledge of procreation and sexual propagation. It is one of the knowings of the existent things, and its basis is from Divine knowledge. So then let us explain to you first its form among the existent things, and after this let us bring it out for you in Divine knowledge - because the basis of each knowledge is from Divine knowledge, as everything other than God is from God. He said, *And He has subjugated for you what is in the heavens and what is in the Earth, all together, from* Hu. This is knowledge of interpolation coursing throughout everything; and it is the knowledge of flesh-conjoining and nikāḥ; and there is (this coursing interpolation in anything) physical, and meaningful, and Divine.

al-jāthiyah 45:13

And learn that when you want to know the truth of this, you should consider first sensory knowledge, then Nature-based knowledge, then spirit-based meanings, then Divine knowledge. As for the sensory, know that it is where, when God desires to bring out an individual from two, those two birth it. And it is not correct that there come out from the two a third, as long as the rule of a third did not consist of the two

> As with 'no three but He is their fourth', Ibn al-'Arabī is making the point that the child is different from the two parents, even though it is a 'third' member.

- meaning, each one of the two comes to the other, skin to skin, for joining nikāḥ. When the two join in a special way with special conditions, where the site is receptive to procreation, the seed is not spoiled - if it is received - and the seed is receptive to the commencement of the image form in it; these are the special conditions. As for the special facet, it is where the two apertures, female and male, should meet and the fluid should descend - or breeze in the case of *jinn* - from passion; then certainly there will appear a third, and it is called a child, and the two are called parents. The appearance of the third is called pregnancy, and the meeting of the two is called 'married nikāḥ' and 'mounting'; this latter physical process occurs among the animals.

As for our statement 'in a special way with special conditions', it is what comes from every male and female meeting in nikāḥ: a child - and necessarily - except when what we mentioned happens; and we will explain it in meanings more clearly than this, as what is sought is clarity.

As for Nature: the heavens when they rain water, and the Earth when she receives the water, she swells - it is her pregnancy - and *puts forth growth, from each pair delight*. It is this way for the pollination of the date palm and tree. *Of everything We have created pairs* - for procreation.

al-ḥajj 22:5
al-dhāriyāt 51:49

As for the meaning: it is where you recognize that the things are of two kinds: primes and composite mounts. Knowledge of the prime is prior to knowledge of the composite. The knowledge of the prime avails of definition, and knowledge of the composite avails of demonstration. When you want to know the being of the universe, whether it is from a cause or not, you rely on two primes - or on what the principle is for two primes, like antecedent conditions. Then you take one of two primes as an initial axiom, and you carry (ḥamala) the other prime over to it, using a methodology of the predicates 'by him', 'from him'. You say, 'every New thing'. This thing named is the nominal subject (mubtadā'), because it is the one which you start (badā'ta) with and the first objective complement which you set down in order to convey to it what you are predicating 'by it', 'from it'. It is a prime, because the governing noun is under the rule of the prime.

ḥamala, a word also used for carrying in the womb, pregnancy

So, necessarily, you will know by definition a meaning of New-thing and a meaning of 'every' which you attach as a governing noun; and you make it like the boundary wall when it is encircling, because 'every' requires a confinement by the convention of the language. So when you know the New-made, at that moment you carry over another prime: it is your statement, 'it has a cause'. So you predicate 'by it' 'from it', and necessarily you also know the meaning of 'cause' and its intelligibility in conventional usage - and this is the knowledge of the primes availing of definition. There arises from these two primes a composite form, just as arose the form of the human being from living-being-ness and articulation; so you say about it, a composite articulate-living being.

The composition of the two primes by carrying one of them to the other does not produce anything, rather it is a claim requiring of the claimant proof of its validity, so that the predicate can be verified based on the objective complement by what is predicating by it from it. One may take this safely from us, as it applies only to a claim - based on our method of making an allegory, fearing too much length. This book of mine is not the place for the grammatical topic of 'evaluating meaning'; that is rather a pursuit of semantics. Necessarily, each prime is a known; and what is predicated by it from the prime objective complement is also known, either by demonstration intuitively or by senses by examination referring to both of them.

Then you seek another antecedent basis to govern what you implemented in the first, and necessarily it is one of the two primes mentioned that are in the two prior bases; thus it is 4 in the composite form, but it is 3 in the meaning dimension - as we shall discuss it, God willing. If it were not this way, it would not produce a result, ever.

We say about this issue, which we are describing as being analogous to the other basis, 'the world Newly made': you search in there for knowledge based on the definition of the prime in what you are searching for in the first antecedent - that is, 'What is knowledge of the universe?' You carry the New to it with your statement, 'Newly made'. This Newly-made, which is carried over for this antecedent, is an objective complement for the first, when you carried the cause to it; so you repeat the New in the two antecedents and it becomes the connector for the two. Thus, when they are connected, that connector is called a facet of the evidence, and their joining is a proof and a demonstration. The result is that the Newly-made of the universe necessarily has a cause. So the pretext is the Newly-made, and the consequence is the cause. The consequence is more general than the pretext, because a precondition in this kind of knowledge is where the consequence be more general than the cause, or equal to it; and if it were not so, it would not be valid. This is for intellectual matters.

And as for its procedure in Laws, if you want to know an example: the nabīdh (a particular pressed juice) is forbidden, by this method. You say, 'Every intoxicant is prohibited; and the nabīdh is intoxicating, so it is prohibited.' You express this as you express the intellectual matter, as we made an example for you. So the consequence is prohibition, and the pretext is the intoxication. The consequence is more general than the pretext obligating the prohibition. Prohibition may have another cause than intoxication, for another matter, like the prohibition of robbing, stealing, and crime; and all of them are pretexts for the existence of the prohibition of prohibited things, so in this particular facet it is valid.

We have clarified for you by approximating the evaluations of meaning and by clarifying that the resultant products in fact come about through the entering-into of the two antecedents - which are like the parents - in the sensory dimension, and that the two antecedents are composed of 3, or something with the rule of 3. It may be that the sentence has a single meaning in the governance and the precondition; thus, the resultant product comes about only from the prime. If it were even, not accompanying a 1 (e.g. 4+1) as a special accompaniment, then nothing would come into authentic being - ever. 'Partners associated with God' (an even number) is falsified in the world's being, but the verbal act is established for the 1 (in 2+1) - and, in fact, from its being, the sites of being (2+1's) manifest from sites of being. So we have explained for you that even though the acts of the creatures emerge from themselves, no act would emerge for them at all, in fact, if not for God (who is the One accompanying).

This scale (of Law establishing responsibility for actions) combines formally the government of actions belonging to the creatures and the discovery of which of these actions are to be attributed to God. It is His word, And *God created you, and what you do* - that is, He created what you do. So He relates the action to the creatures and its being brought about to God. The word khalaqa may have the meaning 'bringing out' and may have the meaning of 'measuring out', just as it may have the meaning of 'creating action' - as in His word, *I did not have them witness the creation of the heavens*; and it may have the meaning of 'created beings' - as in His word, *This is the creation of God.* *al-ṣāffāt 37:96* *al-kahf 18:51* *Luqmān 31:11*

As for this entering-into in the Divine knowledge, and procreation: learn that nothing comes from the dhát of the True at all in the place where She is a substantive dhát. No, another matter is related to Her: related to Her as dhát is that She is All-Capable of bringing creation out, according to the people of Sunnah, the people of the True. Otherwise, related to Her as dhát is that She is a First Cause; but this is not the position of the people of the True, nor is it a valid position. This is something we do not need; but my interest in emphasizing this point was on account of an antagonist opposing the people of the True, in order that we would have him acknowledge that the being of the world is not attributed to this dhát ʃ as a substantive. No, they attribute the world to Her through the existence of Her being a First Cause. This is why we cited their statements.

The relation is where He is All-Capable; so simultaneously there is a situation of three. There is His desiring the creation of this intended entity to be, so certainly there is the attending to the intention to bring the entity about by means of capability (according to intellect) and by means of the statement (according to revelation) that it become. Therefore, the creation comes into being only from the prime 3, not from the 1. Indeed, the One (1) of the *hu* does not accept any second, because She is not the 1 of the counting numbers. So the emergence of the universe in the Knowing of the Divine is based on three intelligible truths.

The '1 in the many' is not the same as the 1 in 1 2 3. Ibn al-'Arabī is showing that the creators are Divine names - here Knowing (something will be), Desiring (something to be), and Able (to make something be).

This principle of three flows throughout the procreation of existence, one from another, because the root is based on this form.

This amount is enough for this chapter. The intent has been achieved by this discussion - because this art, for example, with the family of God, does not bear more than this amount of argument. And this book is not based on reflective knowledge; rather, it is part of knowledge 'received by instruction' and 'drawn nigh'. No other scale is required than this, even if there is in there an anchor - *al-najm 53:8* because it is not altogether free from reflective knowledge. But (the latter comes) only after validation of the premises, such as knowledge of their primes (the 3's of the premises) by the definition, which is not denied, and of the premises by the demonstration, which is not rejected. In this context, God says, *Had there been with the two (the heavens and the Earth) a god besides God, they would have been spoiled.* *al-anbiyā' 21:22* This is what we have been saying in this chapter. And this verse and ones like her compel us to mention this art, but (only) in the context of kashf, as the family of God do not occupy themselves with this art - that is, the knowings - so as not to waste time. The life span of the human being is precious; thus it is appropriate that the human being not cut into one's time, which should rather be spent sitting with one's Cherisher and speaking with Him - as He made Law for you to do.

al-aḥzāb 33:4 *And God speaks the true, and Hu is the guide to the way.*

وَاللّٰهُ يَقُولُ الْحَقَّ وَهُوَ يَهْدِي السَّبِيلَ

The 15th manuscript ends.
And all praise belongs to God!

وَالحَمْدُ لِلّٰهِ

Chapter 22

An Alighting Place

On ma'rifah of the manzil and the manāzil (pl. an alighting place of alighting places), and the arrangement of the whole of cosmic sciences

An Alighting Place

Chapter 22

Wondrous the accounts of the sky-joined souls!
Indeed, the alighting places are a night cloud
journeying through the alighting places.

How is there ascent from lowland to the heights,
except by the compelling Presence of
the Higher than every high?

The art of decomposition is during their ascent
toward the delicate obscurities and
the matters of the lofty One ʃ.

And the art of composition is upon their return,
by the splendor of being to the shadows of the abyss.

by: bi-sanā (by means of). By the Be! of being, we return to the shadows (this world of three dimensions) of the abyss (this body).

إعلم

Learn, may God assist you, that knowledge connected to God does not accept multiplicity or steps arranged, as it is something which is not acquired or won. No, His knowledge is exactly His dhát, just as is everything that is connected to *hu*, such as the adjectives and names He is called by. The knowings of everything other than God are ordered, confined, whether they are knowings gifted or knowings earned. They will not be without this ordered arrangement which we have cited. This arrangement is knowledge of a prime, firstly; then a knowledge of the composite; then a knowledge of the compounding. There is no fourth. If it is based on primes which do not accept composition, it is known as prime; and similarly for the rest, because each known necessarily is prime or compounding, and the compounding self-evidently depends on a prior knowledge which is composite - and so at that moment it may become a compounding knowledge.

That is, such that 'make composite' (tarkīb) is composable, ready to be inserted as an ingredient in something which will then become compounding (murakkabah).

With this, you have learned the step arrangements of all of existence-based knowings. So let us now clarify for you the enclosure wall of the manāzil in this manzil. They are a great multiplicity - not countable. We will limit ourselves in their regard to what is specially linked by our Law and distinguished by the Revelation, not whatever is linked to the manāzil in which there are commonalities with other revelations, shared by us and others - that is, the rest of the knowings of religions and sects (al-millal wa'l-naḥal). We sum them to nineteen matrix steps (ascending stairs). Among them is one that branches off into manāzil, and among them is one that does not branch off. Let us cite the names of these steps, and let us give them the name manāzil. It is this way that we were taught them in the Divine Presence, and courtesy is prior.

The manāzil (pl.): a manzil is 'a place of alighting or descending and stopping or sojourning or abiding or lodging or settling: a place where travelers alight in the desert' (Lane).

For 'matrices' below: ummahāt, from ummahat (sg.) and umm - mother. Then umm al-qurā, the mother of the towns - Makkah, 'because it is asserted to be in the middle of the Earth; or because it is the qiblah of all, or because it is the greatest of towns in dignity' (Lane). And umm al-nujūm, the Milky Way, 'because it is the place where the stars are collected together in great multitude' (Lane). And umm al-ṭarīq, the main part (or track) of the road, with small roads or tracks stemming from it. This is the sense Ibn al-'Arabī uses, translated here as 'matrices': the ummahāt are a large collection of elements (here, the alighting places), sometimes with one of the ummahāt identified as the main element but standing in for the collection, as a metonym.

The nineteen steps

Now let us cite the title-names of these manāzil and attributes (and adjectives) of their masters and their Pivots, who verify for themselves, and their states, and what belongs to each of these states, such as the attribute. Then after this we shall cite, if God so wills, each type of these nineteen; and we shall discuss some of what is encompassed there by the matrices (individually) of the manāzil; not by the manāzil themselves (individually), because there is yet another manzil containing a quantity, exceeding one hundred, of manāzil of signs and pointers containing lights of radiant majesty; and containing thousands, and some less, of manāzil of the utmost encompassing hidden mysteries and special radiances of majesty. Then we follow what we cited with what corresponds to this number for these manāzil of created beings, Old (eternal) and New (transitory). Then we cite what is connected to some of the meanings of this manzil, in the mode of approximating and shortening - if God so wills.

A citation of their title-names, and adjectives of their Pivots

Among them:

1 the manāzil of praise and laudation, for the masters of the disclosures provided by kashf, and the opening (fatḥ)

2 the manāzil of symbol and puzzle, for the people of reality and figurative meaning
3 the manāzil of entreaty, for the people of pointing and gesturing from a distance
4 the manāzil of actions, for the people of states and union
5 the manāzil of beginning, for the people of apprehensions and gestures
6 the manāzil of transcendence, for the people of direction with regard to viewers, and discovery
7 the manāzil of approaching, for the strangers and the divines
8 the manāzil of expectation, for the people of burqas on account of Divine radiances
9 the manāzil of blessings, for the people of the movements
10 the manāzil of oaths, for the people of overseeing among the spirit-beings
11 the manāzil of eternity, for the people of tasting
12 the manāzil of ipseity, for the people of vision by sights
13 the manāzil of the lām and the alif, for the enveloping received by taking on the Divine characteristics, and for the people of the mystery which is not disclosed
14 the manāzil of stability, for the people of knowledge of natural and spirit-being chemistry
15 the manāzil of annihilation of beings, for the 'special ones' (ḍanā'in) who are numb
16 the manāzil of intimacy, for the people of peace among the people of upper rooms
17 the manāzil of threat, for those who cleave to the standing support of the Throne most majestic
18 the manāzil of testing, for the people of unperceived mysteries
19 the manāzil of command, for the ones who verify for themselves with truths of a secret of *Hu* in them.

Later in this chapter, in the detailed description of each of the manāzil, Ibn al-'Arabī presents nos. 11 and 12 (translator's numeration) in the reverse of the order given here.

ḍanā'in: in the hadīth, 'God has special ones among His creation.'

As for their adjectives

1 The ahl (family) of laudation have pride in their full bloom;
2 and the ahl of symbol have salvation from being thwarted;
3 and as for the divines, they have the loss of direction in the desert devoid of signs, because of taking on Divine adjectives (and names, one after the other);

In the Kashshāf of Zamakhsharī, the utterly devoted 'divines' are the hidden Pivots.

4 and as for the people of states and juncture, they have the attainment of the eye;

5 and as for the people of pointing, they experience confoundedness when the message is propagated;
6 and as for the people of discovery, they have error and hitting the mark, and they are not ones protected (from disasters);
7 and as for the strangers, they have brokenness;
8 and as for the people of the burqas, they have fear;
9 and as for the people of movement, they have the vision of the causes;
10 and as for the overseers, they have reflection;
11 and the ones appointed to positions of power, they hold the defined punishments;
12 and the people of vision, they have the repudiation;
13 and the people of the concealed, they have peace;
14 and the people of knowledge, they have the authority over the known;
15 and the people veiled, they are waiting for it to be lifted;
16 and the people of peace, they are in the place of (protective) fear of being tricked (makr) by God;

cf. al-anfāl 8:30 and al-ra'd 13:42 - the word makr in reference to God has no negative connotation but means that He is a better planner than those who plot against Him and against His people.

17 and the people of arising on the Day of Arising for Judgment, they sink down sitting;
18 and the people of inspiration (*her inspiration to what is wronging her and what makes her right* ۞ *al-shams* 91:8), they have the decision;
19 and the people of verification for themselves, they have three recompenses: a recompense of faith, of disbelief, and of hypocrisy.

As for the citations of their states

Learn that God has fashioned
1 the alighting places, for the visitor descending
manāzil al-nāzil
2 and the stronghold for the mature, strong in intellect
mu'āqil lil-'āqil
3 and the collected fold (cf. ṭayy, as the Earth is folded for traveling great distances in a moment) for the one saddled and ready to be launched on the journey
al-marāḥil lil-rāḥil
4 and the highest signs, raised for the one who knows
al-ma'ālim lil-'ālim
5 and the dividing line of a distributor, for the division
maqāsim lil-qāsim
6 and a readying of the disasters, for the back-breaker
al-qawāṣim lil-qāṣim
7 and a clarifying of the protections, for the protected

al-ʿawāṣim lil-ʿāṣim
8 and a raising firm foundations, for the seated
al-qawāʿid lil-qāʿid
9 and an arranging the scouting posts, for the one lying in wait
al-marāṣid lil-rāṣid
10 and a subjugation of the mounts, for the rider
al-marākib lil-rākib
11 and a bringing near the places of exit, for the departing
al-madhāhib lil-dhāhib
12 and a writing of praises, for the praiser
al-maḥāmid lil-ḥāmid
13 and a making easy the sought goals, for the seeker
al-maqāṣid lil-qāṣid
14 and an initiation of recognitions, for the recognizer
al-maʿārif lil-ʿārif
15 and an establishment of the halts, for the one halting to learn
al-mawāqif lil-wāqif
16 and a making rough and rugged the travel, for the wayfarer
al-masālik lil-sālik
17 and a designation of the ritual stages, for the performer
al-manāsik lil-nāsik
18 and a tongue-tying of the seer, for the vision witnessed
al-mashāhid lil-shāhid
19 and a stealing of the calves, for the one put to sleep
al-farāqid lil-rāqid

The citation of the descriptions of their states

He *exalted beyond* made for
1 the descending visitor, measuring;
2 the mature and intelligent, thinking;
3 the journeyer (rāḥil), saddling up and setting forth;
4 the knowledgeable, witnessing;
5 the distributor of allotments, strength to endure troubles;
6 the disaster (qawāṣim) contended with, exertion and struggle;
7 the protector (as in protection from disaster), assistance;
8 the one sitting it out, recognizing (things as they truly are);
9 the one lying in wait, standing still;
10 the rider, being borne;
11 the one departing, being caused;
12 the praiser, being responsible;
13 the seeker, being accepted;
14 the master, having good fortune;
15 the halter, having amazement;
16 the wayfarer (sālik), being returned;
17 the performer of ritual, an object of worship;

18 the seer, having judged;
19 and the one put to sleep, having protection.

With this we have cited the attributes of these nineteen kinds in their states, so we may discuss what each kind includes with regard to matrices of the manāzil. Each manzil of these matrices includes four kinds of manāzil: the first kind is called the manāzil of indications (to the Divine); the next is called the manāzil of definitions (and legal principles); the third kind is called the manāzil of the distinctive (and specially chosen ones); and the fourth kind is called the manāzil of the mysteries. And the multiplicity is uncountable.

The fourth section of the Openings Revealed in Makkah, on the manāzil which are outlined in this chapter, spans eight books, and there Ibn al-'Arabī will describe in detail these degrees (darajāt), the masters (arbāb), and the ones of this art (shā'n) - together with the different tastings and hence different characteristics of these alighting places. Because the people of this art have their own experiences, the titles and adjectives and sequences of the alighting places will differ.

So let us restrict ourselves to the nineteen so we may discuss the numbers of what is folded in with regard to the matrices. And this is its first:

folded: from root tayy - cf. Latin root -plic in implic- ated, complicated, multiplica- tion.

1 manzil of laudation

He (of the family of laudation) has the manzil of the opening - opening the two secrets - and the manzil of the first opening keys; and we have about it a piece we called the Mafātiḥ al-ghayūb (*Opening Keys of the Unseen*); and a manzil of strange wonders; and a manzil of subjugating the intermediating spirits (in the barzakh); and a manzil of the upper-realm spirits. And we have about one of its meanings a poem; this is our statement:

A manzil of laudation and vying for glory is
many manāzil having no end.

Do not search in the exalted heights for a praising;
the referents the people use for
praising are in lowly soil.

Whose soul is thirsty for fighting the lower self
drinks from the most sweet waters.

One is (I am) saying, a slave is not praising when he is described by qualities of his master. This is poor manners. And one is not praising the master when one describes him with qualities of his slave so humble. It is up to the master to descend and alight below, because doing so is not imposed on him. Thus, His descent to the attributes of His slave is a gracious condescension on His part to His slave so that He may make him rejoice. The majesty of the master is much greater in the heart of the slave than that he should be pointed to from afar, had he (the master) not descended. It is not for the slave to be described by attributes of his master, neither in his presence nor among his fellow slaves. Nevertheless, he authorized the descriptions of these qualities, when he said, 'I am the master of the children of Adam, no boast.' And He *exalted* said, *This house of the hereafter, We gave it* - that is, We transferred ownership of it - *to the ones who do not intend high arrogance on the Earth* - because God made the Earth to be lowly and tractable; and the creature is tractable, and the lowly does not claim high elevation. Whoever transgresses one's measure is destroyed. They say, 'Amr will not be destroyed as long as he knows his measure.' *al-qaṣaṣ 28:83*

One says, 'having no end' - meaning, there does not belong to the slave, concerning his 'ubūdīyah (slavehood), any limit one reaches where one would then return as a lord, just as there does not belong to the lord any boundary ending at which he would then return as a creature. So the Lord is Lord infinitely, and the creature is creature infinitely. This is why 'the referents the people use for praising are in lowly soil': the soil is even lower than the surface of the Earth. And one says, 'Only the thirsty knows the pleasure of water.' One is saying, one only knows the pleasure of being described by 'ubūdīyah who tastes the pains associated with being described by rabūbīyah (lordliness). The creation (people) need to feel this. An example is Sulaymān, when he asked God to make him the nourisher of the creatures so he could nourish them physically by his own hand. He amassed whatever he had with him, all the food he had at that time. One of the ocean animals came out and demanded her daily food. He said to her, 'Take from this measure your daily food.' She ate and ate until she got to its end; and she said, 'Give me more; you have not fulfilled my daily sustenance, because God gives me every day ten times this much, and there are other animals larger than me with greater daily sustenance.' So Sulaymān turned for forgiveness to his Lord; and he learned that it is not in the capacity of creation to have that which is appropriate only to the Creator. You see, he had asked God for a dominion not appropriate for anyone after him. He then asked to be released from his request when he saw the situation, while the animals gathered together from every direction to seek their daily sustenance. He was not able for it at all; so when God accepted his new request and released him from the old one, he found a pleasure in that whose measure cannot be measured. *ṣād 38:35, He said, My Cherisher, forgive me and give me a dominion not appropriate to anyone after me.*

2 manzil of symbols

Learn, may God give you success, that even though it is itself a manzil, it encloses manāzil. Among them, a manzil of the Oneness; a manzil of the First Intellect, and the tremendous Throne overlooking all, and the arrival from the Mist to the Throne, and knowledge of tamaththala (as when Gabriel took on the image of a well-proportioned man for the Annunciation); and a manzil of the hearts and the veil (the body); and a manzil of the settling into balanced parts of the fahwānīyah, and the night-cloud Divinity, and the provision of prophesy, and eternity; and the manāzil which are not stable for themselves nor stable for anyone there; and a manzil of the intermediating membranes (barāzakh), and Divinity and the augmentation and the protective jealousy; and a manzil of loss and wild emotion; and a manzil of lifting the doubts and the profusion of treasures; and a manzil of coercion and disgrace; and a manzil of the Vast Earth.

Address of the True, face to face, in the intermediary world. And see the critical edition 5:44.

When I entered this manzil, while I was in Tunis, there erupted from me a cry which I did not realize came from me. All who heard it fell unconscious; and whoever was on the roof terraces - the women of the neighborhoods looking at us - fainted, and some of them fell from the terraces to the courtyard of the house, from the top of the house - but none were injured. I was the first to get up. We had been in prayer behind an imām, and I did not see anyone who was not thunderstruck. After a while, they got up. I asked, 'How are you doing?' They said, 'How are *you* doing? You gave a cry that caused all this to the group praying.' I said, 'By God, I had no idea that I screamed!'

And consider: 'ubūdīyah *f* is an utter abasement, purely so, essential, belonging to the slave - the slave is not tasked to stand with her, because she is exactly one's dhát. Then, when you stand with her truth, your standing so is a worship; and none stand with her except the one who lives in the Vast, Divine Earth, who encompasses the New and the Old. Thus, this is an Earth of God; whoever stands in her verifies for oneself a worship of God. And God annexes (in the sense of joins or attaches without subordination of one to another; 'correlation, or reciprocal relation, so that one of the two cannot be conceived without the other, as in fathership and sonship') you to the True. He *exalted* said, *O My slaves, the ones who are faithful; indeed, My Earth is vast - therefore worship only Me* - that is, in her (the Earth). And for me, I have worshiped God in her since the year AH 590; and we are today in the year AH 593 (the story is elaborated in Chapter 351).

al-'ankabūt 29:56

And some of what is encompassed is a manzil of the strange verses, and Divine wisdoms; and a manzil of preparation and adornment, and the command by which God grasps the heavenly orbit; and a manzil of remembrance and negation. About these manāzil I said:

manāzil of existence in being;
manāzil, all of them symbolic.

manāzil for the intelligent, mature ones there;
indications, all of them conceivable.

When the seekers come in search
to obtain some thing, they are recompensed with it.

So you slaves of existing things, take that
which was sent to you and pass on.

The 'symbol' and the 'enigma' (alghaza) are a speech-unit which gives, in its literal sense, not what the speaker really intends. It is this way for the manzil of the world in being. God did not create it for itself, rather He created it for Himself - so the people are occupying themselves with other than what the world was created for; so the search contradicts the intent of its Creator. This is why a group of the knowledgeable 'ārifīn - and their state is much better than any below them - say, 'God created us for us'; but the one who verifies for oneself - and the real creature - does not say this. Instead, one says, 'He created us for Him, but not from a need He has for me. I am an enigma of my Lord, and I am His symbol.' Whoever recognizes the information imparted by enigmas recognizes what we mean. As for one's word,

alghaza is 'he concealed a meaning different from that which he made apparent.'

When the seekers come in search
to obtain some thing, they are recompensed with it.

- here jūzū is from the passive form mujāzāh (recompensed). One says, 'Whoever seeks God for something, then that is just what he seeks; and he will not get anything more than that.' And one's statement is, 'Who worships God for something, then that thing is his object of worship and his lord; and God is not responsible for him, and he belongs to what he worships.' And one's statement is ḥūzū - that is, 'to obtain' what you came for; that is, it is the reason you came. So 'pass on' (jūzū): this is, rūḥū (depart) from Us - because you did not come to Us, and this was not for Us.

3 manzil of entreaty

This manzil encompasses manāzil: among them a manzil of intimacy of the counterpart; a manzil of being nourished; a manzil of

Makkah (for Makkah, and hands, below - consider al-fatḥ 48:24, *And it is He who has restrained their hands from you and your hands from them in the midst of Makkah*) and the circler of the Ka'bah, and the curtains; a manzil of curtained enclosures and being tested; and a manzil of gathering together and separating, and preventing; and a manzil of the intoxicated ones and the sanctified. And about this manzil, I said:

For you (the name), O Supremely Compassionate
(al-Raḥmān), you have manāzil,
so answer the call of the True,
obediently, you someone.

The mursalāt (ones sent) raise their hands to you;
you hope for bestowal, but the
petitioner does not respond.

You are the one who said the evidence is in
its excellence,
but we have against it witnesses and proofs.

If not for your being distinguished in truth,
the manāzil would not be proud of you, most
high, descending to alight at his side.

One is saying, the call of the True to His creatures is actually a language of names of His by which He is sought, and this creature in this moment is under their authority. And the mursalāt are the subtle natures of creation raising their hands to what is in front - the (Divine) names - to give generously to the one seeking them, these names. The 'answerable one' is actually the one who has the guardian role over the names, such as the All-Knowing who has precedence over the All-Informed, the Esteemed, the Counting, and the Separator: this is why someone said,

You are the one who said the
evidence is in its excellence.

The truth which makes it special is its encompassing what is underneath in rank - the Divine names. Consider: the Measurer is in the rank below the One who Desires (something to *Be! and it is*), and the Knower is in the rank above the One who Desires, and the Living is above all; so the manāzil which are under the encompassing of the All-Comprehensive Name (Allāh) take pride in His descent to them, when He answers their petition (in the third part of the night).

4 manzil of actions

This comprises manāzil, among them a manzil of excellence and inspiration; and a spirit-based manzil of night ascent (while the Night Ascent was bodily); and a manzil of tenderness; and a manzil of destruction. About this manzil I say:

Belonging to the manāzil of the
actions is a lightning flash,
and their winds churn the clouds into a gale;

And their darts pierce the worlds,
and their swords slice the existences into sections.

Her command is cast to the verified inaccessible;
so the eye sees, but the attainment is distant.

Concerning actions of the creatures, people are divided in two: a group sees the actions as coming from the creatures, and a group sees the actions as coming from God. To each group this seems correct, based on their beliefs; it is like a flash of lightning for them, giving them the idea that the party the action was denied to still has some attributable relation. But each group has clouds coming between them and the attribution of the action to the party it was denied to. The statement about their cloud-clearing winds is that they are strong ('a gale') - that is, the reasons and the indications which arise for each group in attributing actions to that party are strong, when looking at the party. Their darts are described as piercing the souls who so believe, and similarly their swords as slicing them into sections.

And the poem's statement that they are 'cast to the verified inaccessible' is, they are shielded by a forbidding shield which prevents the opposer from leaving a mark there. So with this they all remain with what God had intended: He said, *We have made seemly for each community their activities.* And the statement 'the eye sees' is saying, the senses see that the action belongs to the creature; and the human being finds this in oneself, in that one makes a choice. And one's statement, 'the attainment is distant': that is, it is put in relation to something beyond what the senses provide, and the Self is distant from the attainment - except there is a flash of lightning giving a relationship to that action for the party it was denied to, unable to be unacknowledged.

al-an'ām 6:108

5 manzil of beginning

This comprises manāzil: among them a manzil of roughness and swimming orbit; a manzil of descents, and knowledge of Divine tawḥīd; a manzil of intense kindness; and a manzil of truth and fright. And about this manzil I say:

For the beginning are seers and indicators,
and it has manāzil to alight on
when the rider dismounts.

Encircling the eye of the new ones is the wise
property of hu.
God extends hu to aid, the Gracious, the Doer.

There is no relation between anyone and
the Divine,
except clinging and being attained.

Do not listen to the statement of the ignorant:
'The structure of being is truths and falsehoods.'

The structure of being is truths witnessed;
and other than being, there is the impossible, the false.

One is saying, with 'the beginning' of the beings there is a vision of them. They are not themselves - then they become. And for 'it has', the pronoun refers to the beginning; and 'when the rider dismounts' - that is, when you track from where it came, you find it to be from the one who brought it into being; and this is why it has permanence. He *exalted* said, *What is with God is permanent*; so when you 'dismount', you recognize the manzil there, as it is not in yourself. This is a manzil of Divine firstness in His word, *hu is the First* - and from this firstness originates the beginning of the kawn (existence); and from hu comes to pass the new things, all of them; and hu is the Judge over them, and they are slaves under His authority. The attributions are denied Him, because the firstness of the True spreads over the firstness of the creature; and the firstness of existence has no spreading over of anything.

al-naḥl 16:96

al-ḥadīd 57:3

Then there is no attribution but 'by His grace', and no reason but 'He so ruled', and no time but 'the eternal now'. This is the argument of the Tribe. Anything remaining which is not included under the enclosure of these three is blindness and confusion. This is how the author of Maḥāsin al-majālis (The Beautiful Places in the Mystical Sessions), Abū'l-'Abbās bin al-'Urruf al-Ṣanhājī, explained it.

And the statement of one who says 'The structure of being is truths and falsehoods' is not correct - because 'false' is void, and being is true. Being was sought for benefit when the ruling force belonged to the void; and Being is the True, the One whose Being is

Himself. And every void which is then found is found only through a being that can be described only as another's, not your own; and the One who beneficially provides being is Himself Being. As for 'the impossible, the false', that is something which has no being - not its own being nor another's being.

6 manzil of transcendence (tanzīh)

This manzil comprises manāzil: among them a manzil of thankfulness; a manzil of wrong; a manzil of proclamation; a manzil of victory and gathering together; and a manzil of profit and loss and transformations. We have about this:

The manzil of transcendence and holiness has
a secret spoken, its property intelligible,

A knowledge returning to transcendence
its property,
the holy Garden of Firdaws, and
its garden towering high.

The transcendence of the True, clarified, is come
to pass;
hu did not speak, so one's attempt
is a swerving error.

One says: who truly transcends is the one who makes himself transcendent, for himself. In fact, he considers transcendent the one who is allowed to have what he considers Him transcendent above. He is the created being. This is why the declaration of transcendence rebounds onto the declarer of transcendence. He said, 'It is rather your actions that rebound to you.' So the person whose action is to declare Him transcendent, his declaration rebounds onto himself! His context is a transcending above a situation in which a belief about God would arise that is not appropriate for the True. From here he utters, 'subḥānī' (Exalted beyond am I!). He does so to glorify the majesty of God. This is why one said, 'its garden towering'. It is the descent of the transcendent to the place of the creature who is trying to declare its Creator transcendent. *And God speaks the true, and hu is the guide to the way.* *al-aḥzāb 33:4*

7 manzil of nearing

This manzil comprises manzilayn (dual): a manzil of breaking the fabric of the conventional and a manzil of the oneness of *Be!* About it I wrote a poem:

The manāzil (pl.) of nearing have an
imposition / He took upon Himself, known,
and she has the final decision over
existence's very being.

When the stipulated imposition comes on the Day
of Judgment
and her Jabbār (Forceful Restorer) settles and
is triumphant, all being submits and serves.

No, the souls will not reap their fruits,
except the one produced while you were embodied.

And hence the opportunity for fulfilling a deed tasked ends with the transference to the other world (except for one last command: to bow). For the first verse, sharṭ is a stipulation or imposition taken on oneself or made obligatory on oneself - here the Divine stipulation that al-Raḥmān will prevail over all other names, such as Wrathful and Vengeful. For Jabbār, 'As for the Fire, she will not be filled until He places His Foot there and she says, "Enough, enough, enough." Thereupon she will be filled up, and some of her will be knit into others. God will not be oppressive to anyone of His creation.'

One is saying, nearing to one of the attributes of the New ones - because they accept drawing nearer, and its opposite. The True is the Near, even though He attributes to Himself drawing even nearer to the creature. The verbal nouns here are 'nearing' and drawing even nearer. When he says, 'stipulated imposition', it is a reception to influence; usually, the true situation is not known or revealed except in the next world. He is saying, the souls have no fruits except what they planted during their life in this world - whatever was good or bad. They 'draw nearer' based on their practices; so *the one who practices the weight of a mote of good will see it, and the one who practices the weight of a mote of bad will see it.* (al-zalzalah 99:7,8)

8 manzil of expectation

This manzil also comprises manzilayn (dual): a manzil of the Divine path and a manzil of audition. About it I composed a poem:

The manāzil appeared to the
expectant desert nomads,
and their plucking is in the hand of the
one approaching ever nearer.

So pluck from the near branches their fruits;
do not pluck from the distant branches.

Do not depart from your balance; stay attached.
You will see in the middle of the
way the nomadic truths.

One is saying, the human being does not expect and anticipate what comes about, because nothing is expected except it appears first to you in your inside.

> Henry David Thoreau writes in Natural History of Massachusetts (1842): 'The scarlet oak must, in a sense, be in your eye when you go forth. We cannot see anything until we are possessed with the idea of it, and then we can hardly see anything else. In my botanical rambles I find that first the idea, or image, of a plant occupies my thoughts, though it may at first seem very foreign to this locality, and for some weeks or months I go thinking of it and expecting it unconsciously, and at length I surely see it, and it is henceforth an actual neighbor of mine. This is the history of my finding a score or more of rare plants which I could name.'

It protrudes from its unseen (which made it firm) into the inside of the one who anticipates it. Then its outward emergence is expected in the seen world. It becomes more close to being acquired. It is His word, *Its fruits so close* - that is, close to the plucking hand, *al-ḥāqqah* 69:23 saying, Keep to the balanced path, do not swerve from it. Balance here is your persistent connection to your truth of 'ubūdīyah *f*, not leaving her as the arrogant ones do. And whoever is an intermediary between the two paths surveys all, 'hand over the brow'. As soon as you lean toward one of them, the other becomes unseen.

> For quṭūfuhā liyad al-muqarrab dāniyah, see ḥadīth #14736, from the section of ḥadīth transmitted from Jābir, in the collection of Aḥmad ibn Ḥanbal: 'From Jābir, who said, "At noon or afternoon prayers, when we were with the Messenger ﷺ in our rows for the prayer, the prayer of noon or afternoon, suddenly Messenger reached out for something. Then he went back from the people. When the prayer was completed, Ubayy bin Ka'b said to him, 'You did something during the prayer that you have not done before.' He said, 'Displayed to me was the Garden, with its flowers and blooms; and I reached out for some grapes at picking-distance, to bring some to you all, but I was prevented (lit. between me and it was an interposition); and had I brought them to you, everyone between the heaven and the Earth could have eaten from them without lacking a thing. Then, displayed to me was the Fire; and when I came across its scorch, I went back from it.'"'

9 manzil of blessings

This also comprises two manzilayn (dual): a manzil of gathering together and separating,

Ibn al-'Arabī throughout uses these concepts jam' and tafriqah for the Qur'ān, which gathers (jam') verses and signs together, and for the Criterion (furqān), which separates (tafriqah) things in order to clarify.

and a manzil of intermediating adversaries. It is a manzil of kingdom and forcefulness. About it I say:

manāzil of blessings have a light that radiates;
the light is looked for in the inner core of the hearts.

In the blessings is an increase for every seeking seer,
and they have an overflowing
yearning for the soul of being.

If the secret heart of the seeker of wisdom verifies
the truths of the blessings, one will
be alone in the ascension.

So praise to God who in His Being has
entities seeing and hearing!

The manāzil of blessings are increases, and they are the result of thankfulness.

This is a key text Ibn al-'Arabī devotes Chapter 120 to and often cites: la-in shakartum la-aziydanna-kum, 'If you are thankful, We shall increase blessings for you' ۞ Ibrāhīm 14:7.

The True called Himself with the name Thankful (al-shākir) and Exceedingly Thankful (al-shakūr) only so that we would do more of the practice which He made Law for us that we should do - just as the True increases good fortune because of thankfulness from us. Thus, each one of the two parties, the creature and the True, eagerly awaits more after being thankful.

Here one is saying, if you the seeker of wisdom verify increase, you become alone in situations you strive to have no one else share in, so that the increase will be of this kind. With the masters of this station, their situation will be one of careful observation of the state they are seeking.

10 manzil of oaths and swearing

The VII form of fahaqa, conveying the sense of light splitting into rays and dispersing forth, connected to the imagery of Chapter 8.

This manzil comprises manāzil: among them a manzil of compassionate address heard face to face in the intermediary world; and a manzil of spirit-based shares; and a manzil of the written-down; and a manzil of the light-fall; and a manzil of the poets; and a manzil of the spirit-being ranks; and a manzil of the All-Soul; and a manzil of the Pivot; and a manzil of anfihāq of the light into the unseen world; and a manzil of the ranks of the articulate souls; and a manzil of different paths; and a manzil of affection; and a manzil of inspired knowledge; and a manzil of living souls; and a manzil of the middle prayer. About this I say:

manāzil of oaths in the length of
their principles in the world of the earth,

Flowing through the orbits of good fortune over one
who establishes the Sunnah and the obligatory,

Their knowledge is an inheritance of their ʿayn,
and their wisdom is in the length and the width.

The poem is saying, the oath is the product of suspicion; and the True uses the creation (e.g. *by the Sun* ❁ al-shams 91:1) with regard to what they have, not with regard to what He has. And this is why the True did not charge the angels, because they are not part of the world of suspicion. It is not for the creation to swear an oath on something from creation. It is our position; and if one swears by the creation, with us, it is a disobedience. There are no reparations if one breaks the oath, but one should turn for forgiveness to the True for what happened to one - nothing else.

The True swears an oath by Himself when He swears, by citing created things and apocopating the name (citing only the first of multiple correlations, e.g. *by the Lord of the heaven and (by the Lord of) the Earth*) indicating with that the bringing out of the name in places in the Majestic Book, like His word, *By the Cherisher of the heaven and the Earth,* ❁ *by the Lord of the Easts and the Wests.* All of this is a sign in the places where there is no literal citation close to the (apocopated) name. It is unseen there, for some matter that He desires - recognizing it whomever the True teaches it to, such as a prophet or a friend inspired. The oath is an indication of the greatness of the thing sworn by, and there is no doubt that it is mentioned in the oath; one sees, another does not see. Included in that is the raised and the lowered, and the one He is pleased with and the one He is angry at, the loved and the detested, the grateful and the ingrate, the existent and the non-existent. And none knows the manāzil of the oaths except the one who recognizes the unseen world. Thus, there predominates in one the estimation that the Divine name here is the personal pronoun. We have already informed you that the unseen world is length and the seen world is width.

al-dhāriyāt 51:23
al-maʿārij 70:40

11 manzil of innīyah

Ibn al-ʿArabī will later define innīyah: 'The truth in the mode of absolute reciprocal relation. They are the ones focused solely on the Tablet, the ones witnessing the Pen, the viewers of the Nūn, the ones dipping into the ink receptacle of the *hu*, the ones who speak for the I, the articulators of the unification coming from the ring. If you ask, 'What are these words which you cited?' - We say: As for the Tablet, it is a place for the registration and recording fixed by a known limit. As for the *hu*, she is the unseen truth. As for the Nūn, he is synoptic knowledge. As for the I, it is your speaking by you. As for the Pen, analytic knowledge. As for union, the two essences become 1 essence, either a creature or a Cherisher; it happens only in numbers and in the physical, and that is a spiritual experience (ḥāl). As for the ringing, the synoptic address is a kind of forcefulness, because of the intensity of the inrush.

Comprising manāzil, among them: a manzil of Sulaymān but no others among the prophets; and a manzil of the complete cover; and a manzil of difference in the created beings; and a manzil of the Spirit; and a manzil of knowledge lores. About it I say:

An innīyah, purely apart, seen in a vision,
her being with the Men has many manāzil.

Existence vanishes when a form shines brilliantly
as a form ʃ in tajallī,
her signs comparatively more excellent.

You see you in you, her being in her epithet
behind the shadows; her being
for you is an enveloping.

Saying, the Divine truth ʃ described with an epithet of transcendence: when she is witnessed, every eye entity but her is annihilated. If her vision is superior in a single person on account of your states and in different persons on account of their different states, this is because the truth is that the seer of us only sees himself - just as she sees, of us, only herself. Thus, each truth is a mirror for the other:
al-shūrā 42:11 'the faithful is a mirror for his sibling.' *There is nothing like His like.*

12 manzil of eternities (duhūr, pl. of multiplicity for dahr)

This manzil encloses manāzil, among them: a manzil of precedence; and a manzil of majesty; and a manzil of Spirit-beings in celestial orbits; and a manzil of Divine command; and a manzil of childbirth; and a manzil of weighing; and a manzil of the joyful gift from the meeting. About it I say:

Of the manāzil there is something assigned,
like the time period, because time is illusory.

An Alighting Place

Chapter 22

The circlings indicate it by their orbits,
and it has the expending and the great position.

One is saying, as timelessness is an illusory matter - illusory with regard to the True - the time period as well, with regard to the True, is an illusory matter. Time is an imaginary segment notched in orbital movements, because the timeless now, like the time period, belongs to the creation - so understand.

13 manzil of lām-alif

This is a manzil of intimacy; and most of it is harmony, not difference. He *exalted* said, *The leg is interlaced with a leg. To your Lord on that Day is the driving.* It comprises manāzil, among them: a manzil of the two oceans joined and two things joining; and a manzil of the nobility of the Muḥammadī (based on Muḥammad - here corresponding to the lām) which is toward the side of the manzil of the Everlasting (ṣamadī, based on the ṣamad - the Everlasting, and the One in whom refuge is found - here corresponding to the alif). About it I say:

For lām-alif, see Volume 1, Chapter 2.

al-qiyāmah 75:29,30

manāzil of the lām in the verification and the alif,
when there is a meeting; a disconnection
in the state - and the two link up.

The two are the indication for the one who said, 'I am indeed
the secret of being, and I am its 'ayn.' Thus the two

Are good fortune indicators, as they point with their state,
not like the one who points with his argument; so the two are severed.

One is saying, even though the lām-alif links and knots and becomes one entity, it is outwardly twinned among the letters in the place of the twenty-eighth position between the wāw and the yā', the two which have sound forms and weak forms - 'the weak letters'. As there is with the alif some weakness, and as there is with the lām only soundness, there occurs a relationship between the alif and these other two letters, the wāw and the yā'; and the sound one is next to the other sound letter, and the weak one is next to the other weak letter - so one of their hands is open liberally in kindness / and the other is closed tightly in her opposite.

The lām-alif has no form in the prime order; no, the prime is unseen in her. The step-level of her state is between the wāw and the yā'. He (the lām has changed gender) takes the place of the zā (here with no ') and the ḥā', dry ṭā'. The lām-alif has in his unseen the step-level of 7, 8, 9; and he has a manzil (mansion) of the Moon between full and crescent. The membrane (barzakh) continues to accompany him in his absence beyond perception and his emerging visibility. He is 24th, as he has the 7 by the zā, the 8 by the ḥā', and the 9 by the ṭā' (7+8+9). The day has 24 hours; and in whatever hour you practice him, your work will be accomplished, by weighing down the deeds' arm of the scale - because lām-alif belongs to the calligraphic letters, not to the Nature-based letters, because he has no Nature-based letter except the lām (see Chapter 2, p. 173 for an initial discussion).

He is among the lingual letters, an intermediary between the throat (guttural) and the two lips (labial). The alif is not one of the Nature-based letters, so only a single letter takes her place - and that is the lām from whom the alif is generated, when she is rendered fully vocalized by his vowel. If she is not rendered full, she appears as a hamzah (the '). This is why some of the experts take the alif to be a half-letter and the hamzah to be a half-letter - in conventional writing, not in natural speaking.

Then we return and say, The lām is knotted with the alif, as we said, and becomes a single 'ayn. Indeed, its two legs indicate that they are two; then the expression of his name lām-alif indicates that it is two. It is a name composed of two names themselves: the single 'ayn is the lām and the other the alif; but when they come out in the format of a single 'ayn, the observer cannot differentiate them, and one cannot distinguish which of the two legs is the lām so that the other will be the alif. The calligraphy writers differ here. One of them looks after the vocalization; and among them one looks at what begins the etched writing, making it the first. They agree in putting the lām before the alif, because the alif here is born from the lām - no doubt. And it is the same way with the hamzah following
al-ḥashr 59:13 the lām in His word; for example: la'antum ashaddu rahbatan, *You are certainly more intensely to be feared* - and others.

This letter - I mean the lām-alif - is a letter tangled in verbs. The outward active word does not become clarified by the hand of creation, so to whom does it belong? If you argue, 'It belongs to God' - you are correct. If you argue, 'It belongs to the created being' - you are correct. If not for the latter, tasking would be invalid. And attributing the deed arising from God to the creature is this: he used to say, 'It is your actions returning to you.' And God says, Āl-i-'Imrān 3:115

What you do of good, do not cover it up; and, fuṣṣilat 41:40

Do what you like; He sees what you are doing. al-aḥzāb 33:4

And God speaks the true.

Āl-i-'Imrān 3:115 here is the Warsh recitation (2nd person plural instead of 3rd person plural)

And in this way, whichever stem you deem to be the lām or the alif, you are correct. According to the grammarians - and according to everyone else who points to the governance belonging to one of the legs apart from the other - if the syntactical governing process differs in the placement of the shape (and so alif or lām being first makes a syntactical difference) in order to verify the format, then this is not valid; and that proponent is cut short, not confirmed - even though another among the people of this pursuit disagrees about this and he is proven, as he presumes. The argument with him is like the argument with his opponent. The matter is contradictory and complicated, unless God lights up your insight and guides you to the even way.

14 manzil of regulation

This comprises manāzil: among them a manzil of counted good fortune; and a manzil of removing harm; and a manzil of absolute shirk. About this I say:

The manāzil are regulated by the
grammatical rest-stop;
and the emergent outweighs the hidden i.e. the surd u of kun

And indicates by the eye-witness (i'yān) the eyes
('uyūn) of the
bursting water of the spring (ma'īn)

And indicates by lightning strikes the clouds
carrying rain,
when flashes over a clarifying light.

Learn, may God assist you, that one is saying the stabilized things 'regulate the manāzil'. Whoever stabilizes, grows; and he emerges visibly to every 'ayn based on her truth. Do you see what the allegory of rapid motion gives you, what you are given with the rapidity of movement of ambiguous things? The observer of the thing judges contrary to what that thing really is - because it is moved rapidly. One says about the fire which is in the ember or at the tip of the wick, when its movement is speeding widthwise, 'It is making a long

In Chapter 72 Ibn al-Arabī describes this phenomenon of light-writing

line' - or, when the circle of fire is seen in the air, 'It is circling rapidly.' The reason for this is the lack of stability. So when the manāzil are stable, they point to what is around them - such as Divine knowings.

Consider light-writing with a sparkler.

15 manzil of vision

It is a single manzil, a manzil of annihilation of existence; and in there is annihilated 'who never was', and there persists 'who never disappears'. About this I say:

A phrase from the Andalusian Ibn al-'Arīf. This phrase is the 'he' of the poem.

In annihilation of existence is a manzil,
his spirit in us descended.

He is a night of my power, having
no light and no shadow.

He is an 'ayn of light exactly, purely;
no shifting from it does he have.

I am the imām, in truth,
a king in the first origin.

With him are the keys of my command,
entrusted to you and discharged.

My spears are tall; I am
not in Virgo, in the Spica Virginis.

The place of the True in you is
eternal, unchanging.

He is the compeller of spirit,
and he is the leader most just.

There is no resemblance to the light;
no - compared with the Sun, he is more perfect.

I am from him certainly,
in a secret place most excellent.

In the eye of the eye, I lead upward;
and in the command of the command, I send down.

One is saying here, the state of annihilation is neither light nor light-blocking; it is like the Night of Power. Then the poem says that this is the illumination of truth and the shadow of truth, because it is the root which has no opposite; and lights accept blocking, but this does not accept anything.

And the poem's statement, 'I am the imām' means, his vision is toward the True from a particular perspective which is from him to me. And he is 'in the first origin', and from that position there occur differentiation and multiplicity and numbers in forms. He takes the tall spears as an allusion to the efficacy of the Self-Standing *f* in the world, and she has stability. This is why he said 'unchanging'; and he has dominance and balance and does not accept resemblances. In the vision of the dhát, it is upper; and in the Divine command, it is sent down as an imām in the world.

16 manzil of affection

This is a single manzil, and about it I said:

The manāzil of affection are well loved
and known by this epithet.

Say to the one who slept to arise there: 'Rise,
she is guarded by the safe one.'

For *arise*: from 'arrasa, they alighted 'in the last part of the night, for a rest, and took a nap, or slight sleep, and then departed' (Lane) - as also in laylatu'l-ta'rīs, the night in which Messenger slept and then ascended with the isrā'. The 'arūs is the ceremony of presenting the bride (the 'árif) to the bridegroom.

She is halted in even duality
and turned away from the torment of the odd (witr).

This manzil is weddings, happiness, joys, and one of the ones God granted graciously to His Prophet Muḥammad, saying, *He has put affection in their hearts; and if you spent all that is in the Earth entirely, you would not have put affection in their hearts - meaning, affection for you; but God put affection in them* - meaning, love for you and responding to and complying with you. al-anfāl 8:63

17 manzil of testing

It comprises manāzil, among them a manzil of spirit-based strife; and a manzil of strategies of the felicitous - how they defeat the wretched, and vice versa; and a manzil of existence before the human being. About it I say:

When I understood the loves of my heart,
I tried to understand my words.

Their manāzil by your vocalization are only
my misfortune,
coming on account of that, and bad fortune.

I counseled the self, 'Do not look at them,
and be not intimate with their incoming
thoughts, against my counsel.'

I spoke them; perhaps I gained some existent thing;
they were my existence itself, my vocalization itself.

One is saying, they are on my tongue when I am asking of them, and in the black of my eye when I am looking at them, and in my heart when I reflect on them and when I yearn for them. They are with me during every state I have; and they are my eye, but I am not their eye - as there is not with them from me what is with me from them.

What is so strange is that I crave them,
and I ask everyone I see about them
while they are with me.

I strain my eye like an astronomer to observe
them, when they are as close as the black of
my eye.
My heart yearns for them while they
are as close as between my ribs.

18 manzil of threat

This is a single manzil, comprising the wrongful and adhering to existence. About it I say:

The threat is for two houses, both
of them for the one who
abandons the journey to the straighter path.

When you verify for yourself the perfection of his being
and walk along the higher-order steps,

They return in good fortune before you, so your
good fortune is
in the Fire; and it is the good fortune
of each generous one.

A spirit-based manzil is a torment of souls, and a body-based manzil is a sensory torment. It is only for the one who opposes the way of the Law outwardly and inwardly. If one is successful in being evened out, and grace comes in first, one is protected from that - living in good fortune in a fire of the lower-self struggle belonging to a Garden of the seer.

19 manzil of command

This comprises manāzil: a manzil of the intermediary (barzakhī) spirit; a manzil of instruction; a manzil of the night journey (cf. isrā'); a manzil of relations; a manzil of tamā'im (pl. - the taw'īz worn against the evil eye, making the child 'complete', tamām); and a manzil of the quṭb and the two imāms. We have about it:

> From Chapter 73: 'If you ask, "What is the fahwānīyah?" - We answer, The address of the True face to face (with nothing intervening) in the realm of the imaginal; and it is his word about the human being: that you worship God as if you see Him; and from here, you will know the *hu*.'

The manāzil of the matter of fahwānīyah of dhát -
by Her we reach my joy and my dhát.

How I wish I could stand by Her, my
life prolonged,
and not disappear at the moment of the meeting!

The soothing of the eye for the one who chooses
is yours,
when She protrudes from the protruding front
of the secret conversation during the prayer.

The Divine command is from a discursive attribute, and it is closed off from the friends in the point of view of Law-making and what there is in the Divine Presence *f* of a task-based command, unless it is made Law. There remains with the friend only the audition of Her command. When the prophets command, there is with the friend upon hearing it a pleasure flowing in one's being; but there remains for the friends the Divine conversation which has no command in it - only discussion and speaking.

All who say - among the people of kashf - that they are under a Divine command in their movement and their stillness, doing and not doing, inconsistent with a Muḥammadī Law obligation: the command has become confused in them, even though they are truthful about what they are saying - that they heard. It is possible that the Divine tajallī appeared to them in the form of His Prophet, so they conversed with His Prophet ﷺ; or to their ears came the address of His Prophet. That is when the Messenger is the connector of the command of the True by which God commands His creatures. It may be possible that they heard from the True in some Presence that same command which had come first with His Messenger ﷺ, so they would say, 'The True has commanded me' - no, it is with regard to them a notification that they have been commanded. This relation of someone to a new command has expired with the advent of Muḥammad ﷺ, and especially with the commands from God that are part of sharī'ah. Thus, with the friends concerning this there is an anchored stance.

That is, these Friends may visit the site of the original revelation, but they will not become confused and not think that there will come to them some new command.

With this we have brought up the nineteen kinds of manāzil, so let us now discuss the special distinction of the attributes of each manzil. So we say this as a link.

Link

Differences between the list here and the corresponding list earlier in the chapter are also present in the source Arabic.

1 The special distinction of the attributes of the manzil of laudation: connection of knowledge with what has no end.

2 The special distinction of the attributes of the manzil of symbols: connection of knowledge of characteristics of numbers and names; and it is the words and the letters. In there is knowledge of magic.

3 The special distinction of the attributes of the manzil of entreaty: knowings of pointings to and ruses.

4 The special distinction of the attributes of the manzil of actions: knowledge of the now.

5 The special distinction of the attributes of the manzil of beginning: knowledge of the start and the destination, and knowledge of the firsts of every thing.

6 The special distinction of the attributes of the manzil of transcendence: knowledge of the slipping off and the removing (of sandals).

7 The special distinction of the attributes of the manzil of nearing: knowledge of the indications.

8 The special distinction of the attributes of the manzil of expectation: knowledge of the relations and the attachments.

9 The special distinction of the attributes of the manzil of blessings: knowledge of the reasons, and the preconditions, and the causes, and the proofs, and the reality.
10 The special distinction of the attributes of the manzil of oaths: great knowings.
11 The special distinction of the attributes of the manzil of eternity (dahr): knowledge of azal (the everlastingness) of al-bāriyu' (the Creator from no template), as wujūd.
12 The special distinction of the attributes of the manzil of innīyah: knowledge of dhát.
13 The special distinction of the attributes of the manzil of the lām-alif: knowledge of the relation of existence to the Bringer into existence of existence.
14 The special distinction of the attributes of the manzil of regulation: knowledge of Presence.
15 The special distinction of the attributes of the manzil of annihilation of existence (in the manzil of vision): knowledge of the heart of entities.
16 The special distinction of the attributes of the manzil of affection: knowledge of conjunction.
17 The special distinction of the attributes of the manzil of threat: knowledge of context sites.
18 The special distinction of the attributes of the manzil of understanding: knowledge of *There is nothing like Him.* *al-shūrā 42:11*
19 The special distinction of the attributes of the manzil of command: knowledge of the object of worship.

17, 18, and 19 were listed earlier by Ibn al-'Arabī as testing, threat, and command; here, they are threat, understanding, and command.

Link

Learn, that for each of the nineteen manāzil, there is a kind among the enabled beings. Among them there is an angelic kind, and they are a single kind (1), even though their states differ. Knowledge of bodies is 18: orbits, 11 categories; elements, 4; generators, 3. They have another facet accepting the core (jawhar) from the enabled beings in the Divine Presence (11+4+3+1). This belongs to the dhát, and *hu* is the 1st.

Then 2nd is the happenstance occurrences, and they belong to the adjectives.

3rd - the time period, and it is for timelessness.
4th - site, and it is for the *settling on* (ṭā-hā 20:8), or the descriptive categories.
5th - grammatical annexations for the annexations.
6th - the set places for the fahwānīyah.
7th - the 'how many' names there are.

8th - the 'how are they', for the tajallīyāt.
9th - the effects of generosity.
10th - passives, for the bringing out in the forms of belief systems.
11th - the special ones; they are for the oneness.
12th - confusion; this is for the attribute of descent and joy and credit and such things (i.e. the ḥadīth qudsī, where God says He descends in the third part of the night; and 'I rejoice in the repentance of one of you'; and *Who will loan God a goodly loan?* ۞ al-baqarah 2:245).
13th - the life of the existent things, because of the Living.
14th - ma'rifah, belonging to knowledge (the All-Knowing).
15th - ideas suddenly coming into mind, belonging to desiring (the Desiring).
16th - sights, belonging to the Seeing.
17th - hearing, belonging to the Hearing.
18th - the human being, belonging to the complete (and universal being).
19th - the lights and the light-blocking, belonging to the Light.

Link

About the correspondences of the nineteen manāzil: their correspondences in the Qur'ān are the alphabetic letters which are in the first part of the chapters. They are fourteen letters in five steps (14+5): single, double, triple, quadruple, quintuple (e.g. kāf, hā', yā', 'ayn, ṣād). Their correspondences in the Fire are the nineteen angelic treasure-troves.

> From Chapter 343: 'God has divided this composite, kind mercy into well-known parts, providing them to Gabriel as 600 parts (wings) - God providing by them merciful kindness to the family of the Garden and making in His Hand nineteen parts; providing kindness with these p arts to the family of the Fire who are her family; repelling with them the angels of torment, who are nineteen - just as He exalted said, over them nineteen' ۞ al-muddaththir 74:30.

Their correspondences in the world of effects are the twelve zodiacal watchtowers and the seven glistening stars. Their correspondences with the Qur'ān are the letters of the basmalah. Their correspondences with the Greats are the twelve nuqabā' and the seven abdāl - and among these seven are the four awtād (Pegs), the Two Imāms, and the one quṭb (Pivot). The correspondences to these manāzil in the Divine Presence and in the existents are many indeed.

Learn that the manzil al-manāzil (alighting place of alighting places) is an expression for the manzil which combines all of the manāzil together which appear in this world, from the Throne to the moist Earth, and he is called the imām al-mubīn (the clarifying imām). God says, *Everything We have counted in an imām mubīn*. His word 'counted' is an indication that He did not entrust in there anything but finite knowings. So we consider, Is there a confinement to one of her numbers? They jump out from the fence, despite their being finite, because in it is everything that is - from the day God created the universe until the state of this world is wrapped up and the population transfers to the next world. *yā-sīn 36:14*

Then, I asked someone reliable, among the ones who know God, whether there is a limit to the matrices of these knowings which this imām al-mubīn (the clarifying leader) encompasses. He replied, 'Yes.' Then he informed me - the reliable, safe, truthful friend - and he made me promise that I will not mention his name - that the matrices of knowings that include every matrix (umm, mother) there, a vast quantity not countable, fully reach by number to 129,600 kinds of knowings (360^2), each kind encompassing numerous knowings; and they are expressed as manāzil.

So I asked this reliable one whether anyone in the creation of God had been informed of them and had encompassed them with knowing. He said, 'No.'

Then he said: '*No one knows the armies of your Lord except hu*; and since the armies are not known to anyone but hu, and there does not belong to the True any opposition necessitating these armies in order to face them except an individual of ins (human-types) and *jinn* (concealed-types), so one is amazed at the great number of the army of the True; despite the paucity of numbers of ones opposing.' He said to me - 'Do not be amazed, *by the Cherisher of the heaven and the Earth!* (This verse is said as an oath, such as 'By God!') There has come to pass something even more amazing.' I asked, 'What is it?' He replied to me, 'What God cited with regard to two of the wives (Ā'ishah and Ḥafsah) of Messenger of God.' Then he recited, '*If you two back each other against him, then God is his protector, and Gabriel, and the righteous faithful; and after that the angels are his supporters*. This is stranger than the story of the armies.' Yes, the mysteries of God are wondrously strange indeed! *al-muddaththir 74:31* *al-dhāriyāt 51:23* *al-taḥrīm 66:4*

When he had said that to me, I asked God to teach me some more about this issue and what this great thing was that had God make Himself face against them, and Gabriel, and the integrated faithful, and the angels. I was informed of it - and I never felt so happy by anything as by learning this! I learned on whom the two women stood for support and who gave them power. And if God had not mentioned that He Himself would be there for victory, the angels and the faithful would not have been able to stand against the two. I learned that there had come to the two some knowledge of God, and I learned the effect they had on the world after the two were given this power. This is part of the knowledge which is 'like a

The ṣāliḥ is someone whole, whose inward and outward (deeds) are integrated.

deeply concealed form' (from the ḥadīth, 'This is part of knowledge which is like a deeply concealed form, no one knowing it except the ones who know God; and when they articulate it, only the distracted people refuse it').

I thanked God for what He entrusted to me, and I guess that not a single one in God's creation stands on what these two women stood on!

Below, the ḥadīth is this: 'We (I) have more claim to doubt than Ibrāhīm, when he said, "Cherisher, show me how you will enliven the dead." He said, "Do you not believe?" He said, "Yes, I do - but in order to ease my heart." And God be kind to Lūṭ; he was taking refuge at a strong pillar. And if I had been in the jail for the same length of time as Yūsuf, I would have responded to the invitation (to leave, before being declared blameless).' Then the question is, What rukn shadīd (strong pillar) did Lot have that Muḥammad ﷺ says he had, while Lot cried out. 'Would that I had power to suppress you, or that I could take myself to some strong pillar'? The commentators often identify the angelic messengers who identify themselves in Hūd 11:81 as his power, but in this context Ibn al-'Arabī is saying that the angels and the integrated faithful and so on would not be enough. We may then consider the other human beings present: the daughters. (Here, the plural 'Lot's daughters' refers to women in the community of the prophet, as Lot's own two daughters would be referred to in the dual.) The qawm (people; here, the men) say they have no right to women (mā lanā fī banātika min ḥaqq - because they were not heterosexual). And so, Lot had his two daughters, and the offending men had no right to women.

Hūd 11:80 Lot was saying, *Would that I had against you some power, or I could take refuge at a strong pillar.* But there was with him a strong pillar, yet he did not recognize it (This clause may also be read, 'yet he did not recognize him', or hu: lam yakun ya'rifa-hu.). The Prophet had testified that he did have that strong pillar and said, 'God be kind to my brother Lot; he was taking refuge at a strong pillar.' 'Ā'ishah and Ḥafṣah recognized *hu*. And if the people knew the knowledge these two were flush against, they would recognize the meaning of this verse:

And God speaks the true,
al-aḥzāb 33:4 *and hu is the guide to the way.*

Chapter 22

وَاللَّهُ يَقُولُ الْحَقَّ وَهُوَ يَهْدِي السَّبِيلَ

al-aḥzāb 34:4. Transliterated: wa allāhu yaqūlu'l-ḥaqqa wa huwa yahdiya'l-sabīl. This is the verse Ibn al-'Arabī places at the end of hundreds of chapters, and this passage is our clue to its importance.

CHAPTER 23

The Pivots

On ma'rifah of the protected Pivots, and mysteries (of the alighting places) of their protection

Chapter 23

God has a wise reason / *He hid*
in my being, but it is not an 'ayn
such that you could see her.

He created the organic body / *to be an abode for*
play and affection,
and He built her and provided for her effusively and
fashioned her as the clay in His Hands to form Adam.

Then when He had balanced and straightened her,
He brought a Spirit from His Side to make her alive.

Then when the True verified her in knowledge,
He loved him (Adam) and yielded him to her desire.

He said to Death, 'Go, take My devoted slave' -
thus, He called him to Him by that
which vacates her (the body).

And He gave tajalli to him; and he said, 'My God,
Where is my intimate companion?' He
said, 'What, have you forgotten her?'

How could I forget an abode in which You made
of her power
some of Your power? She is the one
who is beyond compare!

O my God and my Master and my Support,
I am passionate only for the idea of her.

She taught me what she desires from us,
by means of the tongue of the messenger
from her higher realm.

She crisscrossed our days in delight
in You, O my Master, so nothing is sweeter than her.

He said, 'Restore him to the abode of his love;
the Spirit spoke truly - he truly does love her.'

Thus we were returned, ever young, intoxicated,
ever enraptured, to her abode freely provided.

The previous abode was characterized by taklīf, having to do things in order to be ultimately felicitous. Here suknā is in the semantic field of the ḥadīth which describes the situation of the man paying for the divorced woman's housing.

And He built her according to the beautiful
proportioning of her mighty power,
and He shone radiantly for her by means
of what He strengthened her with.

إعلم

Learn, may God assist you, that this chapter comprises the discussion of the slaves of God called the malāmīyah (from lawm, blamed). They are Men who have been freed from the responsibility of sacred authority (wilāyah is the authority which certain people have by virtue of being friends - awliyā', sg. walī - of God), in their farthest degrees. There is none above them except the degree of prophethood. This is called the position of closeness in (sacred) authority; and their verse in the Qur'ān is *contrast eyes (hūr) guarded in the pavilion* - alerting us, under these categories of women in the Garden and their contrast eyes, to the souls of God's Men who are appropriated to Him, and to their being protected, and to their being confined by Divine jealousy in guarded pavilions in the corners (the zāwiyah) of the world - lest one catch a glimpse of them and be occupied with them. No, by God! No glimpse of creation should be occupied with them. But it is not in the ability of the creation to be concerned with and support what this group from the True do, because of the elevation of their position; thus, the creatures halt before matters they will not reach, ever.

al-Rahmān 55:72. The word hūr is a synecdoche starting from the contrast of black and white in the eyes.

Their visible forms are in pavilions of conventional activity and ritual practices, such as outward practices and perseverance in required and voluntary practices. They are not known to break conventions and perform miracles; nor are they grandiose, and they do not call attention to themselves by the pious show which is the custom of the common people - however, they are never hurtful to them. They are the hidden, the guileless, the ones the world is safe from, the ones concealed from the people they live among.

Messenger of God ﷺ said from his Lord, 'The most beloved of my friends, according to me, is the believer whose back is light, giving full due to the ṣalāt (prayer), most sincere in worship of one's

light: In Lisān al-'arab: 'with little money', someone not weighed down by burdens

Lord, obeying Him in secret and in public, and concealed among the people' - meaning, they are not recognized among the people by some grand worship act, and they do not profane the sacred, secretly or publicly.

One of the Men said about their description, when he was asked about the 'árif - he said, 'They are muswadd in the face, in this world and the next.' If what he meant is what we discussed about the states of this Tribe, then he meant iswadād: becoming blackened in the face, utterly consumed in this world and the next by the tajallīyāt of the True to him. Human beings, with us, see in the True mirror when He gives tajallī to them only their self and their position. The 'árif is a being among beings, and a being, before the light of the True, is light-blocking (ẓulmah, dark); so one sees only the blackness of the 'árif, because the face of a thing is its truth and its dhát. And tajallī does not persist continuously, except for this Tribe in particular; and they are with the True in this world and the next, as we have described it - that is, with the continuous tajallī; and they are the Primes. *cf. suwād, black*

Or, if he meant by taswīd (roughness, root tasawwada), siyādah (mastery); and he meant by 'face', the truth of the human being - that is, that this one has mastery in this world and the next - then it is grammatically possible. But this is then only for the messengers, specifically, because mastery is their completeness - while this person is among the friends and so is lesser - because the messengers are compelled in the outward in order to make Law, and the friends do not have this.

As we saw, the messengers are given strength and are compelled to be powerful in the outward (e.g. political) world in order to propagate the message and its Law.

Do you see? God, when He completed the religion, He commanded him, in the chapter in which God announced to him his death Himself, sending down, *When comes the help of God and the victory, and you see the people entering the dīn of God in droves, then celebrate with the praise of your Lord and ask for His forgiveness* - that is, occupy yourself with tanzīh of your Lord, and the praise of Him with what is appropriate for Him. He detached himself with this command from this world, as he had then completed what was wished of him; and this was propagating the message and seeking with istighfār (asking forgiveness, astaghfiru'llāh) that he be veiled from His creation, in a curtain of His preserving care, to be ever separated apart from His creation. He had been in a time of propagation and guiding and occupying himself with conveying the message. There were times when 'there was no space for any but his Lord'; and the rest of his moments were with what he had been commanded to do, such as looking after the affairs of the creation. Thus, he would return to *al-naṣr 110:1-3* that single moment which he stole away from the moments of his occupation with the creation, even though it was from a command of the True to be so occupied. Then His word is, *hu is oft-turning (innahu kāna tawwāb)* - that is, the True will turn to you with an invitation to return, the creation having no access to you, from one perspective. And when Messenger of God ﷺ recited this chapter, Abū Bakr the Truthful wept عليه السلام - but only him, none of the others sitting there. He knew God Himself had announced the death of Messenger of God ﷺ to him, and he was the most knowledgeable of the people about him. The ones present were shocked, wondering at his weeping, unaware of the reason.

al-naṣr 110:3; tawwāb is turning often toward the creature so that the creature may turn back to God.

The greatest of the friends, when they are left alone to choose for themselves and for their souls, not one among them chooses visibility at all, because they know that God did not create them for their own sakes, nor for anyone in His creation to cling onto them, from the first intention. He created them for Him, *exalted beyond*. Therefore they occupy themselves with what they were created for - for Him. If the True makes them visible - not by their choice - with what is produced in the hearts of creation for them (such as love and need), then that is for Him, *exalted beyond* - they did not have anything to do with it. If He veils them, He does not make for them in the hearts of the people any standing, magnifying them only for His sake; thus, that is for Him, and they make no choice for themselves simultaneously with the choice of True - because He is their chooser, necessarily. Thus, they choose to be veiled from the creation and to be cut off, apart with God. As their state veils their rank even from themselves - so how much more so from others! - it is then designated for us that we explain the manāzil of their being safeguarded and protected.

The first intention for the creation is 'I am a treasure, concealed; but I love to be recognized.'

Among the manāzil of their being safeguarded is the fulfillment of the required rituals in community and mixing in with people in every country in the dress of that country. Such people do not frequent a particular place in the mosque but change their places in the mosque in which there is the Friday prayer so that their selves will be lost among the crowds of people. When the people speak, they will speak with them, and they will see the True watching over them in their speech. When they hear the speech of the people, they hear this way; but they have few sittings with the people - except with neighbors - so they will not be noticed and stand out. They respond to the needs of children and widows, and they play with their children and their spouse as pleases God; and they joke, but not saying anything except the truth. If they are recognized in some place, they move on to another place; and if they cannot move, they make demands on whoever recognized them, and they pester them with the needs of the people until they start to dislike them.

And if they have the station of shifting into different shapes, they transform - just as do the spirit-beings taking shape in forms of the children of Adam (as Gabriel shifted into the form of Diḥyah), and one does not recognize that the spirit-being is an angel, for instance. And Qaḍīb al-Bān was like this. And this, all of it, is because the True did not want to make that person visible or famous, in a way one is not aware of.

This Tribe is given this rank with God, as their hearts are safeguarded from there being other than God entering them, or that they would cling to any of the beings in existence other than God. They have no majlis (a place of sitting, a session in court, a sitting place for the audience of the king, a place to gather to hear a speech) except with God and no conversation except with God. By God they stand and by God they observe; and they are the riders to God, onward to the final transformation. Of God they speak and from God they take; and in God they put their trust, and with God they dwell; and they recognize nothing but Him, and they see nothing but Him. Their souls are safeguarded from themselves, and they know not their own selves; and they are veiled in the most unseen parts of the unseen. They are the 'special ones' (ḍanā'in) of the True, extracted (as butter from milk) to be purely for Him. They eat food and walk in the markets, but they walk covered up and eat behind a veil. This is the state of this Tribe discussed in this chapter.

A generous completion to this chapter

- And from this presence the messengers are sent. We say, From this presence the messengers are sent - the peace of God be upon them all together - with making the Laws. The True honors with them these malāmīyah following them, standing with their command as one entity, taking from them what the prophets and the messengers made Law; and the friends take from them what they follow. They are the followers 'upon insight' and the ones who know whom they are following - and why they are following. They are the ones who recognize the manāzil of the messengers and the paths of the way based on God, and their destinies are with God.

And God speaks the true, and Hu is the guide to the way. al-aḥzāb 33:4

The 16th manuscript ends.
And all praise belongs to God!

Chapter 24

Existence-Based Knowledge

On ma'rifah of what comes from the existence knowledges, and what is included in it of strange wonders, and who reaches them among the people, and the step-levels of their Pivots, and mysteries of the sharing between two Laws, and the hearts desirous of the breaths, and their origin, and at what number end their alighting places

Existence-Based Knowledge

Chapter 24

I was amazed at the malk being brought
back to us as a kingdom (mulk),
and about the King illuminating the
possessions for those He possesses.

Osman Yahya notes: 'The malk is the milk, and the mulk, according to Ibn al-'Arabī, is the true Possessions, the essential, the completeness of the thing. It is a quality of God alone. The milk is the grammatical annexation to the thing - and this, according to Ibn al-'Arabī - is related sometimes to God and sometimes to the creature. Linguistically, there is no difference between the mulk and the milk.' For mulk ul-mulk below, Osman Yahya notes that this phrase was first coined by Ḥakīm al-Tirmidhī and is used here as a symbol of the anchoring bond between Creator and creation.

That is a mulk ul-mulk, if you are well ordered,
with pearls strung; part of our knowledge
path cleared away (through prose).

Ibn al-'Arabī is speaking of the pearls distributed in a nazm - well-ordered, well-arranged poetry - and here as manthūr, which is prose.

Take from the Being of the True a knowledge
wholly apart,
so one may take this knowledge as
Someone wishes from you.

If you are like me, my analogue in knowledge,
you have seen that the one who is a
duplicate of the world is part of you.

The perfectly complete human being (insān al-kāmil) is a duplicate of the universe.

Is there in the upper realm anything to face against
Your command?
Your swords are annihilated in
humankind - annihilated.

If you can perceive, my beloved, His Being,
and who you are, you are a master:
the sign of the malk.

The God of Creation comes to you as a manifold;
you do not come to Him, if you
verify for yourself, as a mulk.

إعلم

Learn, may God assist you, that God says, *Call on Me, I will answer you* - thus, when you recognize this, you recognize that God is Cherisher (rabb) of every thing and is every thing's King. Everything other than God is cherished - belonging to this Cherisher - and a kingdom belonging to this King, the True. The only meaning of the fact that the world *above, al-ghāfir 40:60* is the kingly dominion belonging to God is that He is the executor of him, according to what He wishes, with no restriction, and that he is the site and object of the effect of the King, his Master - *His Majesty exalted!* The variegation of forms and states that the universe undergoes is the discharging execution by the True in him, according to what He wishes.

Then, when we see God saying, *Your Lord has prescribed on (made incumbent upon) Himself kindness*, He is making His Self share with *al-an'ām 6:54* His creature in obligation. Even though He is the one who obligated Himself what He obligated, still His word is right, and His promise is true - just as humankind obligated themselves with the initial vow (alastu bi-rabbikum, *'Am I not your Lord?' And they said, 'Yes!'* ❁ al-a'rāf 7:172); it was not the True who obligated them. Only then did God obligate on humankind fidelity to their vow which they obligated on themselves; thus, He commanded them with fidelity to their vow. Then, we see Him not answering except after the call of some creature - as He made Law - just as the creature does not answer the True until the True calls it to whatever He calls it. He *exalted* said, *So let them respond to Me*. There commences, for the *al-baqarah 2:186* creature and the world - which is the kingly dominion belonging to God - a Divine execution on the sheltered Side (like min ladunhu, from His Side) of what is required by the reality of the world seeking essential being, and another execution of what is required for establishing the Law.

As the matter is as we said - that is, given that the True answers the command of the creature when it entreats Him and asks Him, just as the creature answers the command of God when He commands it - this is His word, *Be faithful to My covenant as I am faithful to your covenant* - thus both are associated with each other in the legal *al-baqarah 2:40* case. And as the True makes a legal demand concerning His dhát that they be lowly toward Him, whether He made Law to His creatures some deed or did not make it Law, similarly they make a legal demand for the continuance of the existence of their being, that the True safeguard them, whether the True made Law what He made Law or did not so make Law. Then, He makes a Law for the creature some deed that, when it does it, He makes it a Law on Himself that He will recompense this creature for doing what it had been obligated to do. So then the elevated Divine Side starts to look like a mulk (possession) belonging to this mulk (kingdom), which is the world, because of what the creature receives - like a gift given after being asked for. Therefore, a quality becomes applied to the world expressed as a mulk ul-mulk. Thus, He is a King of all, a King by virtue of His commanding His creatures; and He is a mulk (kingdom, possession, subject to a king) by virtue of what He is commanded to do by His creature! You see, they say, *My Cherisher! Forgive me!* - just as the True says to the creature, *Establish the ṣalāt (prayer) for My dhikr (remembrance).* What is from the Divine Side with regard to the creature is called an imperative ('*Establish the ṣalāt!*'), and what is from the creature's side with regard to the True is called an entreaty (a du'ā': '*Please forgive me!*'), as a courtesy to the Divine. But, in fact, it is an imperative command; thus, the definition comprises both commands together as one.

al-a'rāf 7:151 (note the imperative)

ṭā-hā 20:14

The first one to adopt this term mulk ul-mulk, to my knowledge, is Muḥammad bin 'Alī al-Tirmidhī al-Ḥakīm; and I have not heard this phrase from anyone except him. Perhaps someone came before him with this terminology, but it did not reach me. In any case, the matter is correct. The issue of God being obligated, according to the intellect, is a matter of disagreement among the people of examination among the theologians. Someone argues for it and another argues against it. As for God being obligated: according to the revelation, no one would deny it except one who is not a believer in what has come as revelation from God.

annexed: e.g. motherhood connects a mother to a child

Learn that in any two annexed (iḍāfah) words there necessarily occurs to each one of the two something that provides for the annexation. When you say 'Zayd', he is a human being - no doubt; and one does not think anything but this. And when you say "Amr', he is a human being; and one does not think anything but this. Then, when you say 'Zayd, son of 'Amr', or 'Zayd, slave of 'Amr', there is no doubt that there has occurred newly for Zayd the noun of son-ship, as he is the son of 'Amr; and there has occurred for 'Amr the noun father-ship, as he is the father to Zayd. The son-ship of Zayd gives father-ship to 'Amr, and the father-ship of 'Amr gives son-ship to Zayd. So each one of the two annexed words newly creates for its owner a meaning that did not describe him before the annexation. And similarly for 'Zayd, slave of 'Amr'; thus, slavehood provides that Zayd should be the owned and 'Amr the owner. So ownership creates in 'Amr the name 'owner of Zayd', and the 'being owned by 'Amr' creates in Zayd the ownership of 'Amr. One says about him, 'owned' - and said about 'Amr is, 'owner'. It did not belong to either one of the two intelligibly, in these names, before the annexation came about.

Therefore, the annexation 'human being' is implicit in 'Zayd' (the human being).

True is True, and human being is human being. When you say, 'The human being', or, 'the people are creatures of God', you have said implicitly, 'God is the King of the people' - necessarily. If you posited in your mind a removal of existence from the universe altogether (the universe as a kingdom is no more), the existence of the True would not be removed with the removal of the universe. What would be removed is the existence of the meaning of 'the King' from the True - necessarily. But as the existence of the world effectively and practically is anchored by the Being of the Knower - the True (who knows that there will be a world) - the name malik (king, generally) belongs to God timelessly. And if the 'ayn of the world is non-existent with regard to the core being, still its intelligibility (that God knows it will be) is something concrete, anchoring the name mālik (the king who possesses the kingdom). Thus, the world is a possession belonging to God as being and as fore-known destiny, virtually and effectively - if you would understand. No, do understand!

There is no spatial interval between the True and the world which can be thought of at all except the differentiation of features and truths. Thus, '*God was and there was nothing with huw*' - *exalted beyond*. It never ceased to be this way, and it never will cease to be this way: '*nothing with huw*'. So His being 'with' is with us, as is appropriate to His majesty and as is fitting for His majesty. And had He not related about Himself that He is with us wherever we may be, the intellect would not have inferred that being 'with' could be attributed to Him - just as the sound intellect cannot understand just what 'with' means when the True attributes to Himself being with us. What is to be understood as His being
al-shūrā 42:11 'with' this one or that, He who nothing is like Him? He *exalted*
al-ḥadīd 57:4 said, *He is with you wherever you are*; and He said, *I am with you two;*
ṭā-hā 20:46 *I hear and I see* - to Moses and Aaron.

We say, the True is with us to the extent and definition He said and with the meaning which He meant. We do not say, 'We are with the True,'

So while we do not say we are 'with God', we may say on the authority of the text that God is 'with us'.

because it is not so transmitted, and the intellect does not provide it. Thus, we have no intellectual perspective or revealed text providing that we are in fact with the True. As for the one who rejects absolutely 'where' from Him, among the people of al-islām, he is deficient in al-īmān,

As in the ranking, in the ḥadīth of Gabriel, of islām (submission to God's will), īmān (faith: not in the usual sense in English of belief, but, according to another ḥadīth, 'a knowledge in the heart, a voicing with the tongue, and an activity with the limbs'), and iḥsān (right action, to do what is beautiful). A mu'min (who is faithful, who accepts the revealed text) accepts that God is 'with us'.

because the intellect rejects from Him any intelligible 'where', whereas the revealed text established in the Sunnah (the ḥadīth below) - but not in the Book - has established absolutely the expression of 'where' with regard to God. So do not overstep and do not extend analogically, but apply the phrase and the concept in the context in which the Lawgiver applied it.

Messenger of God ﷺ said to the black woman who had been slapped by her master, 'Where is God?' She pointed to the sky; and he accepted her pointing and he said, 'Release her, because she is a believer (mu'minah).'

> *In Musnad ibn Ḥanbal, a man from a people 'recently in the period of ignorance' asked the Prophet ﷺ about certain issues, the last of which he described as follows: 'I had a female slave who watches over my flock, in front of Uḥud and Jawānīyah, and I came upon her one day when a wolf had left with a sheep from her flock. I am a man who is a child of Adam, getting angry as they get angry, and I gave her a slap. I came to the Prophet, and it had become a distressing matter to me, so I asked, "O Messenger of God, should I not free her?" He said, "Bring her to me." I brought her to him and he said to her, "Where is God?"' Continuing with another version of this ḥadīth, from Abū Dāwud: 'He said to her, "Where is God?" She pointed to the sky with her finger. He said to her, "And who am I?" She pointed to the Prophet and to the sky, meaning, "You are a messenger of God."' The Prophet declared her one of the faithful (a mu'minah) and she was freed.*

The one being asked about 'where' is the most knowledgeable of the people of God, and he is a messenger of God ﷺ.

But some of the superficial 'ulamā' interpret her pointing toward the sky - and the acceptance of the Prophet ﷺ of such from her - as being because the god that had been worshiped was on the Earth. This is an interpretation of the ignorant, because of something he does not know; we have learned that the 'arab used to worship a star in the sky called Sirius, a practice made a sunnah for them by Abū Kabshah, believing that the star was a lord of lords. This is how it was spoken of in their conversations. And this is why He said, *He is the Lord of Sirius*. If they had not worshiped a star in the sky, this *al-najm 53:49*
interpretation would have been permitted to this interpreter.

This Abū Kabshah who had begun the worship of Sirius was one of the grandfathers of Messenger of God ﷺ on his mother's side. And this is why the 'arab used to relate Messenger of God ﷺ to him and would say, 'What are you doing, son of Abū Kabshah?' when he started the new worship of one god, just as his grandfather had started the new worship of Sirius.

Among the Pivots of this station who was before us was Muḥammad bin 'Alī al-Tirmidhī al-Ḥakīm, and among our teachers, Abū Madyan - God be kind to him. He was known in the upper world by the name Abū'l-Najā (the Deliverer); the spirit-be-

ings called him that. He used to say, God be pleased with him, 'My
al-mulk 67:1 sūrah of the Qur'an is *Blessed is the One in whose hands is the mulk*.' This is why we are saying about him that he is one of the two leaders (al-imāmayn), because this is the station of the Imām.

mudṭarr: 'compelled, constrained, impelled, to do something, against his will' (Lane)

Then we say that as the True is the answerer of His creature who has been compelled into doing something it is calling to Him about, and asking Him about, it (the creature) becomes like the governor. And this is why Abū Madyan used to give a sign with his statement and say about something, 'mulk ul-mulk'. As for the correctness of this annexation, let the creature verify for itself in every breath that it is a mulk belonging to God without any interpolation into this state of any presumption that would diminish it. Then when the creature is in this position, at this moment it is true that He is a mulk for it. But if there is any wafting pollution coming from presumption, and that is if you claim for yourself that you possess something coming from His Presence - some matter God turned over to you, that you now call a mulk of yours, your possession - then you do not have this position. It is not correct for this person to say about the True that He is a mulk ul-mulk, even though the matter truly is this way. This one has removed himself with his claim that he is unaware of the fact that he is a possession belonging to God and of his neglect (of this fact) during some situation (when he should have been aware) - so he will need a giant mass on the Scale (on the Day of Judgment), the person in this position, his hand never withdrawn, his eyes raised (in fear)!

Link

As for mysteries of sharing between two revelations (Laws), it is
ṭā-hā 20:14 like His word, *Establish the ṣalāt for My dhikr (remembrance)* - and this is the station of the Seal of the Friends, and among the seal's Men today are Khaḍir and Ilyās. It is the affirmation by the second of what was confirmed by the first in the mode in which it was confirmed, despite the differences of the time period, validating the one who came before and the one who came after. The context did not alter, nor the state, so the tasking occurs for the second exactly as it occurred for the first. As the mode which brought them together did not become restricted by time period - and the derivation of it, as well, is not altered with the time period - sharing is possible in the single Law with two individuals. However, the expression differs in its time and language; unless the two articulate in one moment in one language, as did Moses and Aaron, when it
ṭā-hā 20:43 was said to them, *Go, you two, to Pharaoh; he has transgressed.* Despite
ṭā-hā 20:44 all of this, it was said to the two, *But speak to him with a gentle speech*;
al-qaṣaṣ 28:34 so He used the grammatically indefinite in His word, 'a speech', and especially since Moses was saying, *He is better than me in speech*

- that is, Aaron. It could be that the two were different in how they expressed their speech during one session, so they gathered together in one station; and this is being sent out in one time to one person with one message.

Even though a situation like this is denied by this community of my friends and my teachers, such as Abū Ṭālib al-Makkī and whoever argues with his argument, we do make the argument; and I argue for it, and it is authentic according to me because God does not repeat a tajallì to one individual and does not share it to two individuals - given the Divine infinite vastness. In fact, the 'like things' and the 'similar things' are presumed so by the observer and the hearer only because of the similitude of one moment to another, which is difficult to distinguish - except for the people of kashf and the proponents among the theologians who argue that the chance event does not persist over two time periods.

And part of the Divine vastness is where God is the One who *gave each thing its character-creation* and differentiates each thing in *ṭā-hā 20:50* the world with some matter, this matter being the one thing which differentiates it from another; and it is the 1-ness of each thing. Thus, two do not join in a single mix. (If the 1 is removed from 1000, for example, it ceases to exist, and 999 is found instead; what distinguishes the two is the 1.)

Abū'l-'Atāhīyah said,

In every thing there is a sign
indicating that it is one.

And this is nothing but the one-ness of everything.

Two never join together in some way by which there would be differentiation; and if there were a commonality shared between them, there would be no differentiation - but it is differentiated, intellectually and as seen by kashf. Part of this manzil in this chapter is recognizing the large brought to the small, and the wide brought to the narrow, without the wide becoming narrowed or the narrow widening; that is, nothing alters from its status - but not according to the facet which is argued for about this by the people of examination among the theologians and the philosophers, because they argue for their joining together in the definition and in the true dimension, not in the physical body, because one getting larger and another smaller has no effect on the total truth (the combined total volume) of the two. (This was discussed in Chapter 15.)

And also part of this chapter is the statement of Abū Sa'īd al-Kharrāz, 'God is not recognized except by His joining together of two opposites.' Then he recited, *Hu is the First, and the Last, and the* *al-ḥadīd 57:3* *Outward, and the Inward*

Consider the Möbius strip (a non-orientable surface), with one surface (and therefore having an outside which is exactly its inside) and no beginning or end (and therefore having a first which is exactly its last).

- meaning, from a single perspective, not from different relational perspectives as the people of examination among the superficial scholars ('ulamā' al-rusūm) see it.

Learn that certainly there is the descent of Jesus ﷺ and certainly there is his ruling us with the sharī'ah *f* of Muḥammad ﷺ - God revealing her to him, as he is a prophet, because the prophet does not take the Law from other than his messenger. Thus, the angel who is a messenger comes to him giving him information about the Law of Muḥammad, which he ﷺ came with and which was inspired in him as an inspiration. Jesus will not make a determination of things being lawful or forbidden except as it would have been determined by Messenger of God had he been present. When Jesus ﷺ descends (again), the independent judgment (ijtihād) people had to use will be withdrawn. He will rule among us only with the Law that he had in the time of his message and of his turn of worldly authority and what he was knowledgeable about with regard to the Divine revelation which came to him. He is a messenger (rasūl) and a prophet (nabī), and with regard to the Law which Muḥammad ﷺ had, he is a successor to him with it. And he may receive knowledge from the spirit of Muḥammad ﷺ through kashf, since he obtained from him (the rūḥ Muḥammad) what God made Law for him, in that he should rule with his spirit (the rūḥ Muḥammad) in his community, ﷺ. Thus, Jesus ﷺ is a Companion and a Successor from this perspective; and from this perspective he ﷺ is the Seal of the Friends.

One of the panoramic excellences of the Prophet ﷺ is where the Seal of the Friends is in his community as a prophet and an honored messenger - it is Jesus ﷺ and he is the best of this Muḥammadī ummah. Ḥakīm al-Tirmidhī has given information about him in his book Khatm al-awliyā' (Seal of the Friends). He testified to Jesus' excellence over Abū Bakr the Truthful and others, because he (Jesus) - even if he was a friend in this ummah, and in the Muḥammadī millat - he was himself really a prophet and a messenger. Thus, on the Day of Arising he has two gatherings: he gathers with the group of the prophets and the messengers under the banner of the prophecy and the message, and his apostles who are his successors - he has successors like the rest of the messengers; and he gathers also with us as a friend in the group of friends in this ummah, under the banner of Muḥammad ﷺ as a Successor to him - in the first place in front of all the friends in the epoch of Adam until the last friend there will be in the world. God has com-

The millat is the particular cultus and local form of the religion.

bined in him the sacred authority of friendship (wilāyah) and the outward, visible prophethood.

None of the messengers on the Day of Arising will have a messenger who follows him except Muḥammad ﷺ, because there will be gathered on the Day of Arising, following him, Jesus and Ilyās, peace be upon them both, even though every one in the halting place from Adam and below him is under his ﷺ banner. Thus, this is his universal banner; but our discussion above about the banner was for the banner specific to his ﷺ community.

And belonging to the Muḥammadī wilāyah specifically with this Law sent down to Muḥammad ﷺ is a special seal. He is at a rank below Jesus عليه السلام in our time; and I saw him, too, and met with him. I saw the sign of seal-hood which was on him. There is no walī after him except he refers to him, just as there is no prophet after Muḥammad ﷺ except he refers to him - like Jesus when he comes down. The relation of each walī who is after this seal until the Day of Arising is the relation of each prophet who will be after Muḥammad ﷺ in prophecy, like Ilyās and Jesus and Khaḍir, in this ummah.

Thus, I have explained to you the station of Jesus عليه السلام when he descends, so say what you like: if you like, say it is sharīʿatayn (dual) belonging to a single entity; and if you like, say a single sharīʿah.

Link

As for the hearts who are impassioned by the breaths: since they are treasure-troves of animal-based (animate, living, ḥaywānīyah) spirit-beings, they are impassioned by the Compassionate breaths - because of a co-relation. Messenger of God ﷺ said, 'A breath of the Compassionate comes to me from Yemen.' Indeed, the animal spirit is a breath; and, indeed, the source of these breaths - according to the hearts passionate for them - is the Supremely Compassionate Breath / which is from Yemen, for the one who is exiled from his land. And his settling and living there is impossible, so in her his grief is relieved and the heavy blows are repelled. And he ﷺ said, 'God has breezes, so open yourselves to the breezes of your Cherisher.'

The manāzil of these breaths end at the number 330 breaths, in each manzil of her manāzil which is her sum-total, the product of multiplying 330 by 330. Thus, what comes out as the product is the number of breaths which are with the True from His name the Compassionate in the human world. And what I have verified is that she has manāzil exceeding this measure by 200 manāzil in the presence of the fahwānīyah (where the Divine address occurs in the barzakh realm, face to face) alone; so when you multiply 330 by 530, what comes out as the product after the multiplication is the number of breaths of compassion in the human being world, each breath of hers a distinct Divine knowledge - from a Divine tajallī specific to these manāzil, not belonging to any but them. Thus, whoever smells the waft of these breaths recognizes their measure.

I did not see anyone who was one of her people being someone recognized among the people. Most of them are from the country of Andalusia, and I met one of them in the Holy House in Jerusalem and in Makkah. I asked him one day about the issue. He had asked me, 'Do you smell things?' - and I knew that he was one of the people of this station. He assisted me for a time. And I had an uncle, a brother of my father, his full brother - his name was 'Abd-Allāh bin Muḥammad bin al-'Arabī - who had this station physically and in the meaning dimension. I saw this myself in him before I had come back to this path, during the time period of my ignorance.

al-aḥzāb 33:4

And God speaks the true,
and Hu is the guide to the way.

وَاللَّهُ يَقُولُ الْحَقَّ وَهُوَ يَهْدِي السَّبِيلَ

Chapter 25

The Peg

On ma'rifah of the Peg (cardinal direction, four directions around a central pivot) singled out, of lengthened age. And mysteries of the Pivots who are differentiated into four kinds among the people. A secret of the alighting place and the alighting places, and who enters it (the secret) among the people.

The Peg

Chapter 25

Events have a defining limit and
a place of ascension,
after an exoteric and an esoteric
meaning come together.

The 'four kinds of knowledge' are based on a ḥadīth: 'There is in fact no verse but she has an (outward) exoteric, and an (inward) esoteric, and a limit, and a place to ascend to.'

In the 'ayn (entity) of the 1 m is
a secret no one knows;
only step-levels manifold - he makes them happen.

He is the one who brings out the numbers, all
of them,
while he is the one who has no place in the counting.

His circle arena is narrow, wide; thus, his form
is like
a gazer in differently configured mirrors
at the moment when he is figured.

circle arena: the space inside which a trainer at the center holds the tether of a running horse, thereby marking a circumference. It is narrow when vertical, wide when recumbent (when the alif lies down to become a bā'). Notice that the alif upright is a pivot around which beings may turn.

He does not try to gain abundance
when his step-levels are
granted it; he is prevented by transcendence.

In this way is the True, if you have confirmed His
form f
with Himself and with You (pl.); she
exalts herself and she lowers herself.

إعلم

Learn, sincere friend, may God assist you, that this watad (Peg) is Khaḍir, the companion of Moses ﷺ, whose life span God has extended to today. I had seen someone who saw him, and with regard to his true standing a strange affair happened to me - and it was with my teacher Abū'l-'Abbās al-'Uraybī, God be kind to him. Some disagreement circulated between me and him concerning an individual whose joyously awaited appearance had been announced by Messenger of God ﷺ He said to me, 'He is so-and-so, son of so-and-so' - and he named for me someone I knew by name but whom I had not seen, though I had seen the son of his paternal aunt. I was a little hesitant and did not accept his statement - I mean, his statement about him - because I had been 'upon insight' about his situation. But there was no question that the teacher, his color changing to red, suffered inside. I did not realize this, because I was at the beginning of my journey on the path.

Say: This is my way. I call (invite) people to God upon insight, I and whoever follows me ⁂ Yūsuf 12:108

I left him to go to my house and was on the way when I met someone I did not recognize. He greeted me first, with a salām that was caring and concerned. He said to me, 'O Muḥammad, trust your teacher Abū'l-'Abbās about what he said to you about so-and-so.' He named for me the person who was cited by Abū'l-'Abbās al-'Uraybī. I said to him, 'All right.' I knew what he meant. I returned in due time to the teacher to let him know what had happened; but when I reached him, he said to me: 'O Abā 'Abd-Allāh, when I mention something to you that your mind is prevented from accepting, do I need to have Khaḍir intervene and tell you, "Trust so-and-so about what he said to you"? How can this work out well for you, if each time you hear something from me you hesitate?' I said, 'Would that the gate of returning for forgiveness be opened!' He said, 'The acceptance of returning has already happened.' So I learned that this man was Khaḍir; and of course I asked the shaykh about him: was it he? He said, 'Yes, that was Khaḍir.'

Then it happened to me another time. I was in Mursā Tūnis (El Marsa, Tunisia) in the hold of a seaship, and I was seized with a stomach cramp. The boatsmen were sleeping. I stood at the side of the ship and kept staring out to sea.

Ibn al-'Arabī uses the word which in another morphological form is muṭṭala', 'place of ascension'. Note Ibn al-'Arabī's citation sequence in the first line of the poem, which corresponds to 3 ('defining limit'), 4 ('place of ascension'), after 1 ('exoteric'), 2 ('esoteric'). The first encounter has a ḥadd, a definition, in that his teacher defined the person as Khaḍir. Now we have the place of ascension.

I saw an individual far away, illuminated by the Moon - it was a full Moon night. He kept approaching on the face of the water until he reached me. He stood with me and lifted one foot, standing on the other. I saw the sole untouched by wetness. Then he stood on it and lifted the other, and it was like that too. Then he spoke to me in a language he had; then he gave salām and departed, going toward Minārah (Mnara), a cove on the seashore, by a hill - a distance exceeding two miles between me and him. He cut across this distance in two or three steps, and I heard his voice celebrating God behind the lighthouse.

And then I walked to my teacher Jarrāḥ bin Khamīs al-Kinānī, who was one of the leaders of the people stationed at Mursā 'Aydūn. I had come from him the day before this night of mine; and when I arrived at the city, I met an integrated man, and he said to me: 'How was your night last night on the boat with Khaḍir? What did he say to you, and what did you say to him?'

After that time, I left on a journey to the shore of the Mediterranean Sea, and with me was a man who denied that integrated ones could break the fabric of convention to perform miracles. I entered a mosque in ruins, isolated, to pray the ṣalāt al-ẓuhr there, I and my friend. Suddenly a group of travelers from far away also entered into that mosque, intending what we intended - to perform the prayer. Among them was the man who had spoken to me on the sea, the one I was told is Khaḍir. There was also a man of great measure (shukhayṣ), greater than him in stature; and he and I had had a friendly meeting before this. I got up and gave salām to him, and he returned salām to me and was happy to see me. He went in front of us to pray. When we had finished the prayer, the imām went out and I followed. He was going to the gate of the mosque, which was on the western side overlooking the Mediterranean Sea, in a place called Bakkah.

The travelers are munqaṭiʿīn, cut off from everyone else. And note that certain letters in Arabic are 'cut off', because they do not join in ligature to the following letter.

I was going to speak with him (the man of great measure) at the gate of the mosque when suddenly the man (the one about whom was said, 'He is Khaḍir'), having picked up a small mat which had been in the niche of the mosque, spread it in the air a measure higher than seven arm-spans from the Earth. Then he stood in the air on the mat, doing the nāfl (extra) prayers. I said to my friend (the great man), 'Are you seeing this and what he is doing?' He said, 'Go to him and ask him.' So I left my friend waiting and went to him. When he had finished his prayer, I gave him salām and recited a poem to myself:

The lover is distracted from the
air by his inner secret,
loving the One who creates the air and subjugates it.

The intellect ('aql) is like the hobble ('iqāl) binding the camel's legs, allowing one to move enough to forage, but keeping one from wandering off and hurting oneself and others.

The 'ārifūn, their intellects are a hobble,
keeping them from every worldly
thing; they are content, pure.

They are from His Side greatly honored,
but to humanity their states are
unknown and covered over.

He addressed me, 'O you, I only did what you saw me do for the sake of this denier,' and he pointed to my friend who had been denying that the fabric of convention could be broken - he was sitting in the courtyard of the mosque looking at him - 'so he would know that God does as He pleases with whom He pleases.' So I turned back to the denier and I asked him, 'What do you say?' He said, 'After seeing, what is there to be said?' Then I returned to my great friend, where he was waiting for me at the gate of the mosque, and after conversing with him for a time I asked him, 'Who is this man who was praying in the air?' I did not mention to him what had happened to me with him before. He replied to me, 'This is Khaḍir.' Then he became silent, and the group left. We left for Rūṭah, near Cadiz, our intended destination, he somewhere with these integrated ones among the prime isolates. It is in the vicinity of Bushkunṣār on the shore of the Mediterranean Sea. This is what happened to me with this watad, may God benefit us by having seen him! He has some of the knowledge of the Divine Side and some of the compassionate kindness to the world as befits someone at his step-level. And God has spoken highly of him!

On whom We bestowed Kindness from Our Side; and We taught him knowledge from Our Side : al-kahf 18:65

A man among our teachers met Khaḍir, and this was 'Alī bin 'Abd-Allāh bin Jāmi', one of 'Alī al-Mutawakkil's people, and Abū 'Abd-Allāh Qaḍīb al-Bān, who settled in Miqlā outside of Mosul, in his garden. Khaḍir had clothed him with the khirqah (cloak) in the presence of Qaḍīb al-Bān. The shaykh clothed me with the khirqah in the same place where Khaḍir had invested him in his garden, and in the same format, with the state which had flowed through Khaḍir flowing through him during his investiture of me with the khirqah.

I had been invested with the khirqah of Khaḍir in a way far removed from this, from the hand of our friend Taqī'l-Dīn 'Abd al-Raḥmān bin 'Alī bin Maymūn bin Āb al-Tawzarī, and he had been clothed from the hand of Ṣadr al-Dīn, 'Teacher of teachers in the lands of Egypt'. He is Muḥammad bin Ḥamawīh, and his grandfather had been invested with the khirqah from the hand of Khaḍir.

From that time on, I argued for the investiture of the khirqah, and I invested people with it as I saw Khaḍir do; but before, I had not argued for the khirqah as conventionally understood today, because the khirqah with us was rather an expression for mystic conversation, courtesy, and taking on Divine characteristics. This is why you did not see the investiture of the khirqah as a connection with Messenger of God ﷺ, but you saw it as being for mystic conversation and courtesy. It was expressed as the 'clothing of taqwá'. There was a practice among the people of states, when they saw someone among their friends who had a deficiency in some matter and they wanted to perfect him in his state. This shaykh would merge with him; and when he had merged with him, he would take the robe which he had on at that very moment and in that very state and take it off and drape it on the man whose state he wanted to complete; thus, this state would suffuse over him and it would be perfected for him. This is the investiture which was recognized by us and which was transmitted from the ones who verify for themselves, among our teachers.

mystic conversation: in Turkish, sohbet; in Arabic sahbat. 'The libāsu'l-taqwá' al-a'rāf 7:26

In manuscript Q there is 'would verify', and in the margin with another handwriting a mark saying (both merge and would verify are) 'correct'.

So learn that the Men of God are in four ranks: Men who have the outward, Men who have the inward, Men who have the limit, and Men who have the place to ascend to -

> *As in the poem opening the chapter, from the ḥadīth, 'There is in fact no verse but she has an (outward) exoteric, and an (inward) esoteric, and a limit, and a place to ascend to.'*

because when God locked out the lower beings of creation from the gate of prophecy and message, a gate remained for them of understanding directly from God what had been revealed to His Prophet ﷺ in His Majestic Book.

> *Ibn al-'Arabī has described this as the people who go 'to' that place in which the revelation was delivered by Gabriel to the Messenger ﷺ and hear it as if for the first time and as if it were being delivered directly to them.*

And 'Alī bin Abī Ṭālib, God be pleased with him, used to say, 'The revelation has been cut off after Messenger of God ﷺ, and there remains nothing in our hands other than what God nourishes daily: understanding of this Qur'ān.' And our friends have come together in agreement - the people of disclosing kashf - on the validity of a report from the Prophet ﷺ saying about the verse of the Qur'ān, 'There is in fact no verse but she has an (outward) exoteric, and an (inward) esoteric, and a limit, and a place to ascend to.' Belonging to each of these step-levels, there are Men; and for each division of these circlers, there is a quṭb (pivot-point); and around this quṭb an orbit turning for this kashf of the four levels of the Qur'ān.

This is Abū Ṭālib al-Makkī's rizq, which is the daily sustenance and the nourishment of the hearts.

I came upon our teacher Abū Muḥammad 'Abd-Allāh al-Shakkāz, one of the people of Bāghat in Granada, in the year AH 595. He was among the greatest of the ones I met on this path. I did not see anyone like him in ijtihād (self-exertion to decide cases of Law) *al-aḥzāb 33:23* on this path. He told me: 'The Men are four. *Men who are true to what they promised God* - they are the Men of the outward. And *Men who are not diverted by trade or sales from dhikri-'llāh* (the remembrance *[al-nūr 24:37]* of God and the recitation of His names) - they are the Men of the inward, sitting for the majlis in the jalsah (gathering place, court; and the session) with the True in conference. And the Men of the Heights - they are the Men of the limit. God said, *And on the Heights, Men* (who have nothing in them to sway the balance to the Garden *[al-a'rāf 7:46]* or the Fire) - the people of smell and differentiation, released from attributes: they have no attribute. Among them is Abū Yazīd al-Basṭāmī. And Men who, when the True calls them to Him, come to Him on foot; because of the quickness of the response, they take no time to mount an animal to ride. *And announce to the people the ḥajj; they should come to you on foot*. They are the people of the place which is ascended to.' *[al-ḥajj 22:27]*

[Margin: When greeted, 'How are you this morning?' he replied, 'I have neither morning nor night.']

For *muṭṭala'*, Lane cites: 'A place to which one ascends, a place of ascent from a low spot to a place that overlooks.'

The Men of the outward are the ones who have governance over the world of the Mulk and the seen kingdom, and they are the ones who were hinted at by the shaykh Muḥammad bin Qā'id al-Awānī. It is the station which was abandoned by the shaykh, the grand intellect of his time, Abū'l-Su'ūd bin al-Shibl al-Baghdādī, as a courtesy to God. Abū'l-Badr al-Tamāshkī told me, God be kind to him: 'When Muḥammad bin Qā'id al-Awānī' - he was one of the Primes - 'met with this one, Abū'l-Su'ūd, he said, "O Abā'l-Su'ūd, God has divided the kingly possessions of the Mulk between me and you, so why are you not executing your governance over them as I am doing?" Abū'l-Su'ūd responded, "O ibn Qā'id, I grant you my portion. We have left the True to execute all our affairs."' It is His word, *So take Him as an agent*, the executor of affairs; thus, he was complying with the command of God. *[al-muzzammil 73:9]* Abū'l-Badr told me, 'Abū'l-Su'ūd said to me, "I was given the governance of the world fifteen years ago" - from the date of his statement - "and I quit it, and I have not heard anything about it since."'

As for the Men of the inward, they are the ones who have governance in 'the unseen world and the Malakūt', the higher angelic realms. They call down the higher spirits with their inner energies for what they desire. I mean the celestial spirits associated with planets, not the angelic spirits. In fact, this is because of a powerful Divine prohibition necessitated by the station of the angels; God reported about it in a statement of Gabriel عليه السلام to Muḥammad صلى الله عليه وسلم, saying, *We (angels) do not descend but by the command of your Lord*. *[Maryam 19:64]* Whose descent is by a command of his Lord, it has no effect on him specifically, and he will not descend by a direct invocation. Fortunately, the celestial spirits may be invoked by means of Divine names and incense smoke and suchlike, because it is a descent of meaning, which resides in the Malakūt. For the one who sees images, it is image-dimensional (khayālī), residing in the Jabarūt - because the celestial bodies themselves stay in their places in the sky. But for the distant flinging of their rays to the world of 'existence and pollution' (the biological Earth), God has made effects that are familiar to the 'ārifīn similar to having thirst quenched after drinking water, and being filled up after eating, and like seeds growing after the advent of the season of rain and sunshine. They recognize these as a wisdom set down by the Knower, the Wisely Apportioning One, Majestic and Sublime, a wisdom opened for these Men in the inwardness of the Books sent down and in the purified manuscripts and the speech of the people, all of it, and the order of the letters and the nouns from a perspective of their meaning dimension - which are for them only, singled out by the Divine.

Ibn al-'Arabī's examples, such as thirst quenched and seeds growing, are inward matters, and the influence of the celestial bodies is invisible.

As for the Men of the limit, they are the ones who have the governance of the world of fire spirits, the barzakh world, and the Jabarūt, because they are under compulsion (jabr; cf. Jabarūt). Do you see that they are forced (maqhūr, cognate jabr, coerced) under the dominion of the ones with comet tails? - they are a circling group, among them the meteors of piercing light. The Fire spirits are coerced only by their own kind, by comets. With these Men there is an invoking of their spirits and making them present. They are the Men of the Heights, and 'the Heights' is a wall partitioning the Garden and the Fire, a barzakh, *within, compassion throughout, and without, all alongside, torment*. It is a boundary limit between the land of felicity and the land of wretchedness, a land of the people of the vision of the Divine and a land of the veil.

al-ḥadīd 57:13

These Men are the happiest of people in recognizing this wall, and they have a vision of the imaginary line separating every two extremes - as in His word, *Between the two a barzakh they do not breach*; thus, they do not overstep the limits. They are the Men of the Kindness that *vastly encompasses everything*. They have an entrance in every presence, and eyes raised up; and they are the 'ārifīn who recognize those attributes which distinguish each being from another created being, by intellect and by physical perception.

al-Raḥmān 55:20

al-a'rāf 7:156

And as for the Men of the place of ascension, they are the ones who have governance in the Divine names; so they call them down, as God wills - and this is not for anyone else. By them they call down everything under the governance of the three other Men - the Men of limit, of inward, and of outward - and they are the greatest of the Men. They are the malāmīyah. This governance is in their power, but they do not display anything of it. Among them are Abū'l-Su'ūd and others, and they - in being obviously weak and displaying only typical behavior - look just like the general population.

See Chapter 23.

There was with Abū'l-Su'ūd concerning these Men something distinguishing; in fact, he was among their greatest. Abū'l-Badr heard him, according to our mode of transmission 'lip to lip', saying: 'There is among the Men of God one who speaks according to the sudden thought, but he is not actually with the sudden thought - that is, he does not know whose it is, and he does not try to get to know it.' When 'Umar al-Bazzāz and Abū'l-Badr and others described for us the state of this shaykh, we saw it to be flowing along with the states of this elevated category of Men of God. Abū'l-Badr told me, 'He used to recite a verse (of Abū Tammām) a lot; we did not hear anything else from him.' It was this:

He put his foot / firmly in the mire of death
and said to her, 'From beneath your
arch is the Day of Resurrection!'

He used to say, 'What is there but the five prayers and waiting for death?' And underlying this sentence there is a great knowledge. And he used to say, 'Man to God *exalted* is like the bird flying: mouth busy and feet flailing.' This, all of it, is the greatest of states of the Men with God, as the greatest of the Men is the one who puts in each place what is appropriate to it. And the situation of this transitory world is such that it is not possible for you, if you verify for yourself, to apply yourself to anything except what this shaykh cited: the five prayers and waiting for death. And when some man appears in this transitory world applying himself differently, it is clear that he is therefore merely a soul unenlightened - and inescapably so; unless he was commanded to do what came out from him, and they are the messengers and the prophets, peace be upon them. And it may be that some of the inheritors of the prophets (the awliyā') might be told at the moment to do something; but this is a hidden trick God plays, because it is a splitting off from the station of 'ubūdīyah (slavehood) for which humankind was created.

Ibn al-'Arabī is cautioning his friends against 'taking matters into their own hands', because absolute, slave-based passivity ('ubūdīyah) is the true nature of the human being - not rubūbīyah (being a nourisher, a lord, a master).

As for a secret of the manzil and the manāzil, it is the manifestation of the True in tajallī in forms of everything other than Him; and if not for His tajallī to everything, no 'thingness' of anything would come about. He *exalted* said, *Indeed, Our word to a thing,*
al-naḥl 16:40 *when We desire it, We but say to it Be!* - so His word *when We desire it* is

the Divine attending to and facing-toward for bringing about this thing. Then He said, *We but say to it, Be!* Thus, the very listening of this thing to the address of the True is the coming into existence of the thing. It corresponds to the distribution of the 1 to the degrees of the numbers. The numbers appear until no end, with the presence of the 1 in these many degrees. If not for the presence of the 1 there, the entities of the numbers would not appear, and they would have no name. If the 1 appears with his name '1' in this degree (e.g. his name '1' in the degree '5'), the number would not manifest itself. Thus, itself and his name never come together, ever. You count: 2, 3, 4, 5, to infinity - and as soon as a 1 is subtracted from a particular number, the name of that number disappears and its truth disappears. Thus, the 1 in its dhát preserves the being of the numerical entities - and by his name, they become voided.

The '1' is in each number: when it is gone, the number disappears. See Chapter 2.

The count starts with 2 because 1 'is the one who has no place in the counting'.

In this way, when you say, 'the Old,' the New vanishes; and when you say, 'God,' the world vanishes.

See this translator's understanding of Chapter 2 in 'Gut Bacteria and Geometric Algebra' in JMIAS 54, 2013. Ibn al-'Arabī's two examples of 'alif x alif' or '1 x 1' were the following: when God creates the khalīfah, from behind whom He acts, Adam becomes visible and God becomes invisible; and, as in the response to the sneeze of Junayd of 'Praise belongs to God, Cherisher of the worlds,' with the advent of the 'Old' praise, the 'New' worlds become invisible.

And when you empty the world of its safeguarding by God, the world has no being, so it vanishes; but when the safeguarding of God suffuses through the world, the world continues existing. Thus, by His self-manifestation and His tajallì the world continues. On this path are our friends, and it is a prophetic path; and the theologians among the Ashā'irah too are on it - they are the ones who argue for the extinction of the accidentals by themselves, and this is why it is true that the world depends on God for its continuation during every breath, and God continues to be a Creator forever. For others among the people of speculation and examination, this station is not a fact for them. A group among the people of examination who are superficial scholars reported to me that a number of philosophers stumbled upon this truth about creation depending on the Creator for continuation, and I saw it as a school of Ibn al-Sayyid al-Baṭlūsī in the book he authored on this art.

These are the vicissitudes, which are all non-'essential' phenomena.

Manuscript B has a note here: 'A group of the philosophers, specifically Pythagorean, and Plato the Divine; and it is the school of our shaykh Ibn al-Sayyid al-Baṭlūsī, the literary scholar.'

And God speaks the true,
and He is the guide to the way. *al-aḥzāb 33:4*

Recognitions

Ibn al-'Arabī's contemporary, whom we met in Chapter 15, was Ibn Rushd (Averroes), perhaps the greatest intellect to transmit and develop the ideas of the ancient Greek philosophers. The question whether the universe is infinite and uncreated or not was asked by the ancient Greeks, and the debate arises in a strange story told by Cardano (1501-1576), an inventor of the imaginary number i. He writes that he heard his father in the study with two spirits who argued this question: the conclusion was that the world is created per singula momenta: 'Each single moment; in this way God created the world such that if for a moment He desisted, right then the world would perish. For this, he (the spirit) brought out from the Disputations of Averroes certain statements, when at that time the book had not been discovered. He referred, and by name, to some books, some that had been discovered and others still hidden. They were all works of Averroes.' (From De Subtilitate, Book 19)

CHAPTER 26

Pivots of Symbols

On ma'rifah of the Pivots of symbols, and their signaling their secrets and their knowings on the path

Signaling: The imagery of talwīḥāt is the garment held in the hand and waved to signal to a distant friend.
'Abd al-'Azīz's note: Written in the margin, by the handwriting of the Shaykh Ibn al-'Arabī: 'The recitation was performed by al-Ẓahīr Muḥammad to me, and Ibn al-'Arabī wrote it.'

Chapter 26

Indeed, the rumūz is a true indication of
the meaning concealed unseen in the inner hearts.

The worlds have rumūz and symbols
to summon the creatures.

If not for the riddle, the statement would be
a disbelief
and lead the worlds to opposition.

rumūz: riddle, gesture, symbolic language; here, 'signals' (such as a nod of a head, a raised eyebrow)

the riddle: i.e. signals and symbols allow multiple interpretations, according to a person's level, and are not taken literally.

They have reckoned with the
signs, and they spoke of
the pouring out of blood and pollution.

Then how about us, as the command appeared
with no covering to be a sustaining support?

Wretchedness arose in us, here, certainly,
and with the resurrection on the Day of Calling.

'Will you make in her one who will pollute and shed blood?' al-baqarah 2:30

But the Forgiving One raises a cover (the kanaf
shielding the one being judged)
to make us eternally happy, rubbing the
noses of the enemies in the dust.

إعلم

Learn, you sincere friend - may God assist you with a holy spirit and give you understanding - that the rumūz and the symbols are not what is meant themselves; rather, what is meant is what they signal to and what they are a symbol for. Their places in the Qur'ān are all allegoric. The announcement of this is His word, *These parables We presented to the people*. So the parables are what carry the meaning themselves, and they are brought out so that one will understand from them what was 'presented' and what is raised up (an image or process) for its account as a similitude - like His word, *He sends down water from the heavens, so the ravines flow, according to her measure, and the torrent carries away*

al-'ankabūt 29:43

'you heat' - tūqidūna (2nd person plural) in Warsh from Nāfi', and yūqidūna in Ḥafṣ

the foam churned up to the surface; and from that (ore) you heat in the fire for the purpose of making ornaments or utensils, there is a foam like it; in this way, God presents (as metaphor) the true and
al-ra'd 13:17 *the false; and as for the foam, it disappears to no use.* It is taken to
al-isrā' 17:81 be like the false - as He said, *The false has come to naught*. Then He said, *And as for what is benefiting to the people, it abides on the*
al-ra'd 13:17 *Earth*, presented as a similitude with regard to the True. *In this*
al-ra'd 13:17 *way, God presents parables.*

The sense of allegoric above is the Greek metapherein, to carry something across. The i'tibār is a bridge linking two worlds.

The phrase ḍaraba al-mithl is 'strike a likeness', translated here as 'to present a likeness', or similitude, or parable.

al-ḥashr 59:2 He said, *So take heed* ('cross over', a'tabarū), *you who have eyes* to see - meaning, they should consider it anomalous, and they should go across, and they should cross over to what is meant by this announcement. And *verily in that is a warning* ('ibratan, a crossing
Āl-i-'Imrān 3:13 over) *for the ones who have eyes* to see - derived from crossing over the wadi (arroyo), when it is traversed.

And this way is pointing and gesture. He *exalted* said to His prophet Zakariyā, *Give me a sign; He said, your sign is that you shall not*
Āl-i-'Imrān 3:41 *speak to the people for three days except with signals* - that is, with pointing - and this is why she pointed to him in response to *They said,*
Maryam 19:29 *How can we talk to one who is a child in the cradle?* in the story of Mary, as she had made a vow to al-Raḥmān that she would cease talking.

For this knowledge, there are Men great in their stature: among their mysteries, a mystery of timelessness (azal), eternity, state, imagination, vision, intermediaries, and things such as these related to the Divine; and among their knowings, distinguished kinds of knowledge of the letters and the (Divine) names, and the distinguished letters - the composite ones (e.g. alif lām mīm) and the prime ones (e.g. ṣād) - of everything in the world of Nature *f*; she is the unknowable Nature. (The word majhūlah, unknowable, also describes the fourteen letters initiating suwar of the Qur'ān.)

As for knowledge of a mystery of azal, learn that the azal is an expression for the negating of firstness to the One who is so described. It is an attribute of God, given His being a god; and when being first is denied Him given His being a god, then He is what is named by every name He calls Himself, timelessly, given His being a Speaker. So there is

al-'ālim - the Knower
al-ḥayy - the Living
al-murīd - the one who Desires something to *Be!* and it is
al-qādir - the apportioning Measurer
al-samī' - the Hearer

al-baṣīr - the Seer
al-mutakallim - the Speaker
al-khāliq - the Creator
al-bāriyu' - the Creator from no template
al-muṣawwir - the Image-maker
al-malik - the King

He continues ever to be the One named with these names. Firstness is negated from Him by definition, so He hears the one who is heard, and He sees the one who is seen, and so on. The entities of the ones heard are among us; and the ones seen are empty, without being non-existent; but He sees them timelessly, just as He knows them timelessly, and distinguishes them, and separates them - all timelessly. They have no being in the wujūd of self and being; rather, they are stabilized entities in the rank of the enabled.

The stabilized entities are the 'things' in 'When He desires a thing, He but says to it, Be! and it is.' These things have no being until they are 'enabled' by God's wujūd. In the case of letters, they are the skeletal form which awaits being moved (vocalized) in the case of the written form, and breathed (by the breath coming through the mouth) in the case of the oral form.

imkān and mumkin are things that are possible; if they are given being, they have been 'enabled'. The terms will be translated as 'possible' and 'enabled' in this passage. The antonym is 'necessary', as in Necessary Being. It is Necessary Being that gives wujūd to anything 'possible', which, when given wujūd, becomes 'enabled' to be.

The enabled being/ has a timelessness just as she has a state present and forever, but never with Necessary Being in herself - which belongs to God only. Then, in the first temporal iteration she returns as possible, and not impossible; and then in the second temporal iteration she returns as enabled. In fact, just as the Necessary Being based on dhát belonging to God is timeless, in the same way the necessary possible (i.e. the possibility of there being a world which will be enabled is necessary) belonging to the world is timeless. 'God', in His step-levels of His Most Beautiful names, denominates 'grammatical substantives' accompanied by their adjectives.

So the 'ayn of the relation of First to *hu* is the same as the relation of Last, and Outward, and Inward to *hu*. (Hence, *hu is the First, the Last, the Outward, the Inward; and hu is over everything, All-Knowing* ❁ al-ḥadīd 57:3.) One does not say, *hu* is the First with regard to such-and-such, nor Last with regard to such-and-such, because the enabled connected to 'necessary being' in its being and its non-being is to connections which are dependent on His Being. If He brings it out, it stays in its possible, enabled state; and if it is emptied and not going to exist, it stays in its to-be-enabled state - as it could be, but will not be. As no adjective enters into the possible, in its core being, after it had been non-existent, it stays in its possibility - just as there does not enter into the Creator, the one of Necessary Being who will necessarily create His creation of the world, any adjective withdrawing Him from His Necessary Being of Himself. One does not think of the True except in this way, and one does not think of the possible except in this way.

If you understand, you recognize the meaning of New and the meaning of Old. After this, say as you wish.

Next, the firstness of the world and its lastness are an annexed matter (the firstness *of* the world), if it has indeed a last. As for being, the world has an end at every time quantum (zaman fard) - and he does indeed end, according to the masters of kashf; and they are unanimous in calculating based on this - just as the Ashā'irah are unanimous that the happenstance ('araḍ) does not last two time periods.

See Time is not Real: Time in Ibn 'Arabi, and from Parmenides (and Heraclitus) to Julian Barbour, Eric Winkel (MIAS 51:2012). Julian Barbour describes Zeno's paradox this way: the arrow does not move through the air to the target; the arrow that is shot is not the arrow that hits the target. There is no continuation of a single arrow across two time quanta.

So 'first' for the world is in relation to what is created after him, and 'last' for the world is in relation to what is created before him. It is not this way for thinking about God's names First and Last and Outward and Inward - because the world multiplies, but the True is Single, not multiplying. It is not correct that He be First 'with regard to us', because His degree is not comparable to our degree, and our degree does not accept His firstness. If our degree did accept His firstness, the name Firstness would be inconceivable for us. In fact, applied to us would be the name Second to His First; but we are not second to Him - *exalted* is He far beyond that - nor is He first to us. This is why the 'ayn of His first is exactly the 'ayn of His last.

On a non-orientable surface (a Möbius strip), a notch for the start is also the place of the end; the surface which we label 'outward' is the same surface we label 'inward'.

This perception is a rare attainment, impossible to imagine for the one who is not deeply acquainted with the Divine knowings which are given by tajallī and sound observation. To it Abū Sa'īd al-Kharrāz used to point with his statement, 'God is recognized by His combining two opposites.' Then he recited,

هُوَ ٱلۡأَوَّلُ وَٱلۡأٓخِرُ وَٱلظَّٰهِرُ وَٱلۡبَاطِنُ

He is the First, and the Last,
and the Outward, and the Inward. al-ḥadīd 57:3

I have clarified for you a mystery of timelessness and that it is a negating epithet.

As for a mystery of forever, it is the negation of lastness. Just as the enabled is denied lastness in the revelation, with regard to the whole - as the Garden and the Resurrection in her are until no end (and so nothing is last) - similarly, firstness in relation to the ranks of beings in time is intelligible in being. So the world in this Divine allegoric sense is not spoken of as having a first or a last (because from the Divine perspective, there was never a time when at least the idea of creation was not; and there is no end); and in the second allegoric expression, He is First (vis-à-vis x) and Last (vis-à-vis y) with two different relations, in contrast - but absolutely for the True, according to the ones who know God.

As for a mystery of the state, it is continuity, and it does not have first or last. It is the ʿayn of being of every being. I have informed you of some of what the Men of rumūz know about the mysteries, and I have been silent about much - because its topic is vast, and knowledge of the Vision and the barzakh and the Divine relation with this Tribe and their discussion of it is lengthy indeed.

As for their knowings about the letters and the names, learn that the letters have their distinguished ones, and they are in three sets: among them the letters written, vocalized (lafz), and mustaḥḍarah

lafz: put the letters into a word and speak them; also write them - and with writing, vocalization means putting the pronunciations as vowels onto the letters making the words; e.g. we vocalize k t b as kitab, and we speak k t b as kitab.

mustaḥḍarah is the Xth form of 'presence' - so 'calling into the presence of', summoning

- and I mean by 'summoned' (or presented, to the mind), the letters which the human being calls into presence, into one's imagination and into one's imaginal realm, and they take on image form. If the letters 'come into the presence' as writing or as letters vocalized, and there is no other rank, then one does with the summoned letters as one does with the written-down or the vocalized ones.

As for the vocalized letters, they are only names (nouns); and this means 'specially invoked' names. And as for the written, they may not be names.

The people of this knowledge disagree about the information of the single letter, whether it acts verbally and makes a verb or not. I have seen among them one who says no, someone from that group

- and no doubt. When I became involved with them in this kind of expertise, I pointed out their mistake in that which they were propounding, and their hitting the mark, and what they were deficient in with their expression.

Among them some affirmed the verb for the single letter; and these too are like the ones who say no, being both erroneous and correct. I saw among them a group, and I informed them of the places of error and hitting the mark; so they acknowledged as the others acknowledged. I said to the two groups, 'Test what I have informed you about that, based on what I have clarified for you.' So they tested it and they found the matter to be as we had cited it, and they were delighted. And had I not promised myself not to let appear from me any transmission from letters, I would have shown them the wonder of some of it.

Below: The 'single letter' idea recurs later in the Futūḥāt. In Chapter 177, Ibn al-'Arabī writes: 'From here you will learn that the ḥarf al-wāḥid (single letter) has an operation - but only with intention - in the way that shi operates in the 'arab language, with the hearer, that you should "adorn" (yashiya) your clothes. It is a single letter. And, qi, that you "protect" (yaqiya) yourself, in this way; and 'i, that you should attend (ya'iya) to what you are hearing, all with a single letter.'

So learn that the single letter, equally whether it is written or vocalized: when 'that which seeks' the 'operating-on' is stripped from the summoning - in writing or in the vocalizing which is imaginal-based - it does not operate semantically or have an effect.

imaginal-based: grammarians of the old 'arab language spoke of the 'operator' ('āmil) which determines the i'rāb (declension) being explicit ('that in which the tongue has a share') and implicit ('that in which the tongue has no share' - i.e. abstract, ma'awīyah).

For example, the single word qi operates grammatically only if what is intended or sought is for you to adorn your clothes. It has no other grammatical meaning.

If the summoning is simultaneous, it does operate - because then it is composed from a summoning, articulated or written. What was hidden from the two groups was the image form of the summoning being simultaneous with the single letter.

Therefore, if you agree with the summoning simultaneous with the single letter and you see the operating-on, you pay no attention to the summoning and the relations of the operating effect of the single letter. And if you agree with the vocalizing or the writing of a single letter without the summoning, where the letter operates on nothing, then you argue for forbidding it.

Wright gives the examples of ru'ūsun, Dā'ūdu.

But there was not a single one of them who had understood the meaning of summoning, nor of these similarly compounded letters of similitudes, such as two wāws and others. So when we notified them about the example of this, they tested it, and they found it to be correct. But it is a repugnant knowledge, intellectually and according to Law.

There is an aspect described below of conjuring spirits for black magic, for example, and this is repugnant to Islam.

As for the vocalized letters: they have ranks in governing, and some of the letters are more universally governing than others - and than most. The wāw is the most universal of the letters which govern, because the wāw has a power over all the letters; and the hā᾽ is the least of the letters in governing; and whatever letter is between these two letters governs commensurate with its ranking, according to what we established in the book *al-Mabādī wa᾽l-ghāyāt fīmā tataḍammanahu ḥurūf al-mu῾jam min al-῾ajā᾽ib wa᾽l-āyāt* (in Book 1, the title is *al-Mabādī wa᾽l-ghāyāt fīmā taḥwī ῾alayhi ḥurūf al-mu῾jam min al-῾ajā᾽ib wa᾽l-āyāt*; here, The Beginnings and the Ends of What Is Embraced - the Pointed Letters: Wonders and Signs).

The letters of the alphabet, when placed in a circle, start with hā᾽ and end with wāw - i.e. they join to form hu.

This knowledge is called the knowledge of the friends, and by it there come about the entities of the beings. Do you see the notification of the True of this with His word, *Be! and it is*? So existence comes out from the letters, and from here Tirmidhī takes it as a knowledge of the friends. And from here, whoever forbids forbids that one use the single letter - because one sees that, with Divine predestination, He did not bring a single letter for the creative process; rather, He brought three letters (the kun): a letter unseen (*u*) and two letters visible (*k* and *n*), as the existence is 1. And if there is an exceeding of 1, the three letters appear. Thus, these are knowings of these Men mentioned above in this chapter. *al-baqarah 2:117*

Most of the Men use this knowledge for this as a columned list, and they err there and are not correct. I have not perceived whether they do this deliberately so that they will leave the people in blindness about this knowledge, or they are themselves ignorant of it; and the latest thinkers are just flowing along the courses of the earlier ones. And a student of Ja῾far al-Ṣādiq argues for it, as do others.

This is the list of the natures of the letters.

رطب	يبس	برد	حر
د	ج	ب	ا
ح	ز	و	ه
ل	ك	ي	ط

ع	س	ن	م
ر	ق	ص	ف
خ	ث	ت	ش
غ	ظ	ض	ذ
wet	dry	cold	hot
d	j	b	a
ḥ	z	w	h
l	k	y	ṭ
ʿ	s	n	m
r	q	ṣ	f
kh	th	t	sh
gh	ẓ	ḍ	dh

Each letter occurring in the column 'hot' is heating, and what occurs there in the column 'cold' is making cold, and similarly 'dry' and 'wet'; but we do not see this arrangement holding true for each use; rather, it operates by convention, like the conventional assignations of numbers (e.g. for magic squares, the jadāwal al-murabbaʿah).

Learn that these letters do not have these invoking-specialties because they are letters; rather, they have them because they are shapes. So, as they possess shapes, they are special because of their shape. This is why their use differs with the differences in penmanship - because the shapes are different. As for the written (letters), their shapes are sensed by the sight; and when their entities are found, and the spirits of their essential life are accompanying, the specialness is - for this letter - due to its shape and its mounting (composition) with its spirit. In this way, if the shape is composed of two letters or three or more, the shape has another spirit, not the spirit which belongs to the letter singly - because if this spirit disappears and the life of the letter stays with it, the shape will not oversee any but a single spirit; and the spirit of that single letter will pass on to the barzakh with the (rest of the) spirits, because the death of the shape is its disappearance in the deletion. This other shape composed of two letters, or three or whatever it is, is not the same as the first letter, which was not compounded (with others) - just as ʿAmr is not exactly Zayd, even if he is like him.

As for the vocalized letters: they are shaped in the air, and this is why they connect with the hearing according to the form in which the speaker articulates them. When they are shaped in the air, their spirits arise. These letters stay on, the air holding their shape, even though their usage has ended - because their use is rather in the first part of what was shaped in the air. Then, after this, they attach to the rest of the communities; and their preoccupation is the celebration of their Lord and ascending upwards - *to Him mount up the words of purity* - and this is the very shape of the words themselves, with regard to their being a shape, celebrating God. And if the words are

i.e. as the sound-vocalization left the mouth, continuing on, where it may become an echo

fāṭir 35:10

ungrateful ones, then this will revert ingratitude's noxiousness onto her speaker, not onto her; and this is why the Lawgiver said, 'A man may speak a word that displeases God not thinking anything will come of it, but he will be thrown by it into the Fire seventy seasons.' So the punishment is made for the one who vocalized her on the occasion but does not become involved with her.

So this word of God glorifies and declares majestic and makes wholly apart the written book in the copy of the Qur'ān (the muṣḥaf), recited with a perspective of closeness to God, while in it is everything the (non-Muslim) Jews and the Christians said with regard to God - including ingratitude and deprecation. But the words of ingratitude return their noxiousness to their speaker - and there are left the words in their domain, charged on the Day of Arising for Judgment to punish their people (the speakers) or give them good fortune.

These letters of the air, vocalized, are not perceived to have a death after their being in existence, contrary to the written letters. This is because the shape / of the written letter and the written word accepts alteration and disappearance, as it is in a place which accepts this (the transitory world). The vocalized shape is not in a place to accept this (having propagated to the other world). And this is why she has permanence; so the hollow interior (of the horn-shaped barzakh), all of it, is filled with the speech of the world, seen by the people of kashf as erect figures.

And as for the summoned letters: they are permanent. You see, the being of their shapes is in the barzakh, not in the sensory realm, and their action is stronger than the action of the rest of the letters. But when the force of their summoning becomes soundly executed and the summoner of them concentrates them - and there remains no room for any other (letters), and the summoner knows what their specialties are such that he summoned them for this reason - then one sees their effect. This is merely a semblance of the action (verb) coming through himmat (internal effort). Even if one does not know what these letters will provide, still the action will occur in being (reality) - while one has no such knowledge of this. And it is like this for the rest of the shapes of the letters in every rank. About this action by means of the summoned letters, someone expresses it - someone who has no knowledge - as himmat and veracity (where one says 'such-and-such will happen' and it does), but it is not like that! (Summoning is magical, while himmat and veracity are sacred and depend on one's good soul.) Even though himmat is a spirit belonging to the summoned letters, the spirit is not the entity of the summoned letter shape. All of this is a presence generalizing over the letters, all of them, letters vocalized and letters written.

So although you know the distinguishing marks of the shapes

by which the effective action occurs theoretically, for their writer or their speaker - and even though the passive object anchoring it is designated (as written or spoken) - you do not know it. I have seen someone who recited a verse from the Qur'ān and did not have any information about her. He saw a strange effect start to happen, while he was fully cognizant, so he returned to his recitation nearby in the text, so as to observe that effect of some particular verse. He started to recite and observe, and he passed along the verse which had had this effect, and he saw the action; then he skipped over her, and he did not see that effect. Then he returned a few times until he had verified this for himself, and then he singled her out to be this object of influence. He resumed every time he wanted to see this object of influence, following this verse; so then there appeared to him that effect.

It is a panoramic knowledge in itself, except that safety in it is rare. So the best is to leave off pursuing it, because it is part of knowledge that God made specially for Himself and for His friends wholly - even if with some people there is a little but in a way other than that in which the integrated ones obtain it; and this is why the one with it is wretched, not happy. Therefore, God make us among the ones who know God!

al-aḥzāb 33:4

And God speaks the true,
and He is the guide to the way.

وَاللَّهُ يَقُولُ الْحَقَّ وَهُوَ يَهْدِي السَّبِيلَ

Chapter 27

Come Connect

On ma'rifah of the Pivots of 'Come connect, I intend your being connected to Me' - it is from an alighting place of the light world.

Chapter 27

If not for the nūr (light), the eyes would not connect
with the ʿayn (entity) of the things
sighted, nor would they see them.

If not for the ḥaqq (True), intelligences would
not connect
with the entities (aʿyān) of the affairs
so as to perceive them.

If strong minds are asked about substantives
with differences enumerated, they will deny them;

And they will say, 'We do not know anything but
a dhát ﷻ
extended to dhāwāt (word particles, and pl. of
dhát) of creation; She makes them emerge visibly.

She is the meaning and we are Her letters;
so as much as She individuates a
matter, She makes it meaningful.'

Ibn al-ʿArabī has spoken of the letters being the skeletons from which meanings arise.

إعلم

Learn, sincere friend - may God fill you with His grace - that God says in His Majestic Book, *soon will God bring out a people whom He loves, and they will love Him*; so His love for them precedes their love for Him. al-māʾidah 5:54 And He said, *I respond to the call of the caller when he calls Me, so let them indeed respond (yastajībū) to Me*. Thus, He preceded His al-baqarah 2:186 answer to us when we call Him over our answer to Him when He calls us. He made the isṭijābah (-type answering, grammatically intensified; yasṭajībū, 'indeed respond') for the creatures because it is more intense than the ijābah (-type answering) - because there is nothing stopping Him exalted beyond from answering. There is no semantic benefit from intensification, but the human being has obstacles preventing one from answering what God has called one to. They are delusion, the lower self, satan, and the transitory world; so this is why one is ordered with isṭijābah ('so let them indeed respond to Me'), because the tenth form (isṭijābah) is stronger in semantics than the fourth form (ijābah). And where is 'extraction' (istikhrāj) compared with 'removing' (ikhrāj)? This is why existence seeks from God help in its actions, but it is impossible for God that He would ask for help from the creation. His *exalted* saying, as a teaching for us, that we should say, *And to You alone do we ask for help*, is part of this chapter. This is why it was said in this chapter, 'Come connect, I intend your being connected to Me' - thus the will to have this be, on His part, precedes. He said, 'Come connect'. When you make the effort to connect, then this is His connection itself through you, and this is why He made her an intention, not a doing.

al-fātiḥah 1:5

Messenger of God ﷺ said, 'God says, "Who approaches Me a hand-span, I approach it an arm-span."' This is a closeness specifically referring to what you approach Him with - for example, actions and states - because the universal closeness is His word, *And We are closer to him than the jugular vein.* ❁ *We are closer to him than you, but you see not.* He makes intervals for closeness to be by the arm-span, because the arm-span is a multiple of the hand-span.

qāf 50:16
al-wāqi'ah 56:85

Lane cites the Miṣbāḥ of al-Fayūmī: 'The dhirā' is divided into six qabaḍāt, hand-fists. The "king's" dhirā', as we saw, may vary: in the Miṣbāḥ, it is seven hand-fists.'

That is, his word 'come connect' is closeness; then there is 'approach Him a hand-span'. Then it becomes clear to you that you do not approach Him except by Him, because had He not called you and clarified for you the path of approach, and taken you by the forelock to the approach, it would not have been possible for you to learn the way by which you would approach - how the way is.

Universally, God is near, as in the cited references, but in a special way - that is, on our part, we are not necessarily near. As explained elsewhere, distinguishing qurba from qarab, the distance from the True to His creation is one; the distance from us to Him varies. This opens a non-metric space, where d(A,B) is not equal to d(B,A).

And if you did recognize the way, you would not have any strength or might to pursue it except by Him - that is, lā ḥawla wa lā quwwata illā bi'llāh (no power and no might but by God).

As nearing comes through journeying and traveling to Him, one of His attributes is Light, in order to guide us to the path - just as He *exalted* said, *He made for you the stars, for you to be guided by them through the light-blocking places of land* - and land is the outward journey, traveling with actions and deeds based on the body - *and sea* - and sea is the inward journey in the meaning dimension, traveling with actions based on the soul. With the people of this topic, their recognitions (sg. ma'rifah) have been acquired - they have not been gifted - and they eat 'from under their feet' - that is,

al-an'ām 6:97

from their working to acquire these recognitions and their struggling (cf. ijtihād) to achieve them.

Ibn al-'Arabī also refers to this imagery in Chapter 71: "'If they had stood with the Torah and the Anjīl, and what was sent down to them from their Lord, they would have eaten from above themselves and from under their feet" ۞ al-mā'idah 5:66 - the "above" being the gifted, such as manna, and the "from under their feet" being the acquired.' Note how for Ibn al-'Arabī even knowledge which is 'acquired' and achieved through one's own efforts (ijtihād) comes from the grace of God.

But if not for the True desiring them to achieve this, He would not have made them take the right course; and He would not have made them work - when the time came that He drove away others, not them (not those with ma'rifah) - with the idea (of acquiring; 'acquiring', using the secondary causes, is fraught with danger, as noted in the verse, *corruption has appeared in the land and sea because of what the hands of the people have acquired* ۞ al-Rūm 30:41); but He called them (those with ma'rifah) with the imperative (*Travel through the Earth* ۞ al-Rūm 30:42). Thus, He prevented the others (those driven away) from connecting, by His preventing them from employing the ropes (secondary causes) which He made to be a path for connection based on the near Presence. And this is why He gave good tidings to the ones (with ma'rifah), saying, 'Come connect, I intend your being connected to Me.' Thus, (Divine) grace preceded for them, so they journeyed.

They are the ones God commanded to wear two shoes (ni'alayn) during the ṣalāt (prayer) - as the settled one does not wear shoes, rather they are put on for walking with them. This indicates that the one praying is walking in one's ṣalāt and speaking intimately with one's Cherisher in the verses with which one is conversing with Him, manzil by manzil; each verse is a manzil and a condition. He said to them, *O you children of Adam, put on your beautiful adornment at each mosque.* A Companion said, 'With this verse com- *al-a'rāf 7:31*
ing down, we were being told to do the prayer wearing two shoes.' This was a notification from God to the one praying that you are walking along the manāzil you are reciting in your ṣalāt from the suwar (of the Qur'ān), as the suwar are also the manāzil linguistically. Al-Nābighat said:

Do you see that God gives you an elevated sūrah ʃ?
Below her you will see every king
blown about here and there?

You are a Sun, and the kings are planets;
when she rises, none of the planets can be seen.

He means, manzilah.

Lane cites sūrah as 'any degree (manzilah) (floor level) of a structure'. Ibn al-'Arabī is introducing the idea that a sūrah of the Qur'ān is a map of the terrain; later, the imagery will emerge wherein an atlas - a collection of maps - is the jam', another name for the Qur'ān. In al-Rāghib's (d. 1109) dictionary of the Qur'ān: 'The sūrah is the elevated manzilah (floor level), as the poet says: "Do you see that God gives you an elevated sūrah - Below her you will see every king blown about here and there?" And the suwar (pl.) of cities, their encircling which encompasses them; the sūrah of the Qur'ān is likened to them, given their having a circling by which the suwar surround the city.'

ṭā-hā 20:12 It was said to Moses عليه السلام, *Take off your sandals* - that is, 'you have come to the house' - because he is speaking to God without an intermediating connector to His word, with no translator. And this is why He gives it grammatical stress, for our recognition, with the verbal noun (maṣdar, here 'a speech', in this next Qur'ānic verse) - so He said, *And to Moses God spoke with a speech.*

from al-nisā' 4:7, kallama taklīman

One who comes to the house removes his shoes. And the rank of the one praying becomes clear with 'the two shoes', as does the meaning of munājah (intimate conversation with God) in the ṣalāt. It is not the meaning of 'speech' that came to Moses عليه السلام, because He said about the one praying, 'One converses' - and conversation is an act performed by two; so it is certainly part of wearing 'two shoes', as the one praying switches back and forth between two truths. And switching back and forth between two matters produces a walk between them in meaning, pointing to the phrase 'wearing two shoes' and pointing to the word of God the Prophet صلى الله عليه وسلم translated as: 'I have divided the prayer between Me and My creature in two halves. One half of her is for Me, and one half of her is for My creature; so for My creature is what the creature asks for.' Then he said the creatures say *al-ḥamdulillāhi rabbi'l-'ālamīn* - heard by your Creator, the One you are conversing with.

al-fātiḥah 1:2 - All praise belongs to God, Cherisher of the worlds.

Then the creature in this ḥadīth qudsī moves from the manzil of its saying something to the manzil of its hearing something, so you will hear what the True is responding with to your speaking. This is the journey, and this is why you wear your shoes to travel with them along the path which is between these two manzilayn (the dual; here, saying and hearing). When you move to the manzil of hearing, you hear the True saying to you, 'My creature has praised Me'. Then you move from the manzil of hearing to the manzil of saying, and you say, *al-Raḥmāni'r-raḥīm*. When you are finished your movement toward the manzil of your hearing, when you reach your house, the True hears and says to you, 'My creature has celebrated Me'. You continue to switch back and forth with speaking in your conversation.

al-fātiḥah 1:3

Then there is another journey from the state of one's standing in the prayer to the state of one's rukūʿ (bowing), so you journey from an attribute of self-standing toward an attribute of greatness.

The first is the standing up of the qayyūm and the alif, and second is the bowing down as an ʿaẓamah, because you say in rukūʿ, subḥān rabbī al-ʿaẓīm wa bi-ḥamdih.

Then you rise - and it is your journey from a station of greatness to a station of substitution; you say, samiʿa Allāhu li-man ḥamidah ('God hears the one who praises Him' - said when rising from rukūʿ back to standing). The Prophet ﷺ said, 'God said on the tongue of His creature, "God hears the one who praises Him."' Then they say, Rabbanā, la-ka 'l-ḥamd ('Our Cherisher! To You belongs the praise'). This is why we take the rising from rukūʿ to be a substitution for the True and a return to self-standing. Then when one goes into sajdah, the 'greatness' (ʿaẓamah) is inserted into Divine rising beyond (ʿalā); so you say in sajdah, Subḥān rabbī al-ʿalā wa bi-ḥamdih ('Exalted beyond is my Cherisher, the Elevated, and I do so by His praise'), because the sajdah is the opposite of the elevated. Therefore, elevation belongs purely to God. Then you raise your head from the sajdah and istawā (settle, sit) seated, and it is His word, *al-Raḥmān ʿalā 'l-ʿarshi 'stawā (The Supremely Compassionate, settled on the Throne).* Then you say, rabbi 'ghfir lī wa 'rḥamnī wa 'hdinī wa 'rzuqnī wa 'jburnī wa 'ʿāfinī wa 'ʿfu ʿannī ('My Cherisher, forgive me, be kind to me, guide me, sustain me, heal me, make me well, and overlook my faults').

The substitute is the creature on whose tongue God says what He says.

ṭā-hā 20:5

All of these are manāzil and watering-hole stops which are performed during the prayer; you are a journeyer from state to state. So one whose state is journeying, forever: how would one not be told, 'Wear your shoes!'? - that is, seek help in your journey in the form of the Book and the Sunnah; they (the Book and the Sunnah) are the adornment of every mosque; of the states of the prayer, and what happens in her, such as the speech of God; and of what one embarks on there, such as ambiguity (experienced while reciting) obscure verses, like a road twisting and turning; and of the fact that during the prayer human beings have God in their prayer niche - therefore, they find *hu*. So all of this corresponds to the thorns and scree on the path, and especially the path of what we are obligated to do. Therefore, one is commanded to wear the two shoes to protect oneself with taqwá with them against what we cited, anything which would harm the feet of the traveler - the two which are, here, being expressed as one's outward (actions performed) and one's inward (states experienced); and this is why we take the two to be the Book and the Sunnah.

As for the shoes of Moses 🕊, they are not these ones - because He, his Lord, said to him, *Take off your sandals, because you are in a* *ṭā-hā* 20:12 *holy valley.* We have been told that the two shoes were made from a donkey's carcass, so combined in them are three things: The first, the hide; it is the 'outward of the matter' - that is, do not stop with the outward for every state inwardly experienced. The second, idiocy - because it is related to the donkey. And the third, its being a carcass, not killed ritually. 'Death' - it died and the hide was used - is ignorance. If you are a carcass, you do not understand what you are saying nor what is said to you; and the 'one in intimate conversation' in the prayer necessarily has the description of understanding what one is saying and what is said to one - and you necessarily become alive of heart, understanding the topics of the speech, immersed in the meanings which are sought from the conversation about them. When you finish your prayer, you give salām (the greeting of peace) to whoever is present, with the greeting of the one arriving (from a journey) - as you are someone who is arriving from being with their Cherisher back to the family home with your souvenirs, for which you will be feted.

We have informed you about the secret of wearing the two shoes during the prayer in the outward matter but not with the meaning of them with the family on the path of God among the 'ārifīn. He 🕊 said, 'The prayer is a light,' and the light is what one is guided by. And the noun ṣalāt is taken from the muṣallā;

Lane, 'He followed next after the foremost (in a race, at the goal line). Hence the saying in a tradition of 'Alī: *sabaqa rasūlu-llāh wa ṣallā Abū Bakr wa thallatha 'Umar.* Following up Messenger of God is Abū Bakr and third is 'Umar.'

he is the second who is near to the foremost of the race, and this is why this topic is translated by 'connecting union' (as in a horse approaching the foremost horse), and one makes it part of the world of Light (as the way to connection requires a guiding light).

For the family of this vision, there is a light of taking off the two shoes and a light of wearing the two shoes; and they are the Muḥammadī-Mūsawī (Muḥammadan and Mosaic) family, directly spoken with from the willow tree, with a language of light like the lamp-niche. It is a visible light, extending the light of the inside invisible olive oil, made from a 'tree of blessed olives', along a middle line, free from directional bias - as the speech to Moses 🕊 came 'from' the tree, but not directionally.

Chapter 27

God is the Light of the heavens and the Earth; the like of His Light is like the niche, within her a lamp; a lamp enclosed in glass; the glass as if she were a brilliant star, lit from a tree blessed, an olive, neither of the East nor of the West, whose oil is well-nigh luminous, as though fire scarcely touched it ❁ al-nūr 24:35.

ٱللَّهُ نُورُ ٱلسَّمَٰوَٰتِ وَٱلْأَرْضِ مَثَلُ نُورِهِۦ كَمِشْكَوٰةٍ فِيهَا
مِصْبَاحٌ ٱلْمِصْبَاحُ فِى زُجَاجَةٍ ٱلزُّجَاجَةُ كَأَنَّهَا كَوْكَبٌ
دُرِّىٌّ يُوقَدُ مِن شَجَرَةٍ مُّبَٰرَكَةٍ زَيْتُونَةٍ لَّا شَرْقِيَّةٍ وَلَا
غَرْبِيَّةٍ يَكَادُ زَيْتُهَا يُضِىٓءُ وَلَوْ لَمْ تَمْسَسْهُ نَارٌ نُّورٌ عَلَىٰ
نُورٍ يَهْدِى ٱللَّهُ لِنُورِهِۦ مَن يَشَآءُ وَيَضْرِبُ ٱللَّهُ ٱلْأَمْثَٰلَ
لِلنَّاسِ وَٱللَّهُ بِكُلِّ شَىْءٍ عَلِيمٌ ٣٥

It is a Light upon Light - that is, a Light 'from' a Light. The substitution of the letters 'from' by 'upon' is for understanding it contextually. And it may be that 'upon' should be part of its subject, because the light of the visible lampshade is elevated, physically, over ('alā, 'flush against') the invisible olive oil. It is the extension from the invisible to the lamp; and if there were not a (fatty) wetness in the oil extending and aiding the lamplight, the lamp would not have this continuously.

In this way, if there were not a wetness in the oil, an extension of taqwá (being mindful of the Divine with regard to one's actions) to the knowledge which the ones who know receive - in His word, *Be aware (have taqwá) of God and He will teach you*, and His word, *If you are aware (have taqwá) of God, He will make for you a Criterion* - then that Divine knowledge would be cut off and not be continuous. The light of the olive oil is inward, inside the olive oil bearing it, flowing out from there as an invisible meaning in one of the foliating rays of the unseen, to keep the light of the niche going.

al-baqarah 2:282
al-anfāl 8:29

To the Pivots of this station belong mysteries: among them, a mystery of extension from one dimension to another; a mystery of nikāḥ; a mystery of limbs; a mystery of jealousy; a mystery of impotence - which is when it does not rise for nikāḥ; a mystery of the circulation of bitter cold; a mystery of the Presence of the True in the mirage (*Their deeds are like the mirage in sandy deserts, which the thirsty man reckons to be water; when he comes to it, he finds nothing, but he finds God there* ❁ al-nūr 24:39); a mystery of the Divine veil; a mystery of the articulate speech of birds and animals; a mystery of maturity; and a mystery of the two friends.

al-aḥzāb 33:4

And God speaks the true,
and Hu is the guide to the way.

وَاللّٰهُ يَقُولُ الْحَقَّ وَهُوَ يَهْدِي السَّبِيلَ

Chapter 28

Do You Not See How?

On ma'rifah of the Pivots of 'Do you not see how?'

Do You Not See How?

Chapter 28

Knowledge of how is an unknown and a known,
but with the Being of the True it
is a characteristic sign.

The outward visibility of existence is a how-
formation; and its inward invisibility is
a knowledge, pointing to the how, so it is hidden.

The strangest thing is that ignorance with regard to
my adjective (quality) -
ignorance of what we humans have - is
actually, in the verification, a known.

Ibn al-ʿArabī uses name, adjective (quality), and verb (action) to describe both grammar and the Divine in the world.

How does he perceive, whose perception
is inability;
how is he ignorant, when ignorance is nothingness?

Inability to perceive is perception. This is Abū Bakr's 'The incapacity of the perceiver to perceive what is to be perceived is perception.'

I become confused about it, and about
my situation; I am not any
but Him, so creation is a wrongdoer
and is itself wronged.

If I say, 'It is I,' He says, 'The "it is" part is I!'
Or if I say, 'It is You,' He says,
'The "it is" is understood.'

So praise is God's; I seek no substitute;
rather the daily provision, by being
measured out, is divided between us.

إعلم

Learn that the questioning matrices are four. They are: whether, which is a question about existence; what, which is a question about the feature which is expressed by what-ness; how, which is a question about the state; and why, which is a question about cause and effect. The people disagree about which of them is correctly used to ask something of the True. They agree about the word 'whether', because it is imaginable that one ask 'whether' of the True; but they disagree about the rest. Among them is someone who forbids, and among them is someone who allows. The ones who forbid - and they are the philosophers, and a group of the Tribe - forbid this intellectually; and among them is one who forbids this based on Law.

As for a form of their forbidding based on intellectual argument, they say that what is sought by 'what' is a question of what-ness, so it is a question of definition; and the True *exalted beyond* has no definition, as definitions are composite mounts of genus and separation into categories, and this is forbidden with regard to the True - because His dhát is non-composite, beyond any matter that would occasion sharing and would then be in genus the same, and beyond any matter that would occasion distinction. There is nothing but God and the creation; and there is no correspondence between God and the world, nor the designer and the designed, nor is there partnership - so there is no genus and no distinction.

The one who allows this intellectually but forbids it based on Law says: 'I do not argue that the definition is composed of genus and separation; rather, I argue that the question is, in its seeking knowledge of the truth of the asked-about object - and certainly everything known or mentioned has some truth which it has itself - the same whether it is based on a truth it shares in common or based on a truth it does not share in common (with other objects). Thus, the question about what is imaginable but does not come from the Law is something we forbid to be questioned with regard to the *al-shūrā 42:11* True - based on His word, *There is nothing like Him*.'

And as for their forbidding the 'how', it is a question starting with 'how' - and it too is divided into two divisions. There is one who argues, 'He *exalted beyond* has no "how", because the state is an intelligible matter additional to His being an essence dhát; and if there arises in His essence an existential matter additional to His essence, it leads to the existence of two necessary existences belonging to the essences of the two timelessly. Proof arises to indicate this to be impossible and that the only Necessary is He in His essence; so "how" is seen to be impossible by the intellect.' And there is one who argues, 'He has a "how", but it is not known; so it is forbidden to ask after, by Law and by intellect, because it departs from the "how"s that are intelligible to us - so we will not know. And He has said, *al-shūrā 42:11* *There is nothing like Him* - meaning, in every thing related to Him compared with what He relates to Himself, saying, "He is according to what was related as an attribute to the True." Even if there occurs a sharing in the phrasing, the meaning will be different.'

As for the question 'why', they forbid it also - because the actions of God are not the effects of something else; and as the effect makes the action necessary, the True would be inserted under an obligator - making obligatory on Him this action, additional over His essence. And others deny absolutely, by Law, the 'why' with regard to His action, where one argues, 'There is no relation to Him except what He related to Himself'; and this is the meaning of my statement 'by Law' - not that there came a forbidding from God against doing everything we mentioned being forbidden by Law (i.e. the forbidding mentioned by these thinkers is not in fact a correct interpretation). All of this is a disordered discourse, not occasioning anything purely separated out as being all correct or all incorrect; it is only so after a great long time sorting. With this we have cited the method of the one who forbids.

And as for the one who allows the question to Him with these inquiries, among the scholars, they are the people of the Law among them. And the reason for their allowing this is where they argue: 'What the Law has confined us to, we confine ourselves to; and what we are obligated to pursue, we pursue - and to be compliant also. And what is not referred to with confinement or obligation is all good: if we like, we speak of it; and if we like, we are silent about it.' And He did not forbid Pharaoh, on the tongue of Moses عليه السلام, from asking him with his question, *And what is the Lord of the worlds?* In fact, he responded with what was appropriate, from that elevated Side. Even if the occasion of the answer was not congruent with the question, this returns to the convention of the one speaking conventionally - that he is not asking except from a composite (sentence containing) 'what'-ness. One agrees that the answer is an athar (a saying handed down as a tradition), not an answer to the one who asks 'what'. This convention does not need to be disputed, so this question is not absolutely forbidden with this wording - as the phrasing is not seeking with itself but is rather seeking what is indicated of meaning which is established. So it is a matter of established convention, and not every group establishes a convention vis-à-vis what the other did. Thus, the disagreement could be in the expression, not in the truth of the matter - and disagreement is expressed only in meaning.

al-shuʿarāʾ 26:23

As for their allowing 'how', it is like their allowing the question 'what'. And they require this with His word, *We shall finish with (and attend exclusively to) you, you weighty ones* - and His words, God has 'an eye', and 'eyes', and 'a hand', and 'in His Hand is the Scale', going up and going down. And this, all of it, is a 'how' - even if there are unknowable concepts, since there is a lack of similarity here.

al-Raḥmān 55:31

As for their allowing the question 'why', it is a question about effect. With regard to His word, *I created the jinn and the ins (humans) only to worship Me* - this 'only to' lām (in li-yaʿbudūni, to worship Me) is the lām of effect and cause, because this comes in the answer of the one questioned with, 'Why did God create the *jinn* and the

al-dhāriyāt 51:56

human being?' Thus, God says to this questioner, 'only to worship Me' - that is, for My worship. Thus, the one who alleges that there is absolute restriction with regard to these expressions: he must give proof. Then, one says to the whole of the legal scholars, who permit and who forbid: 'All of you are arguing, but not hitting the mark. There is nothing you have been arguing for forbidding or for allowing except there is in there some interjected doubt. The best is to halt from decisions of forbidding or allowing.' This is with the mutasharri'īn.

A distinction is made between the ishrāqīn, who are illumined from within and perhaps illiterate, and the mutasharri'īn, who are scripturally and sharī'ah-based.

As for others than the mutasharri'īn, among the wise philosophers: according to them, deep inquiry into this is not allowed unless the Lawgiver allows or obligates it.

As for when there does not come, for deep inquiry into it according to them, any articulation from the Lawgiver - then there is no way to deeply inquire into it actively, according to them, so they halt at the ruling principle; and they do not rule over the one who inquired into it, whether he was accurate or he erred. It is similar for the one who abandons deep inquiry: there is only the ruling principle belonging to the Lawgiver concerning what is permitted to articulate or not to articulate, based on the fact that it is an obedience or a non-obedience. With this, my friend, we have separated out for you the approaches of the people in these questionings.

As for the beneficial knowledge with this, it is that we say: just as He is not like anything - in the same way, things are not like Him. And the intellectual and Law evidence arises to deny likeness and to confirm transcendence, from the path of meaning; and the matter remains to apply only the phrasing to Him which He permits us to apply to Him, in the Qur'ān or on the tongue of His Messenger. As for its application to Him, it is the same whether or not the creature is commanded to do this absolutely; so one's application is an obedience, obligatory, and the speaker of it is rewarded for being obedient - like His word about the takbīrah (saying God is greater) for the ḥajj: Allāhu akbar (God is greater). It is a phrase whose grammatical measure requires a comparison 'greater than', but He does not get compared. And as for what would be preferred, it would be according to what the speaker sought and commensurate with the command of God for it.

If we use the phrase, either we will say Allāhu akbar and the applied meaning will be in ourselves and what we understand it to mean in the convention of the language; or, we will not apply a definition, using it to worship only according to Law as God intended us to do - without having a picture in our minds based on the convention of the language. It would be like the Persian who does not know the Arabic language. He recites the Qur'ān but does not understand its meaning. He gets the reward of recitation. It is the same way with the 'arab, with what is ambiguous in the Qur'ān and Sunnah, reciting or remembering their Lord: worshiping according to the Law as God wishes, without any leaning toward any particular side, specifically - because transcendence and negating similarity are demanded if one halts one's fanciful conjecturing during the recitation of these verses.

Safest and best for the creature is where you refer the knowledge of this to God, to His intent in applying these phrases to Himself - unless God has informed you of something and what the meaning of these phrases is, from a prophet or a friend who is a Speaker (a muḥaddith), inspired 'upon an explanation from one's Lord' in what one was inspired to or made to speak of. They are permitted; no, it is their obligation to believe what is understood from what he reported based on his inspiration or his speech.

And you should learn that the ambiguous verses are actually sent down as a test from God to His creatures. Thus, He worked to bring good counsel to His creatures about this and to stop them from 'obeying the ambiguous' (mutashābih) as laws - that is, one does not apply them legally to anything, because their interpretation is known only to God. And as for those anchored in their stances in knowledge: if they know it, it is from being notified by God, not from their thinking and their efforts. Because the matter is grave, the intellect is too slight to perceive; there is only Divine reporting. Thus, safety is best - and *all praise belongs to God, Cherisher of the worlds.* *al-fātiḥah 1:2*

ٱلْحَمْدُ لِلَّهِ رَبِّ ٱلْعَـٰلَمِينَ

As for His word, *Do you not see*, and the application of the sight to the 'how's: the meaning is self-evidentially the 'how's and not the means (i.e. not what the means are), because the means refer to the intelligible state which has a relation to the One about whom 'how' is asked. It is God; and not a single one has a vision connected to the Divine power pre-determining things as He brought them out. He *exalted* said, *I did not have them witness the creation of the heavens and the Earth.* *Ibrāhīm 14:24* *al-kahf 18:51*

The 'how' above is that which we are commanded to look with, not at (in English, how one is dressed as opposed to the procedure one uses to get dressed). In fact, this is so that we will take it as a warning and an indication to the One who formed it - that is, made it come into being as having a form. It is the form which the created beings have which is formed. (The words 'how' - kayf - and 'form'

al-ghāshīyah 88:17 - kayyafa - are cognates.) He said, *Will you not look at the camel, how (kayfa) she was created?* ❁ *and to the mountains, how they are fixed firmly?*
al-ghāshīyah 88:19 - and others. It is correct only that we observe that they are; thus, we look at them and the manner in which they differ in their forms.

And if what was meant by 'how' was the moment of creation, it would not be said, 'Look at it' - because creation was not yet existent. So we know that the 'how' meant is for us to observe the things; it is not what the one who does not know presumes about it. Do you see that when He wants the observation which is reflection, He places it next to the letters 'at' - and He does not place it together with the phrasal 'how'? He *exalted* said, *Do they not look at the governance of the heavens and the Earth?* - the meaning being that they should reflect upon it so they will recognize they do not operate by themselves, but Someone else operates them. al-a'rāf 7:185

This observation does not require of you the existence of eyes, like the observation which we considered previously. In fact, humankind is addressed to observe that with their reflective faculty, not with their eye. Among the governances is something unseen, and it is not visible. So we are commanded certainly with the participle 'at' to observe the created beings, not God - to demonstrate by this particle that He is not like them. If He were like them, it would be 'permitted' to happen to Him what is 'permitted' to happen to them, inasmuch as they would be similar. This would lead to one of two forbidden things: either He is like them in every respect - and it is impossible, as we mentioned - or He is like them in some respects and not like them in other respects; so then His dhát would be a composite of two matters. Composition in the Essence of the True is impossible; therefore, similarity is impossible.

What is appropriate for this chapter with regard to the discourse is that it is not feasible to bring all this out entirely in a single chapter, as it would slip too fast into imaginations too weak for it - since in here are obscure issues. But we have scattered it throughout the chapters of this book, so turn your attention to it in the chapters of the book - this chapter being the acquaintance of the whole - and especially as long as there has not occurred to you an issue from Divine tajallì. Thus, halt here to learn, and wait; you will find what I have cited to you, based on what is appropriate in this chapter.

The Qur'ān is full of 'how's, because the formations of 'how's are states; and some of the states are essential, based on the essence of the 'how', and some are non-essential. (How one is dressed is a state, non-essentially; and how one is dressed - as a human being donning clothing - is essential.) The essence-based has for her rule the rule of the 'how' - the same. If the 'how' depends on the 'howness' for its 'how', and if it does not depend on the 'howness' for its 'how' - instead its 'how' is exactly its essence, and its essence does not depend on another, because she is she for herself - then its 'how' is the same way. There is no addition to the 'how' - so understand.

And God speaks the true,
and Hu is the guide to the way. al-aḥzāb 33:4

وَاللَّهُ يَقُولُ الْحَقَّ وَهُوَ يَهْدِي السَّبِيلَ

Chapter 29

Ahl al-bayt

On maʿrifah of a mystery of Salmān the Farsī, who was attached to the people of the house, and the Pivots he inherited from, and a maʿrifah of their mysteries

Chapter 29

The slave ('abd) is anchored to the Lord,
and it has no disconnection from Him; you see a
verbal action, a considered measuring out of destiny.

The name Lord is anchored to the name 'lorded over' (the creature).

And the child is even more richly blessed in the
sublime degree.
The Law has emancipated the child
there with knowledge consecrated.

The children watch closely the wealth of the parents;
you see, they are stingy, miserly.

The children yearn to receive their high place on
the ladder -
and wish to see them (the parents)
with the dead, buried.

The slave: his price is based on the wealth of
his master;
he is referenced to him as someone
freely choosing and compelled.

The slave: his measured value is in the renown of
his master -
so he continues to be, by covering over
the celebrity, himself covered up.

Humility accompanies him in himself always -
so he continues to be with each
breath forcibly compelled.

The children themselves are as they are because of
their parents -
honored, proud; thus, they try to
be made dignified, esteemed.

Below: mawlā, from walī and wilāyah; the mawlā is the emancipator or the emancipated; the son of a paternal uncle and so a freedman, called a mawlā 'because he is in the condition of the son of a paternal uncle, being one under the patronage of his emancipator; i.e., whom the emancipator is bound to aid, and whose property he inherits if he dies having no natural or other legal heir' (Lane). And as Indeed, God is my walī, Who sent down the Book; and He gives authority to the integrated ones ۞ al-a'rāf 7:196 - so God is the mawlā of the ones who are faithful (from al-Rāghib).

Recognitions

إعلم

Learn, may God assist you, that we report a ḥadīth from Jaʿfar bin Muḥammad al-Ṣādiq, from his father Muḥammad bin ʿAlī from his father ʿAlī bin al-Ḥusayn from his father al-Ḥusayn bin ʿAlī from his father ʿAlī bin Abī Ṭālib from Messenger of God ﷺ that he said, 'The mawlā of the people is among them.' And Tirmidhī narrated from Messenger of God ﷺ that he said, 'The family of the Qur'ān are the family of God, His specially chosen.' And He said about the specially chosen among His creatures, *Indeed, over My creatures you have no dominion.* And with every creature of the Divine, if there is any one who directs a claim on you, among the created beings, you have diminished your 'ubūdīyah (slavehood) toward God commensurate with the amount of such claim - because this created being will seek its claim, and it has a dominion over you, so you will not be a pure slave utterly for God.

al-ḥijr 15:42

This is the one who returns, among the ones cut off to be alone, to God. They are cut off from the creation, and their attachment is to journeys, the open spaces, and the shorelines, and fleeing from the people, and departing the kingdom of the living - because they want freedom from all beings. I met a great group of them in my traveling days. In the time period when I reached this station, I had dominion over no living thing; in fact, there was no clothing I wore - I wore only what was doffed from someone who then specifically permitted me to use it. And the very moment I acquired something, I dispossessed myself of it immediately, either by giving a gift or by freeing - if it was something to be freed. This came to me because I wanted to verify for myself an 'ubūdīyah specifically for God. I was told, "ubūdīyah is not authentic until not even one will have against you some writ.' I said, 'And neither God, inshā'Allāh.' I was asked, 'Then how is it authentic for you that God not have a writ against you?' I said, 'The writs arise against the deniers who deny in court some claim, not the acknowledgers; and they arise against the people of claims and properties, not against the one who says, "I have no claim owed me nor property owned by me (which would be subject to writ).'"

As Messenger of God ﷺ was a pure slave, God cleansed him and his family (the ahl al-bayt, the family of the house) with a cleansing and removed from them impurity. It is everything that would sully them, because impurity is filth, according to the 'arab. In this way al-Farrā' the grammarian related. He exalted said, *God wants to remove from you impurity, you family of the house, and purify you with purification.* Affixed to them is the pure only, and necessarily so -

al-aḥzāb 33:33

because the one who affixes to them is the one like them, and they do not affix to themselves any except the one who has the property of purity and holiness. This is the testimony from the Prophet ﷺ for Salmān al-Fārsī: having purity and protection from the Divine, and protection from error - such that about him Messenger of God ﷺ said, 'Salmān is a person of the house among us.' And God testified about them having purity and a removal of impurity from them. And since there is only affixed to them purity, and being wholly apart, and they received Divine grace in a stripping away of the annexation (of impurity to them), what do you think about the family of the house themselves? They are the purified; rather, they are purity itself.

This verse indicates that God has put in partnership the family of the house with Messenger of God ﷺ in His statement, *So God may forgive you what came before of your sins and what comes after.* al-fatḥ 48:2 And what wasakh (something becoming dirty by being seldom washed, or 'by want of care') and filth are filthier than sins and wasakh things? God purified His Prophet ﷺ with forgiveness, and it is not a sin as it relates to us. If there did occur some sin of his ﷺ, it would be a sin in form, not in meaning, because the blameworthy does not attach to him from it, with God - nor with us, by Law. If the property of it were that of sin, there would be with it what is with the sin of blameworthiness, and His word would not be true: *to remove from you impurity, you family of the house, and purify you with purification.* al-aḥzāb 33:33

The honored children of Fāṭimah are all included with the family of the house, like Salmān al-Fārsī and others, up to the Day of Arising, with the property of this verse - that is, with forgiveness. They are the specially purified ones by God, and grace is on them because of the honor of Muḥammad - *blessings and peace, and grace of God be upon him*. The property of this honoring does not appear to the family of the house except in the next world, because they are gathering having already been forgiven. And as for this world: the one to whom comes a (punitive legal) sentence, it is carried out on him. He is like the repentant when the judge has finished with him; he has committed adultery, or stolen, or drunk; the punishment is carried out despite the verification of forgiveness, as with Ma'iz and ones like him - but it is not permitted to speak with blame against him.

According to the account, Mā'iz b. Mālik repeatedly came to the Prophet ﷺ to ask him to purify him. Each time the Prophet told him to go away and ask forgiveness of Allāh. On the fourth appearance of Mā'iz, the Prophet investigated further and it was learned that Mā'iz had committed adultery. Mā'iz asked to be stoned to death as a punishment. The Prophet pronounced sentence and the sentence was carried out. Later, the Prophet came to his Companions and said: 'Ask forgiveness for Mā'iz b. Mālik.' They said: 'May Allāh forgive Mā'iz b. Mālik.' Thereupon the Prophet said: 'He has made such a repentance that if that were to be divided among a people, it would have been enough for all of them.'

It is appropriate for every Muslim believing in God and what He sent down to affirm God in His word, *to remove from you impurity,* al-aḥzāb 33:33 *you family of the house, and purify you with purification*; so one believes that anything bad which came about from the family of the house has been overlooked and forgiven them. And it is not appropriate for the Muslim to affix blame to them, and to any vicissitudes agitating one, to one for whom God has testified to his purity and removed impurity from him - but not because of something they did and not because of some previous good deed; no, it is grace that came first to them from God. al-ḥadīd 57:21 *This is a grace of God He gives to whom He pleases, and God is full of grace and majesty.*

If the report that has come about Salmān al-Fārsī is authentic, he has this degree - because if Salmān had been doing something that was hateful to the outward Law, blame would have been attached to him for so doing. And there would have been attached to the family of the house someone who did not have impurity removed from him; but the family of the house had this quality, to the extent it is affixed to them, and they are declared pure by the revealed text; and Salmān was with them - no doubt. I hope for the end result of 'Alī and Salmān to attach to subsequent people with this grace as it attached to the children of al-Ḥasan and al-Ḥusayn, and the mawlā of the family of the house - because the compassionate mercy of God is vast!

My friend (walī)! When the level of a created being with God is of this status, where someone attached to them becomes honored with their honor - and their honoring is not for themselves, rather God is the one who chose them and clothed them in honored robes - then, my friend, how about the one who is affixed to Someone to whom belongs the praise and the majesty, the honored in Himself and in His dhát? Thus, *hu* is the Majestic - *Glory be to hu, and He is exalted* (subḥānahu wa ta'ālā) - so the one annexed to Him, that is, His creatures who are His creatures, they are the ones the creation has no dominion over in the next world. He *exalted* said to Iblīs, My creatures, so He attached them to Him (with 'My'), *Indeed,* al-ḥijr 15:42 *over My creatures you have no dominion* - and you will not find in the Qur'ān creatures attached to Him except they are felicitous, only. The phrase which comes about others than them is 'creatures' - not 'My creatures'. So what do you think for the declared innocent ones, the protected ones among them, the ones who hold to the limits of their master, the ones who stand in his footprints? Their honor is higher and more complete; and these are the Pivots of this station.

Among these Pivots is the inheritor Salmān, honored in the station of the family of the house; and he was, God be kind to him, among the most knowledgeable people concerning what rights God has among His creatures and what rights (to be claimed, such as ḥadd punishment) they have - and the creation has - and he was the most forceful of them in fulfilling them. About this, Messenger ﷺ said, 'If faith were in the Pleiades, men from Persia (Fāris) would (still) attain it' - and he pointed to Salmān al-Fārsī. And the Prophet ﷺ singled out the mention of the Pleiades and not other stars - a startlingly subtle pointing to the seven fixed attributes, because they are seven stars - so understand. The secret of Salmān, who was attached to the family of the house, is what the Prophet ﷺ gave him - that is, paying off his contract; and with this there is a strange legality. He was an emancipated slave of his ﷺ - and 'The mawlā (emancipated slave under protection of a walī) of the people is among them.' All are the mawālin (emancipated slaves under protection of a walī) of the True; and His kind mercy vastly extends over everything - and everything is the slave of *hu*, and the mawlā of *hu*.

And now that I have explained for you the level of the family of the house with God and that it is not appropriate for the Muslim to blame them for what happened with them at all - because God has purified them - so let the one blaming them know the blaming will revert to him. And if they oppressed him (i.e. some of the descendants of the family of the house), then such oppression is an oppression in his presumption, not an oppression in the matter itself - even if the outward Law (punishment) is carried out. Rather, the rule of their oppressing is with us in the matter itself, similar to the decrees occurring against us in our property or self, by drowning or burning or so on - that is, destructive matters. So something is burned down, or one of his dearest dies or is injured in his person; and this, all of it, is part of what does not conform to his wishes. It is not permitted him to blame the destiny of God or His decree; rather, it is appropriate for him to accept it, all of it, with submission and consent. And if one descends from this level, then (at least) with patience; and if one rises from this level, then gratefulness - because in the fold of gratefulness is a blessing from God for the afflicted. And lagging behind what we have mentioned (the descent to patience or the rise to gratefulness), there is no good - because what is behind it is nothing but irritation, resentment, and a lack of contentment, and bad manners toward God.

So in this way it is appropriate that the Muslim accept all that happens to him coming from the family of the house to his property, person, honor, family, and people. One accepts this, all of it, with consent and handing over and patience; and one does not attach blame to them at all. And if there face them rules established by Law, it does not detract from this; rather, it goes as destiny goes. We are forbidden from connecting blame to them, as God has distinguished them from us by what we do not share with them; we have no standing in any case against them.

As for fulfilling the rights laid down by Law - about this, Messenger of God ﷺ took a loan from the Jews. And when they sought him out for their right, he paid them back in the finest way possible - even the Jew who was insolent with him in words, when he said to his Companions who wanted to avenge him, 'Leave him be; indeed, the one who is owed something has a right to strong words.' And he ﷺ said about punishment, 'If Fāṭimah daughter of Muḥammad stole, I would cut off her hand.' Execution of the rules belongs to God, to execute them however He pleases and in whatever way He wishes, as these are the rights of God (and not ours) - and despite this, God does not blame them.

Our discussion now is on our rights, and it is not for us to seek them. We are the ones who may choose: if we like, we take them; and if we like, we leave them. Leaving is best, generally, so how much more so for the family of the house? We are not blaming anyone, so how much more so someone of the family of the house? So we, when we come down from seeking our rights and we forgive them any claim in that which befell us, we have for this with God the great giving hand and the near position (in the Garden).

The Prophet ﷺ did not seek from us, commanded by God, *anything but affection for the ones near of kin*; and in there is a mystery of the close bonds of the womb. (*al-shūrā* 42:23) Whoever does not accept the request of his prophet requesting something which he is able to do, with what face will he meet him tomorrow when he dies? Or in what way could he hope for his intercession? He did not assist his prophet ﷺ when he sought from him some affection for his near relatives - and how much more so for the people of his house? They are the most distinguished of the near relatives. Then he came with the word muwaddah (from wadd, the tent stake), which means a stable love toward the beloved, because the one who is stable in his love in a matter maintains it there in every state. And if you maintain your muwaddah in every state, you will not hold against the family of the house anything which occurred with them to you, something for which you could prosecute them. You give up, with the giving up based on love and choosing (your love for them) over holding anything against them. The real lover says:

Everything the beloved does is beloved.

He (the poet Miḥyār al-Daylamī) used the word maḥabbah (in maḥbūb, the beloved; love is like a seed - ḥabb, same root - not yet grown), so how much more the state of wadūd (cf. wadd, stable affection)? One of the good tidings is the coming of the Divine name al-wadūd (One with stable affection), belonging to God.

Ibn al-ʿArabī describes in Chapter 178 four words for love: maḥabbah (from ḥabb, a seed of love sown); ʿishq (derived from the hyacinth vine, growing and swirling upwards - light-headed intoxication); hawāʾ (sinking like a downdraft; pounded by the pestle in the mortar - a cognate of hawāʾ); and wadūd (stable affection; muwaddah, like the tent peg pounded into the ground, anchored).

There is no idea about its stability except the arrival of its consequence by action in the next world, and in the Fire for every group with what is required by the wisdom of God for them. And another says about the idea:

I love, because of my love for her,
everything black - such that
I love, because of my love for her, blackness in dogs.

And we have for this an idea:

I love, because of my love for
you, all the Abyssinians;
and I am passionate for your name
- the illumined full Moon.

This is ʿAbd-Allāh Badr al-Ḥabashī, Ibn al-ʿArabī's companion for 23 years; in Book 1 (p. 35), 'we were the four Pillars upon which the world's person and the human being stood.'

One is saying, the black dogs are snapping at him, and it makes him love her even more. This is the action of the lover in love whose love does not give him anything (e.g. reward) with God and does not bequeath him anything from God. Is this not exactly true love and stable, fixed affection?

So if your love for God and His Messenger is true, you love the family of the house of Messenger of God ﷺ. And you see everything originating from them with regard to yourself - including that which does not support your nature or your desires - as a beautiful thing, giving good fortune with its occurrence. And you know from that perspective that you have grace from God, who made you love them for His sake, inasmuch as He mentioned you as one who loves Him, and you come to His attention - and they are the family of the house of His Messenger ﷺ. So thank God for this good fortune, because they mention you in pure languages with the purification of God, a purity your knowledge will not fully reach.

If we see you having the opposite of this state with the family of the house, whom you are needy of, and to Messenger of God ﷺ when God guides you by him, how can I be sure of your love - with which you presume that you love me intensely - attending to my rights or my side, when with regard to the people of your prophet you have this stance regarding what occurred to them? By God, that is nothing but a deficiency in your faith, and some trick of God against you, leading you off to somewhere you do not realize.

The form of the trick is that you say and you believe you are protecting the religion of God and His Law, and you say - to seek your right - that you are seeking only what God permits you to seek; but blame is inserted in this prosecution, and hatred and disgust. You prefer yourself over the family of the house, but you do not realize it. The good medicine against this nigh-incurable disease is that you see yourself with them having a right to claim, and you step down from your right so as to insert in your prosecution what we have mentioned to you. You are not one of the judges of the Muslims such that you have been appointed to set up punishment or bring justice to the oppressed or return a right to its people. And if you were a judge - and certainly so - you can ask the one with a right to forgo his right, if the one on trial is one of the family of the house; so, if you refuse - specified against you at that very moment is the execution of the Lawful decision for him. And if, my friend, God lifts the veil off their levels with God in the next world, you would wish that you were one of their mawālin (sg. mawlā, a client; someone under protection). May God inspire our selves with integrity. So consider how honored is the level of Salmān, God be pleased with all of them!

As we have explained for you the Pivots of this station and that they are creatures chosen of God, most preferred, then learn that theirs are mysteries which God informs us of. The common people are ignorant of them; indeed, most of the elite people are too, who do not have this station; and Khaḍir is among them (the Pivots of this station), God be pleased with them, and he is one of the greatest of them, God be pleased with them; and 'if Moses were alive, he could not help but follow me.' And among their mysteries is what we have already mentioned about the knowledge of the level of the family of the house, and what God has informed us about the elevation of their rank.

And among their mysteries is the knowledge of Divine plotting, where God tricks His creatures with hatred of them (the family) despite their claims of love for Messenger of God ﷺ, and his request for *affection for the ones near of kin*; and he ﷺ is wholly family of the house. But most people do not do what he asked them to, the Messenger of God ﷺ, by command of God; so they disobey God and His Messenger. They love only his near relatives whom they see as being most fine, whose behaviors they love, whose selves they love passionately (meaning, conditional love, not the unconditional love required.) *al-shūrā 42:23*

And among their mysteries is the study of what God made Law for them in this Muḥammadī sharī'ah - where the 'ulamā' are not aware of it, because the legal scholars and the ḥadīth scholars are the ones who take their knowledge 'dead from the dead'.

See the Muqaddimah (Preface. Book 1) for the story where the scholars say 'so-and-so transmitted a ḥadīth from so-and-so.' Someone asks, 'Where is so-and-so?' The answer is, 'He is dead.' Then, 'Where is so-and-so?' The answer is, 'He is dead.' This continues until he says, 'You take your knowledge dead from the dead, but we take our knowledge from the Living (a name of God), who does not die.'

The latter one is upon a preponderance of guessing, as transmission is testimony to someone's reliability, and multiple unbroken chains of transmission are rare. Therefore, when they come across matters giving them knowledge by means of the multiple unbroken chains, this phrase transmitted through multiple unbroken chains is not a key text for what they are ruling on - because the key revealed texts are rare, few. Thus, they take this phrase to the extent of their understanding of it, and this is why they have disagreements. It is possible that there is for this phrase for some matter another key revealed text contradicting it, but it has not reached them; and as long as it has not reached them, they do not worship with it, nor do they recognize which of all the possible facets in the scope of this phrase would be the one Messenger of God ﷺ would have ruled with, making Law. But the family of God take from Messenger of God ﷺ through kashf to disclose the matter of brilliant radiance, and with the obvious revealed text for the ruling - or from God based on clarification which they are upon, from their Lord, and the insight by which they invite creation to God, just as God said, *Is the one who is upon a clarification from one's Lord* .... *Hūd 11:17* And He said, *I call (invite) people to God upon insight, I (Joseph) and whoever follows me*. He did not single himself out with having insight, and *Yūsuf 12:108* he testified for them that they follow in ruling; so they do not follow him except upon insight. They are the 'ibād (slaves) of God, the family of this station.

And among their mysteries too are the people of belief systems hitting the mark in what they believe in about the Divine Side, and what came to them of tajallī such that they would believe this. From where can a contradiction be imagined when there is unanimity on the necessary causes which support it? - because no two disagree about it; rather, the disagreement comes about the cause and why it is called the cause. There is one who argues, 'It is Nature'; and there is one who argues, 'It is eternity'; and there is one who argues, 'It is otherwise.' Each agrees on its affirmation and the necessity of its being. Does this disagreement harm them with this dependency or not? This, all of it, is part of the knowings of the family of this station.

The 17th manuscript ends, followed by the 18th.

At the bottom of the page, there is a samā' (list of names in the audience hearing the written text read aloud). Then, at the end of the list, 'and this is in the tenth of the month of Rabī' al-ākhir, in the year AH 633, in the house of the author, in Damascus; and al-ḥamdulillāh, and His blessings be upon Muḥammad and his āl (synonym ahl, family). With the Prophet ﷺ, āl often means 'his followers, whether relations or others, and his relations, whether followers or not' - and also his wives specifically. And, as we have seen elsewhere in the Futūḥāt, it may include the (tall, towering) figure one sees from a distance, as if in a mirage.

wa'l-ḥamdulillāhi wa ṣalātihi 'alā Muḥammad wa Ālihi

والحمد لله وصلاته على محمد وآله

Chapter 30

The Company of Rider Pivots

On ma'rifah of the first degree and the second degree among the Pivots
who are the composite retinue

The company of mounts and riders (rukbān) are a caravan, and the ḥadīth instructs buyers not to meet the approaching caravans to make purchases before they reach the urban market. Consider, then, that these riders are not to be approached and learned from before, or unless, they bring their knowledge to the community.

The Company of Rider Pivots

Chapter 30

God has creatures who ride
upon swift high-breeds of actions, in the obscure night.

The intentional energies of the lowly rise by them,
before the astounding majesty of
the Prime, who knows all.

An operator in mathematics may be a composite mount, a matrix (rows and columns of numbers) operating on a 'lowly' number to increase its value.

He clothes them and shines brilliantly to them;
He teaches them through cups of the friend.

The one who is full of elevation in lowliness:
indeed, he recognizes the measure of the Great.

With the rank ∫ of New, if you verify her
for yourself,
in fact the New appears in her by the Old.

God has knowings manifold -
in a messenger, and a prophet, and
one who divides shares.

Osman Yahya notes, 'So called because he shares in the Divine inheritance with the prophets and messengers' (III:243).

A dhát delicate, fine - so she is not perceived
by a world of the breaths, breaths of fresh air.

إعلم

Learn, may God assist you, that the noble peoples, in conventional usage, are the composite riders. The poet says: *If only I had against them a people that, when they mounted/They would attack fiercely, a cavalry and a camelry (a company of mounts).*

The cavalry are a company of mounted horsemen, and rukbān is a company of riders mounted on camels. The cavalry in conventional usage is the mounting of riders of the entirety of tribes, 'ajam and 'arab. The dromedary is used only by the 'arab, and the 'arab are the masters of literary language, zeal, and generosity - and since these attributes predominate in this Tribe, we call them the rukbān. Among them is one who rides the nujub (swift, high-bred camels) of stirring, internal energies, and among them is one who rides the swift, high-bred camels of outward operations.

i.e. non-Arab and Arab

This is why we take them to be in two degrees: a first and a second. These are the companions of composition; they are the Primes in this path (because composite numbers are composed of prime numbers). They, God be pleased with them, are in degrees: among them the Pivots, and among them the Imāms, and among them the four Cardinal Pegs, and among them the Alternates, and among them the Headmen (nuqabā'), and among them the Swift Nobles (nujabā'), and among them the people of Rajab (rajabiyūn),

The revered ones of the month of Rajab, the seventh month; also called rajab al-fard, the prime month, because it is a sacred, no-fighting month surrounded by months in which fighting is permitted

and among them the Primes (afrād, sg. fard). There is no group but I have seen some of them and lived with them, in the Western country (Iberia and North Africa), and in the Ḥijāz country, and in the East.

These titles are (singular) quṭb, imām, watad, badal, naqīb, najīb, rajabī, fard. Their numbers are presented in Chapter 73 as 'the family of numbers'. Their letters were presented in Chapter 2 (The Discourse on the Letters: The Terminology).

1 Pivot(s): alif

2 Two Imāms: wāw yā'

4 Cardinal Pegs: alif wāw yā' nūn

7 Alternates: alif wāw yā' nūn tā' kāf hā'

12 nuqabā': based on the Zodiac. Chapter 73: 'They are numbered by the Zodiac orbit - twelve watchtowers.'

8 nujabā': Chapter 73: 'They are the family of the knowing of the eight adjectives - the seven witnessed and the eighth perceived' (the seven adjectives are living, knowing, desiring, powering, seeing, hearing, speaking - in the written name al-Raḥmān: the letter A: knowing; L: desiring; R: powering; Ḥ: speaking; M: hearing; N: seeing; dagger alif: living. Then the eighth adjective is perceived but never visibly seen: it is the hu dhát - corresponding to the primal alif, which emerges only as hamzah).

40 The rajabiyūn are forty in each time period.

This chapter is specifically about the Primes, and they are a Tribe external to the rule of the Pivot - they alone. The Pivot has no governance over them. Among the numbers, they have from 3 to beyond of the primes. They do not have, nor do others than they have, any footing in what is less than the first prime, which is 3.

Prime numbers are positive integers divisible only by themselves and by 1.

Indeed, the 1 basis is the 1 belonging to the dhát of the True; and the 2 belongs to the step-level - and this is the Divine tawḥīd (oneness); and the 3 is the first becoming of existence from God.

The 1 basis is the dhát hu, in the verse qul huwa 'llāhu aḥad (Say: God is One). The 2 comes as soon as there is a view 'back' at the 1. This oneness (tawḥīd; cf. aḥad) is of Divinity, and Divinity implies an object of Divinity (e.g. the Forgiving, the object of forgiveness), so this is the one and only Divine plus the one and only object of Divinity. Then, from 3 comes existence, as in the three letters in kun (Be!).

The Primes in the angelic: they are the guardian angels in the beauty of God and His majesty, the ones external from the subjugating and overseeing dominions (because they are too stunned by Majesty to have any creation-based function), the ones who are inside the world of recording and writing down; they are from the Pen, and the First Intellect, and (down) to subsequent beings. The Primes with the human beings are similar to the guardians among the dominions (as they have been singled out to be only for God - hence their lack of connection with things political). The first of the Primes is 3; but he ﷺ has said, '(The lone rider is subject to Satan, the riding pair is subject to two satans, but) the three make a group' - so the first composite is the 3 and above.

al-thalāthat rakbun, defined as less than a 'company of riders'; once there is a 'group', they have a leader and are safe from Satan.

Here, the numbers placed together to make a composite group commence at 3; the first prime number is also 3. We can say that the 3 is decomposable into 1 and a pair, and that the 3 is divisible only by 1 and itself.

They have of the Divine presences the Presence of Singleness, and in there they are distinguished. They have of the Divine names the Single. And the substance of the incoming thoughts to their hearts is part of the station from which they return to the guardian angels, and this is why their station and what they are granted there are unknowable, resembling what Moses عليه السلام denied to Khaḍir - despite the testimony of God about him given to Moses عليه السلام, and Moses' being informed about him with regard to his level. God attested to Khaḍir, and Khaḍir received a promise from Moses, if Moses wanted to accompany him.

That is, al-kahf 18:70, 'Then follow me, but do not ask me about anything until I speak to you about it.'

Khaḍir knew that Moses عليه السلام did not have the taste of the station which Khaḍir had, just as Khaḍir did not have the taste of what Moses had - that is, knowledge which God had taught him - except that the station of Khaḍir did not give anyone of the creation of God displeasure, based on a special vision he had. The station of Moses and the messengers gives displeasure - with regard to their being messengers commanding something that might cause displeasure (to their communities), not with regard to everything the people saw as extraneous to what they were sent as messengers for (i.e. their characteristics as individuals were fine, but their role as messengers could cause displeasure). The proof of what we are arguing for in this is the statement of Khaḍir to Moses ﷺ, *How can you be patient with what you do not encompass as knowledge?* But if Khaḍir were a prophet, he would not have said to him, *what you do not encompass as knowledge* - and, indeed, what he did was not part of the station of prophecy. He spoke to him in the Primes, each one of the two from his station which he was in.

al-kahf 18:68

As a prime number is divisible only by itself and by 1, so the Primes know themselves and the 1 only. A composite number such as 30, for example, knows 2, 3, 5, 6, 10, and 15 - besides itself and 1.

Then the primes 7 and 13, for example, share no factors except 1 - whereas composite mounts share factors: 6 and 30 share 2, 3, and 6, and so on.

Khaḍir said to Moses ﷺ 'Moses, I have knowledge which God taught me and did not teach you; and you have knowledge which God taught you but did not teach me' - so the two differed and were distinct in what they denied having.

But negation is not part of the affair of the Primes; because they have firstness in the matters (the firstness of a 17 is contrasted with the secondness of a 15, which is composed of 3 and 5, where 15 has a first 3 and a first 5); they are denied themselves, but they do not negate others. Junayd said, 'No one will reach the degree of truth until 1,000 truthful ones testify one is a dualist' - and this is where Primes know from God what others do not know.

e.g. none of the composed numbers find themselves equal to primes, so they are denied; but prime numbers are found as factors in composed numbers, so they 'deny no one' who is a composite.

In Chapter 275, Ibn al-'Arabī will describe people of this station. They are like the letter alif who is connected to the previous letter, e.g. hā and alif make ها, but اه (alif and hā) is unconnected. Since they make these connections, these linkages of one to the One, there are people who will truthfully testify to duality surrounding this person.

They are the people of knowledge whom 'Alī bin Abī Ṭālib *God be pleased with him* spoke of when he struck his hand to his chest and sighed: 'Here indeed are knowings manifold; if only I found for them a bearer!' - because he was one of the Primes. This was not heard from another during his time except Abū Hurayrah, who said something similar to this. Bukhārī brings out in his Ṣaḥīḥ from himself that he said, 'I carried from the Prophet ﷺ two sacks; as for the one, I have disseminated it to you; as for the other, if I disseminated it, you would cut this bul'ūm out of me.' The bul'ūm is the course the food takes (the throat). Abū Hurayrah mentioned that he carried it from Messenger of God ﷺ, so there is a transmission (down the throat) without tasting (digesting). Nevertheless, it is knowledge, as it was heard from Messenger of God ﷺ - but we are rather talking about the one who is given understanding itself of the word of God in oneself, and this is knowledge of the Primes.

One of the Primes was 'Abd-Allāh bin al-'Abbās, the 'Ocean', so called because of the vastness of his knowledge; and he used to say about His - *inaccessible and majestic!* - word, *God is the One who created the seven heavens, and of the Earth (seven) like them, sending down between them the command* - 'If I told you its interpretation, *al-ṭalāq 65:12* you would stone me'; and in another narration: 'you would say I am a disbeliever (kāfir).'

'Alī bin al-Ḥusayn bin 'Alī bin Abī Ṭālib, the Ẓayn al-'Ābidīn *upon him blessings and peace* pointed subtly to this kind of knowledge, with his word - and I do not know whether the two are exactly what was said or similar:

O Lord of the core knowledge! If I make it known,
they will say to me, 'You are one of
the ones who worship the idol';

And the Muslim men would consider lawful
spilling my blood,
regarding as ugly what comes to
one beautifully sound.

He notifies with his word 'worship the idol' his intent, considering the interpretation of his ﷺ word, 'God created Adam flush against H/his image,' by taking the pronoun back to God - 'His'; it is one of the possibilities ('his' is another possibility).

By God, my friend, treat me fairly concerning what I am saying to you. There is no doubt that you are with me about everything which is authentic, from Messenger of God ﷺ in the reports, concerning everything by which his Lord is described - such as joy, laughter, wondering at, becoming cheerful toward, angry at, hesitate, dislike, love.

Allāh afraḥu bi-tawbati 'abdi-hi, 'God takes joy in His creature turning to Him in repentance.'

ḍaḥaka Allāhu min rijalayn, 'God laughs at two men; one killed the other and both of them are in the Garden!'

One example is 'ajiba rabbunā 'azza wa jalla min rajulayn, 'Our Lord wonders at two men: One man stirs from his mat and his cover in the midst of his family and people to his prayer (ṣalāt). So our Lord says, "My Angels, look at My creature, stirring from his bed and his mat in the midst of his family and people to his prayer, preferring what is with Me and affectionate to what is with Me." And one man fights in the way of God and the army is defeated, but he knew what would happen with fleeing and what would be with returning (to fight), so he returned until he spilled his blood, preferring what is with Me and affectionate to what is with Me. So God says to His angels, "Look at My creature, returning, preferring what is with Me and afraid of what is with Me (if he fled), until he spilled his blood."'

illā tabashbasha Allāh, 'except God becomes cheerful toward him as the family of the man who is away becomes cheerful when he returns to them'.

man lam yad'u Allāh, ghaḍaba Allāh 'alayhi, 'Who does not call on God, God is angry at him.'

wa mā taraddatu 'an shay'in anā fā'ilu-hu, 'I do not waver to do something that I do as much as I waver to take the soul of a believer who hates death; I hate his being harmed.'

wa idhā kariha liqā'ī, karihtu liqā'ahu, 'If he dislikes meeting Me, I dislike meeting him.'

idhā aḥabba 'abdī liqā'iy aḥbabtu liqā'ahu, 'If My creature loves to meet Me, I love to meet him.'

When you receive descriptions like these, you are required to have faith in them and affirm them. Then, if breezes suddenly waft from this Divine Presence, in a Divine kashf, tajallī, and ta'rīf (becoming Divinely informed of something) to the hearts of the friends - where they recognize by God's informing and the showing with God's vision some of these matters expressed by these phrases which (already) came on the tongue of the Messenger - we have placed faith, you and I, in this, all of it, when there comes something like this to this friend about God. Would you call him a dualist, as Junayd said? Would you say, 'This is ambiguous; this one is a worshiper of idols! How could the True be described with attributes of the creation? The worshipers of idols did nothing more than this' - as 'Alī bin al-Ḥusayn said. Would you fight him or issue a fatwā to kill him, as Ibn 'Abbās ordered?

What did you believe in and trust when you heard this from Messenger of God ﷺ with regard to God, matters which intellectual evidence says are impossible and prevented from being interpreted? The Ash'arī interpret it in ways which make it transcendent, in their presumption, so where is the fairness? Why do you not say, 'Divine power is vast enough to provide this friend what was provided to the Prophet, such as knowledge of mysteries'? In fact, this is not part of the particularities of prophethood, and the Lawgiver does not restrict this subject from his community and does not say anything negative about it; no, he said, 'There are in my community Speakers, and 'Umar is one of them.' So the Prophet ﷺ has firmly established that there are more Speakers than 'Umar who are not prophets and who may speak the like of this - but not about other subjects, because one is excluded from making legal rulings, such as declaring (actions) lawful and unlawful, since doing so - I mean making Law - is one of the particularities of prophethood.

Being given information about things that are obscure in Divine knowledge is not one of the particularities of prophetic Law-making; rather, it flows through all the slaves of God, including a messenger, a friend, a follower, and a third-generation follower. So where is the fairness on your part, my friend? Is this not present with the legal scholars and the people of opinions, the ones who are the pharaohs to the friends and the devils to the creatures of God who are integrated? God says to the one among us who puts into practice what God has made Law for one, that God will teach you and God will take charge of your education, with knowledge that will be the result of your practice. He *exalted* said, *Have taqwá of God and God will teach you; and God is over everything, All-Knowing*; and He said, *If you are aware (have taqwá) of God, He will make for you a Criterion.* *al-baqarah 2:282* *al-anfāl 8:29*

The concept of taqwá can be glossed as 'put into practice deeds that will protect you from God's wrath, being mindful as you do them that God will call you to account.' These Qur'ānic verses, Ibn al-'Arabī is saying, promise education to anyone with this practice and attitude.

One of the Pivots of this station is 'Umar bin al-Khaṭṭāb, and Aḥmad bin Ḥanbal. This is why he ﷺ said about 'Umar bin al-Khaṭṭāb, mentioning what God had given him of power, 'O 'Umar, Satan will not meet you on a mountain pass except he travel along a pass other than your pass.' He is pointing out his ('Umar's) protection from error, a testimony from the one who is himself protected from error. And we have learned that Satan does not travel, ever, toward us except toward falsehood - and falsehood is a pass other than that of 'Umar bin al-Khaṭṭāb. 'Umar traveled only along passes of the True with the revealed text, and he was among the ones whose rebuking from the rebuker God will not listen to, throughout the entirety of his travels - and the attack is actually on the True (al-ḥaqq).

And then as ḥaqq (truth) is a difficult place of far-aiming search, powerfully hard on the souls to carry, they do not carry it and do not receive it; no, they spit it out and reject it. This is why he ﷺ said, '(The truth is weighty) and the True did not omit any friend (ṣadīq) for 'Umar' (to assist him to enjoin what is right and forbid what is wrong ۞ al-ḥajj 22:41).

And he ﷺ testified (ṣadaqa, i.e. to his truth) - meaning, for the outward and the inward. As for the outward, it is (an assisting friend) for a lack of justice, and for people's love of being the head (on top), and for human beings departing from their 'ubūdīyah (slavehood), and being preoccupied with what is not their concern - and a lack of following through with what they are called to do, because of being preoccupied with themselves and their failings and the failings of the people. And as for the inward, the True did not neglect to provide for 'Umar, in his heart, any ṣadīq (friend, assistant): he had no connection, except with God (and not to less-than-excellent people).

Then a huge disaster: when you say to one from this denying group, 'Occupy yourself with yourself!' he says, 'I am standing up to protect the religion of God, jealously guarding it for Him; and jealousy for God's sake is part of the faith' - and statements similar to this - so he will not calm down, and he will not consider whether all this is a likely possibility or not. I mean, it may be that God taught one of His friends, such as Khaḍir, something of what happens in His creation and taught someone knowings from His Side which would be expressed by this sign, which the Messenger ﷺ articulated - as Khaḍir said, *I did not do it from my command.* (*al-kahf 18:82*) The denier believes in it, he presumes, because it came from Messenger of God ﷺ. But, by God, if he is a believer in it, why is he denying such to this friend, when the Law did not deny its reporting from the Side of the True, such as 'settling' on the Throne, 'descending' in the third part of the night, 'being with' you wherever you are, 'laughing', 'joy', 'cheerful with', 'wondering at', and so on? And there is no report coming from him ﷺ at all restricting this from any one of the creatures of God; in fact, he reported from God that He is saying to us, *You have in Messenger of God a fine exemplar.* (*al-aḥzāb 33:21*) So He opened this up for us; and he commended us toward being consoled by taking him ﷺ as an example (ta'āsī; cf. uswatun ḥasanah, the fine exemplar); and he said, *So follow me; God will love you.* (*Āl-i-'Imrān 3:31*) This is the one who follows him and is consoled by taking him as an example.

And (this is the one) who takes him as an example, when there comes to us from the True an incoming truth, and we learn from His Side some knowledge in which is a kindness, given by God to us freely - and a grace where we become, in this, 'upon an explanation from our Lord'; and it is followed by a vision of ours, and it is our following (the example of) his Sunnah and what is made Law for us. We do not insert anything in there, nor do we mount up a contradiction, making lawful what is unlawful or making unlawful what is lawful. We seek with it the known which we know from the Side of the True, (from) the likes of these prophetic expressions; so we will speak them purely from there - and especially when we are asked about some of it, because God reported from one who had this attribute that he called to God *upon insight.* (*Joseph; see Yūsuf 12:108*) And part of the consoling emulation commanded by Messenger of God ﷺ is that we attach to these meanings these prophetic phrases, because if there were expressions of them which were purer and better than them, he ﷺ would have attached them - because he was commanded to give explanations of what was brought down by him to us. And we do not steer toward anything else for any clarification we want - together with verifying that *There is nothing like Him.* (*al-shūrā 42:11*) So, if we steer to another expression, we make claims about it - for example, I am more knowledgeable with regard to God and more clear from ascribing attributes falsely than Messenger of God ﷺ. And this is just the worst there can be of bad manners! Then indeed, the meaning, inescapably, may become disordered before the audience, as this phrase, which is at variance with the phrase of the one who is the purest speaker of the people - he is Messenger of God ﷺ - and with the Qur'ān, does not point to this meaning with the force of correspondence; so He made Law for us that we be consoled through emulation of him.

Hidden from this denier - who is covering things up, who comes with the like of this - hidden from view is this, all of it; and it is because of two things, or one of them. If he is knowledgeable, envy arises in him (when a friend receives knowledge from the Divine Side); he *exalted* said, *Envy from their selves.* And if he is ignorant, he is even more ignorant of prophethood. *al-baqarah 2:109*

My friend, at Mount Abī Qabīs in Makkah

Abī Qabīs: where Adam and Eve descended, where Adam was buried, and where the Moon was split

one day I met not more than seventy Men of the Pivots of this station. (The masters of) this degree have no students in their path at all, and none travels along a path of training; but they do counsel, give advice, and spread knowledge - and whoever is fortunate takes from them. Someone said Abū'l-Su'ūd bin al-Shibl (a disciple of al-Jīlī) was part of them, though I did not meet him nor did I see him. But I received a scent of his as a fresh breeze and a breath of attar, and I heard that 'Abd al-Qādir al-Jīlī, who was rightfully the Quṭb of his time, testified for Muḥammad bin Qā'id al-Awānī as being in this station. In this way, it was transmitted to me, and the guarantee is on the transmitter.

Ibn Qā'id assumed that he did not see there in front of him anything but the footsteps of his prophet, but this does not happen except with the Primes of the time; so if he was not one of the Primes, he would certainly be seeing the footsteps of the Quṭb of his time in front of him, in addition to the footsteps of his prophet, if he were a Leader. And if he were a Peg, he would see in front of him three footsteps. If he were an Alternate, he would see four footsteps - and so on in this way - except that he is definitely in a presence of following as a station.

al-makhdaʿ in Andalusia is a short-cut (Corriente, A Dictionary of Andalusī Arabic); also a chamber or bedchamber, which figures later in the 58th question of Tirmidhī in Chapter 73.

If he had not stationed in following presences and had swerved there away from the right side of the road, between the short-cut and the road, then he would not see any footstep in front of him. This is a path of a special face which is from the True to everything in existence. From this special face are disclosed to the friends these knowings which the deniers refuse to acknowledge, by which the friends are accusingly called dualists; and they call them dualists because of it, and they deem them unbelievers - the one who believes it when it comes from the messengers! They are knowings themselves, and they are the ones we have mentioned above (e.g. laughing, wondering, becoming cheerful).

See Chapter 23.

To the people of this station belong the management and governance of the world. The first degree of these leave God's governance to His creation, despite their being able and rightfully charged; they are given the ability - they are not so commanded - but it is by chance (it depends on whether they wish to). They put on the veil and enter the pavilions of the unseen; and they are covered over with the veil of habitual practices, and they adhere to worship and dependence on God. They are the Youths (sg. fatā), vibrant, malāmīyah (the blamed/self-blaming) - the ones concealed, free and clear.

al-muzzammil 73:9

And Abū'l-Suʿūd (al-Shibl) was among them. He was, God be kind to him, one of the ones obeying a command of God in His word, *So take Him as an agent* - and the agent has the governance. So when one is commanded, one obeys the command. This is part of their affair. As for ʿAbd al-Qādir (al-Jīlī), the outwardness of his state was that he was commanded with governance, and this is why it came out in him. This is the estimation for people like him. And as for Muḥammad al-Awānī, he used to say that God gave him governance and he accepted it; so he was governed, but not by command - so he was really being tested. He was deficient in realizing the measure which elevated Abū'l-Suʿūd over him. Abū'l-Suʿūd articulated in the speech of the first degree of the composite Tribe.

A quṭb (pl. aqṭāb) is an axis, a pole.

We call them aqṭāb because of their stability. Since this station - I mean the station of utter worship - revolves around them, I do not mean by their being Pivots that they have a constituency under their command, over whom they are the heads and the Pivots. They are more majestic than that and higher, and there is no leadership in them at all in themselves - because they have verified for themselves their utter 'ubūdīyah, and a Divine command is their priority. What they receive, their adherence is to obeying - because of what they have of verification and also of 'ubūdīyah. They are the ones standing with it in a station of 'ubūdīyah, by obeying the command of their Master; and despite choice and chance, or seeking to reach the station, they do not bring it out - except one who has not verified the 'ubūdīyah upon which one is created.

And so with this, my friend, I have informed you here in this chapter of their stations; and there now remains recognizing their roots, and designating the states of the aqṭāb, who oversee the second degree among them. We shall mention this in what comes here after, God willing.

And God speaks the true, and hu is the guide to the way. *al-aḥzāb 33:4*

And there is no Lord but hu!

CHAPTER 31

The Company of Riders

On ma'rifah of the origins of the composite retinue

Endless time leans convexly on us,
and bends affectionately,
and passes on in its force, and does not slacken.

We are passionate for him, and he sings to us;
perhaps eternity
will stir the rhythm of the song.

We appoint you as judge in ourselves -
so rule, if you like, against us or for us.

The rule is his, and this rule does not
belong to the eternity of us.

The even-numbered is my endless time; and the
one who
turns time so, so does he turn and inflect us.

We rode mounted, seeking the original root,
the one who made public the secret on our side.

We have, on our side, of hu what moves us (such
as a vowel, e.g. kun)
and hu has, on our side, what stills us (and makes
quiescent, like a grammatical stop, e.g. kawn).

The movements of endless time in us testify:
indeed, hu said, to hu belongs whatever is at rest.

wa lahu mā sakana, To hu belongs whatever is at rest, in the night and the day; and hu is the Hearer, the All-Knowing ۞ al-an'ām 6:13. Sakana may be from suknā (to take up an abode) or may be from sukūn (rest, grammatical stop, quiescence). The sense of rest may also be of two contraries, such as night and day; then the sense of the verse is 'all who are at rest and in motion' - meaning, everything.

I am the slave, humble (dhalīl), chosen (mujtabā);
and I am a receptacle shaped out (ḥuqq);
and the true (ḥaqq) is not I.

dhalīl recalls the description of Muḥammad ﷺ as adhillat (gentle and easy) with the faithful (al-mā'idah 5:54), as does mujtabā.

إعلم

Learn, may God assist you, that the root factors on which the company of riders are supported are many - among them, the exemption from accountability for movement when they are made to move; this is why they ride mounted. They are the still, quiescent ones (without vowel) on their riding mounts, made to move by the movement (as a verb) of their riding mounts. (One image is the stillness of the rider atop a racing horse.) They are the ones dividing (cutting) what they are ordered to divide by others than them, not by themselves; so they find rest from what they encounter as difficulties of movement, exempt from the boastful claims they get from moving - so much so that if they were proud of dividing the distant intervals in a short time, this pride would go back to the riding mount by which they divided this interval, not to them. They are exempt, and they do not have boastful claims. Their midday customary speech is lā ḥawla wa lā quwwata illā bi'llāh (there is no power nor might but through God), and their verse is, *You did not throw, when you threw, but God threw* - saying to them, 'You did not divide these intervals when you divided them, but the riding mounts divided them.' So they are the ones borne, and the slave has no (right to) leaping assault (unlike the warrior) except on the authority of his master - therefore, he has humility and inability, shame and weakness, in himself.

In an arithmetic sense and in the sense of 'cutting' a distance

al-anfāl 8:17

When they saw that God had alerted them with His word - *To Him belongs whatever is at rest* - and that He dedicated such a person to Himself, they knew that movement contains a boastful claim and that becoming still and quiescent was not similar to making claims: it negates movement. So they said, 'God has commanded us to divide this interval in the meaning dimension and to pierce transversely these deserts one is destroyed in, because if we ourselves were to divide (cut) them, nothing would keep us safe from being lauded for doing so, in the presence of the union (of the two dimensions)

al-an'ām 6:13

This is the ittiṣal (union) we have identified with the inner wedge product, the 1 x 1 = 1. With the operation, these riders were not safe from praising themselves.

- because our selves are naturally thoughtless and seek to get ahead and love to be proud. And we are some of the deficient people in this station, to the extent that it is appropriate that we honor this greatest Majesty (al-jalāl al-a'ẓam). So let us use a riding mount we may divide with, and if she boasts herself, the boasting is for the riding mount, not for the souls (being borne).'

Therefore, they take from 'no power nor might but through God' swift camels (nujub), as the nujub are the most patient in enduring a lack of water and fodder compared with horses and other animals. And the path makes one thirsty and parched, destroying riding

Lane: The heart, the most excellent, applied to the Qur'ān (e.g. the sūrat al-anfāl), and the swiftest, lightest, applied to camels

mounts there who do not have the rank of the nujub; and this is why they take nujub, apart from other animals which they could ride.

> Below, qaṭ' (cut, divide, cut across) is also grammatically the severing of the natural connection between substantive and adjective. For example, 'I passed Zayd, the generous.' The cut removes the implied words: 'I passed Zayd; he is the generous one.' Here, below, the phrase al-ḥamdulillāh (all praise belongs to God) is highly connected. Ibn al-'Arabī elsewhere reminds us that tasbīḥ is celebrating God with His praise (not our own praising), and so the praise and the object of praise are inexorably linked.

It is not correct that the riding mount divide 'all praise belongs to God' (al-ḥamdulillāh), because this dhikr is one of those distinguished by fusion; nor 'Glory to God' (subḥān Allāh), because it is one of the ones distinguished by tajalli; nor 'No god but God' (lā ilāha illā'llāh), because it is one of the ones distinguished by claims; nor 'God is greater' (Allāhu akbar), because it is one of the ones distinguished by comparisons (greater than, akbar min). Therefore, appointed is 'there is no power nor might but through God,' because it is one of the actions distinguished by doing and by speaking, outwardly and inwardly - because they are commanded to act; and the journey is an action, in heart and in body, meaning dimension and sensory. And this is singled out for 'there is no power nor might but through God,' because by means of power and might, one may say (and one is able to say), 'There is no god but God.' And with power and might we say, 'Glory to God exalted beyond' - and others of the entirety of words and deeds.

And as quiescence is the absence of a moving vowel, and absent void is their root, because of His word, *We created you from before, when you were nothing* - meaning, not existent - so they choose still- *Maryam 19:9*
ness over movement; and this is standing up and being established on the foundational root. He *subḥānahu wa ta'ālā* (Glorified is He, and exalted!) alerted them with His word, *To hu belongs whatever is at rest, in the night and the day*, that the people (creation) hand over the *al-an'ām 6:13*
void to *hu*; but they make claims to *hu* when they have become. Now part of the subject of the truths is where the True divests and strips His creation, in this verse, from attaching to themselves what they claim - by His saying, *To hu belongs whatever is at rest, in the night and the day*; that is, whatever is stabilized ('sakana the thing; *al-an'ām 6:13*
fixing it solidly, stabilizing it' - from the lexicon Tāj al-lughah; and the stabilized entities are in the void); and stability is a real matter, based on intellect (because it is understandable), not entity (because it is not something concrete). No, it is based on relation. *And hu is Hearing, All-Knowing*: Hearing your claims about a relationship *al-an'ām 6:13*
between you and what is properly His, you affiliated what is prop-

erly His to yourselves; All-Knowing that the matter is contrary to what you are claiming.

One of their roots is tawḥīd (oneness) in speaking - by Me one speaks, by Me one hears, by Me one sees ('I become the tongue by which one speaks'); and this station is not reached except from the branches of deeds - and they are the nawāfil (extra, voluntary devotions), because the result of these branches is Divine love ('My creature continues to draw near Me with the nawāfil, until I love him'). Then this love gives something to the creature to gain this quality (of 'and when I love him, I become his hearing by which he hears, and his seeing by which he sees, and his hand by which he grasps, and his foot by which he walks'). Now, this quality becomes a foundational root for this category of devoted slaves, concerning whatever they know and make judgments about, such as the judicial principles of Khaḍir and his knowledge (commanding his responses to the three cases, e.g. building the earthen wall to protect the orphans' wealth). Thus, it is a foundational root earned (by extra devotions) - while it is, for Khaḍir, a root given by Divine grace, coming from the kind mercy (raḥmah) which God gave him (i.e. *They found one of Our slaves, on whom We bestowed raḥmah (Kindness) from Our Side ('indanā); and We taught him knowledge from Our Side (ladunnā)* ۞ al-kahf 18:65). And coming from this raḥmah, Khaḍir obtained this learning which Moses عليه السلام asked him to teach him - some of it. Now if you grasp and understand this matter which I am bringing forth, you will recognize the great measure and authority of this Muḥammad-based millat, and of the mother community and her position.

Ibn al-'Arabī uses the word millat here to denote the particular, cultural aspects of al-islām, which is otherwise the universal truth of submission to the Divine.

The basis of the learning Khaḍir had, which even the prophet Moses عليه السلام wanted to learn from him, is the raḥmah of the Divine, which leads to being taught knowledge directly from the Divine Side; and this millat of the mother community is based on the person of Muḥammad ﷺ, who is the arḥama'l-rāḥimīn (the most kind of the kind) and 'was sent as a raḥmah to the worlds' ۞ al-anbiyā' 21:107.

(And you will recognize) that the ripe fruit (third branch) of the blossom (second branch) of the branches (closest to the trunk): their trunk (aṣl, root) - set by Law universally - is the trunk of Khaḍir, which God *exalted* bestowed as a favor to His slave Moses عليه السلام by having him meet Khaḍir and being taught well by him.

addabahu, teach him well (as if from a banquet). The teaching is the tripartite 'I wanted (to scuttle the boat)', 'your Lord wanted (to build the wall)', and 'We wanted (to kill the boy)' - variously attributing the acts according to their praiseworthy or blameworthy status. Khaḍir says, 'I did not do it from my command.'

Thus, brought forth for the Muḥammadī ('ārif) is a branch (ripe fruit) of a branch (blossom) of a branch (closest to the trunk). Your trunk (root) is the trunk belonging to Khaḍir; and someone like Moses ﷺ asks him to teach him the knowledge he has. Now consider the position of this Muḥammadī ʿārif: where is the position set apart and distinguished? Therefore, what is your situation in relation to this by which the root is brought forth, to which these branches refer?

Olive trees on Thassos

Messenger of God ﷺ said, about what was narrated to him by his Lord, 'God says, "The approacher approaches Me with what is most loved by Me - that is, the fulfillment of what I required of him to do."' So this is the root: fulfilling the required. Then He said, 'And the creature continues to approach Me with the nawāfil' - and it is what is additional over the required practices, but of the same kind (e.g. prayers, charity, fasting), such that the required practices become the foundational root for the additional ones, like the khayriyāt nawāfil (the khayriyāt are the good deeds one chooses to do, and choosing the better action) one chooses to perform as additions, such as prayer, charity, fasting, ḥajj, and dhikr. This is the nearest branch to the trunk. Then this action - which is the nāflah (extra deed) - results in God loving you. This is a special love, requited (i.e. conditional, arising in response to the extra devotions); this is not a love of grace bestowed (unconditional), because the love / which is bestowed graciously (without conditions) is root (because the stabilized entities, without doing anything at all, were given the priceless gift of being). The entirety of the people of felicity with God share in her, and she is the one provided to these ones approaching near to God by means of extra devotions chosen.

Thus, this love: she is the second branch, which corresponds to the flower, with the end result for you that the True is your hearing and your seeing, and your hand, and so on. Now (this result) is the third branch, and it corresponds to the fruit which is pinned to the flower; and with this, the creature hears by the True, and articulates by Him, and sees by Him, and strikes by Him, and perceives by Him. This situation is a special Divine revelation, provided to one in this station. The angel (e.g. Gabriel) has no mediating connection between such a person and God, and this is why Khaḍir said to Moses 🕮, *How can you be patient with what you do not encompass* al-kahf 18:68 *as knowledge (khubr)*.

If the messengers are given revelation, it is in fact through an angel between God and His messenger - so Khaḍir had no knowledge of this tasting, concerning how exactly it takes place in the seen world. The dispatch of Law for the Divine rulings customarily comes to the seen world only with an intermediary spirit, who comes down with it onto the messenger's heart or to his exemplar world (Jabarūt) - the messenger not recognizing the shari'ah except by this description. But this is only for the shari'ah, because the messenger has a nearness coming from fulfilling the required practices, and a love from God, and what is the end result of this love; and he has the nearness of the nawāfil and love of them, and what is provided him by his love of them - but as a part of knowledge of God, not part of knowledge of the Law and the execution of the ruling in the seen world. *He does not encompass as knowledge* that which is based on this Tribe - and this part is the one that singles out Khaḍir, apart from Moses 🕮.

And part of this topic: the person based on Muḥammad makes rules. He is the one who has no preceding knowledge of the Law - through the intermediary of transmission, reading the fiqh and the ḥadīth, and understanding of the rulings of the Law; here, the one of this station articulates the knowledge of the rule set down in Law with what one has in the Law sent down from this Presence. But such a person is not one of the messengers; rather, it is a Divine notification and a protection from error - the two provided to this station which message does not enter. This is the meaning of his state- al-kahf 18:68 ment, *What you do not encompass as knowledge*, because the messenger takes this rule only through the descent of the peaceful spirit (rūḥ al-amīn, Gabriel) onto his heart - or in his exemplar world, in his vision in which the angel may take on the likeness of a man (as with the tamaththala of the Annunciation).

As prophethood has been precluded, and similarly messengership, since Messenger of God 🕮 - the (Divine) notification of this person is with what the Muḥammadī Law is in the seen world. If it were in the time of Law-making, as it was in the time of Moses, it would come out as the ruling of this friend - just as it came out from Khaḍir, without an angelic intermediary. Indeed, it comes from the near Presence, as the messenger and the prophet both have the near Presence *f*, similar to what this one has. But such a person does not have Law-making from her; no, Law-making is a prophet's only, through the intermediary of the angelic spirit, and so on.

However, when there reaches the later prophet some Law of the former one which is not his, does this come through the intermediary of the spirit, as does the rest of his Law? Or does it reach him as it reached Khaḍir and this friend among us from the Presence of Revelation? My position is that what reaches him is only what is singled out for him of the Laws of that messenger; and this is why the reliable, just one was true in his word, *What you do not encompass as knowledge.* al-kahf 18:68

We do not recognize an antagonist or an opposer, with regard to what we have mentioned, among the people of our path, nor do we attend to such a person - unless someone of our path disagrees with us. And disagreement with us is unimaginable except from one of two men: A man among the people of God who is confused in the matter and takes the Divine informing to be a ruling - and he allows that the prophet or the messenger was ruling in that way, but in this community. And as for the earlier times, it was a rule for his companion then, certainly, and it is an informing for the messenger through the intermediary of the angel that this is going to be a Law for another. God said, when He mentioned the prophets, *These are the ones God guided, so follow their guidance*; and He did not say to him al-an'ām 6:90 'their guidance' except by the revelation through the intermediary spirit. And the second man is the man who extends the reports analogically. And as for other than these, there is none. And despite this, there has not come to us from any one of them any disagreement about what we have mentioned, nor assent.

'Abd al-'Azīz notes that this potentially confusing word is affirmed in the manuscript. The meaning seems to be that the two neither confirmed nor denied the argument.

Part of the roots of this degree too is that one speaks of what one heard; and no one but they speak of it, with regard to tasting. But one may also speak of it who argues from a basis of intellectual evidence. These (the tasters) take it from a Divine tajallī, and others (the intellect-based) take it from sound examination in conformity with the matter as it really is - and it is the truth. Disagreement in the path occurs, so this path is not this other path - even if they are congruous in step-levels and it is the end goal.

Hu is the Hearer for Himself, the Seer for Himself, the Knower for Himself, and similarly for everything He names Himself by - or one describes Him by, or makes a category for Him, if you are one of the ones who have bad manners toward God in the place they attach an adjective to what is properly related to Him, or a categorical phrase - because He attaches only the phrasal name (i.e. God is the Forgiving, not 'someone who forgives'). Thus, He says,

al-a'lā 87:1
al-Raḥmān 55:78
al-a'rāf 7:180

Exalt beyond (sabbiḥi) a name of your Lord, and
Blessed be a name of your Lord, and
To God belong the Most Beautiful names,
so call on Him with them.

And He said with regard to the mushrikīn (who associate partners with the One God), *Say, Name them.* And He did not say, 'describe them' or 'categorize them'; rather, He said, *Exalted is your Lord, a Lord inaccessible, beyond what they ascribe* to Him; so He freed Himself from the description by phrase and by meaning - if you are among the people of courtesy and intelligence. This is the meaning of my statement, 'if you are one of the ones who have bad manners toward God'.

al-ra'd 13:33
al-ṣāffāt 37:180

The one who opposes us says: 'One knows knowledge; and one is able with ability; and one sees with sight; and similarly for everything that is named, except for the transcendent attributes, because they are not spoken of in this category, such as the Independent and the like - except some of them, because one takes this, all of it, as a meaning established in the dhát of God. She is not *hu*, nor is She other than *hu* - but She is the entities additional over the dhát of *hu*.'

The teacher Abū Is'ḥaq takes the adjectives to be seven roots, entities additional over His dhát - His dhát being described by them. And he takes every noun to be commensurate with the thing its indication provides. He takes the adjectives of transcendence, all of them, to be in the column of the name Living (+1); and he takes al-khabīr (All-Aware) and al-ḥasīb (All-Accounting) and al-'alīm (All-Knowing) and al-muḥṣī (All-Counting) and their brothers in the column of Knowing; and he takes the name al-shakūr (Intensely Grateful) in the column of Speaking. And this is the way he attaches them all, each adjective of the seven (6+1) to what is appropriate for them - that is, the names - in meaning, such as al-khāliq (Creator) and al-rāziq (Sustainer) to qudrat (ability, and hence 'having the power/ability to create, and the power to sustain), and others according to this procedure. This is the argument of this teacher.

The theologians among the Ashā'irah agree that there are still more matters additional over the substance dhát, and they erect proofs for this. Then, despite their agreement on the additional, they do not find a certain proof that this additional-over-the-Essence is a single entity having different principles or not. And if it is additional, surely - or not. Or is this 'additional' a numbered entity?

Their most intelligent do not say anything about it; in fact, one says, 'It is possible that the matter as it is itself refers to a single entity - and it is possible that it refers to different entities, except that it is "additional", inescapably.'

Nothing extra is brought by this speaker except an absence of arbitrariness, because for the Essence - if it accepts a single entity additionally - it is possible that it accepts many additional entities onto its Essence. The earlier generation did not calculate much (and hence was somewhat innumerate), and this is the argument of Abū Bakr bin al-Ṭayyib. The disagreements around this are lengthy, but our path is not founded on this basis - I mean, to refute them and argue with them.

However, our path is to clarify the source-arguments of each group, and from where they take up their creedal positions, and what was given to them in tajallī, and whether this has an effect on their ultimate felicity or has no effect. This is the lot of the people of the path of God based on knowledge of God, and we do not occupy ourselves with refuting a single one in God's creation. In fact, based on Divine vastness, we may firmly erect for them a plea for that error, because God erects an excuse for the one who calls on another god simultaneously with God, using a burhān (demonstrated reason) one sees as being a proof, as one presumes. He - majestic beyond what they say - said, *And who calls on another god with God: he has no burhān for it.* *al-mu'minūn 23:117*

Thus, there is a twist away from conventional understanding; here, because there is in fact no proof for the existence of two gods, one is excused for thinking that there is.

Part of the roots of people on our path is courtesy with God, so they do not name Him with anything but what He named Himself with, and they do not affix to Him anything but what He affixed to Himself - just as He said, *What happens to you of good, it is from (min) God*; and He said about the bad, *What happens to you of bad, it is from (min) yourself.* Then He said, *Say: Everything is from (min 'inda) God's Side.* He said this about two matters when they are combined, not saying 'from God (min Allāh)', heeding the phrase. *al-nisā' 4:79* *al-nisā' 4:79* *al-nisā' 4:78*

As with Khaḍir's tripartite pronominal referents, when something is good, it comes min (from) God; when something is bad, it comes from you; whatever happens (good or bad), it is min 'inda God (from God's Side).

Learn that for the combination of the matter there is a truth differing from the truth of each Prime, as the Prime is solitary and does not combine with anyone else, like the black of ink between the gall producing ink from the ballūṭ tree and the vitriol (neither one of which is black), where He separates what comes from it and what comes out of it, saying *exalted* with regard to a particular ṭā-hā 20:73 group, *For God is better and more lasting*, with a comparative structure - but there is no relation. And He said with regard to another group, al-qaṣaṣ 28:60 designating their traits, *But what is with ('inda) God is better and more lasting*. What is with ('inda) *hu* is not exactly what is from (min) *hu*, nor exactly the core of huwīyah (*f*, hu-basis); and between the two groups is what is between the two step-levels.

It is as one (Abū Bakr) was asked, 'What have you left your family?' He said, 'God and His Messenger.' And another was asked, and he said, 'Half of my wealth.' So he was told, 'Between you two is what is between your two words' - meaning, in the ranking. So when the creature takes from everything other than *hu*, *hu* deems it to be *better and more lasting* concerning God; and when you take it from some facet of the world requiring the veil (veiling the fact it is really not your wealth) and distance (not seeing the Hand of al-Raḥmān on it) and blame (when the wealth is possibly illegitimate), *hu* deems it to be *better and more lasting* concerning 'what is with God' - so the rankings are distinguished.

Then He informed us about the people of courtesy and their position in knowledge of Him and said from His friend Abraham al-shu'arā' 26:78-79 that he said, *The one who created me, and the one who feeds me and gives me water*; and he did not say, 'He makes me hungry.' *And when I* al-shu'arā' 26:80 *am sick* - and he did not say, 'He made me sick' - *He heals me*; so he attached 'healing' to Him and 'sickness' to himself, even though all is from *hu* (min 'inda-hu). But *hu* *exalted* is the One who taught messengers of *hu* courtesy - as sickness is not accepted by the souls, unlike death (which is received, or accepted, by the souls).

In fact, the most excellent among the intelligent 'ārifīn seek death for a pure separation from this genus; and the prophets seek a meeting with God - which death involves. And in this way are the family of God; and about this, no prophet was given a choice for death except he chose it, because in it is a meeting with God. So death is a good fortune for him, and a gracious gift. But sickness is a preoccupation that diverts one from fulfilling what God has obligated you to fulfill, such as the rights of God - because of your feeling pain. It is felt in the place of being addressed to do something, and one feels only the pain in the animal spirit (e.g. breathing, energy level), so the overseeing spirit *m* occupies himself with his body, distracted from what you are called to do in this world; and this is why sickness is related to yourself, and healing or death is related to the True.

Below, the references are to the story told in al-kahf 18:71-82. Ibn al-'Arabī has been citing the relationship between Moses and Khaḍir throughout, and the reader will benefit from a close perusal of the Qur'ānic passages.

It is like Moses' عليه السلام companion Khaḍir did in attaching the scuttling of the boat to himself, as he deemed the boat's being scuttled to be a bad thing (a failing). And he attached the killing of the boy both to himself and to his Lord, as in the killing there was a kindness to the boy's parents - and what was hurtful to them he attached to himself. And he attached the raising of the wall to his Lord, as in the raising of the wall there was some general social benefit and good. He *exalted* said from His slave Khaḍir about the scuttling of the boat, *I wanted to damage it* (because there was after *al-kahf 18:79* the people who owned it a king who was seizing every boat by force) - transcendence attaching to the elevated Divine Side what is outwardly a blameworthy action in convention and in habitual practice. And he said about raising the wall - as he deemed its raising to be a kindness for the orphans, as they would gain some good, which was the treasure - telling Moses عليه السلام, *Your Lord* *al-kahf 18:82* *wanted that they should attain their age of full strength and extract their treasure, as a kindness from your Lord.* And he said to Moses with regard to the boy, 'He had an ungrateful nature.' Ingratitude is a blameworthy attribute - He said, *He is not pleased with ingratitude in His creatures* - and he wanted to tell Moses that God would give *al-zumar 39:7* the boy's parents in exchange one *better than him in purity and closer* *al-kahf 18:81* *in affection* to the family.

Thus, he wanted to attach something that was, concerning the issue, a fault in the view of Moses عليه السلام, as Moses considered him to be one doing something unheard of, and he considered the boy 'a pure soul killed other than as recompense for killing another soul'. Khaḍir said, *We wanted that their Lord give them in exchange* (someone *al-kahf 18:81* better than him in purity and closer in affection). So he brought out the nūn of the plural (fa-aradnā), because in killing him there were two matters: one matter toward good and one matter otherwise - in the view of Moses, and in well-established custom. Thus, what was a good in this action, it belongs to God through the pronoun 'we'; and what was an unheard-of thing, in the outwardness of the matter and in the view of Moses عليه السلام at that moment, belonged to Khaḍir with regard to the pronoun 'we'. The nūn of the plural has two facets, as in there is the combination of a facet toward good attaching the matter to God, and a facet of fault attaching the fault to himself.

He brings this case - occurring in the middle (of the passage, between al-kahf 18:71 and 18:77) not at the extremity - between the boat and the wall cases, so that what was there of fault would come from the direction of the boat case, and what was there of good would come from the direction of the wall case (i.e. the case of the boy shares in something of both extremes). If the case of the boy were at the extreme beginning or end, wisdom would not provide that each facet (wholly bad - boat; and wholly good - wall) would be exclusive and apart, but that it would be like something of good or of its opposite. If it were first and the boat case were middle, what was good in the case of the boy for him and for his parents would not connect, such that it would go past the presence of fault outwardly - it is the boat - and at the moment He *the Beautiful, the Majestic* connected to the good which was in the wall. And if the wall were in the middle, and the story of the boy was delayed, the fault of the boat case would not connect through the connector to the fault of the boy - such that it would pass over the good which was in the wall case, and it would pass without being related. One of the qualities of the presences is that the entities of things alternate - I mean their attributes, when they pass over - so the case of the boy is in the middle, and it neighbors the facet of fault in the direction of the boat, and it neighbors the facet of the good in the wall case; so wisdom is indeed established.

'Abd al-'Azīz notes: 'Added in the margin; otherwise, the "connected" is either passive (it was connected) or a non-Divine, third person singular.'

If you ask, 'Why is God and he himself combined in the pronoun "we" - that is, the nūn of aradnā (we wanted) - when he ﷺ said when he heard one speaker who had combined God and Messenger of God ﷺ in a single pronoun by his saying "and who disobeys the two", (he said) "Wretched speaker, you; say instead, 'who disobeys God and His Messenger'"'? - Know that it is part of the topic we have confirmed; and it is that one not attach to the True anything but what the True attached to Himself, or ordered His Messenger to attach - or someone who was brought knowledge from His Side, as Khaḍir was - to Him as a sacred text. This is part of this chapter. As this speaker above was divested of having knowledge from His Side, and Messenger of God ﷺ did not go before him in permitting the like of this - this is why he was censured. And he said (to him), 'Wretched speaker, you', because it was appropriate for him that he not combine the True and creation in a single pronoun, except by Divine leave, from a messenger, or from 'knowledge from His Side' - and he had neither one of these two situations, and this is why Messenger of God ﷺ censured him.

And Messenger of God ﷺ said in a ḥadīth reported to us about him - in a sentence he spoke where he mentioned God there and he mentioned himself ﷺ - then he combined his Lord and himself in a single pronoun: he said, 'Who obeys God and His Messenger has done well, and who disobeys "the two", he has harmed only himself, and nothing harms God at all.' And he ﷺ *does not speak from (his own) inclination; it is only revelation*

al-najm 53:3-4

revealed; and in this way Khaḍir said, *I did not do it from my command* - meaning everything he did, that is, the cases, and everything he said, that is, the statements he expressed to Moses ﷺ about this - so understand!

'on my authority' al-kahf 18:82

With this, we have clarified for you something of their roots, a sufficiency. The riding mounts are the wanted-aspirants (murād-ūn) and the intensely attracted (majdhūb-ūn), the ones who guard their mysteries in the 'egg', and no air has penetrated

The main tafsīr of the verse following is that the reference to the egg is the inside of the egg before the shell has been broken. The synecdoche is ḥawr, 'houris'.

- like the restricted glance of the ones with black-white contrast eyes, restricted in the pavilion, *as if they were an egg, hidden.*

al-ṣāffāt 37:49

And one of their *m* attributes is that they do not uncover their faces when sleeping, and they sleep only on their backs; they are ever-receptive to learning (which comes down upon them from on high; recall Ibn al-'Arabī's delight in the dreamer of the ṣād dream - recounted in Book 1, Chapter 2 - who saw him lying down on his back, as was the practice of the prophets). They move only by order of the Divine, and they become still only likewise, by His wish. Their wish is whatever He wishes for them. And as stillness is a non-thing, we associate it with a 'wish' without a command; and as moving is an existential thing, we associate it with a Divine command - if you understand!

wish: irādah, as in 'Our word to a thing, when We desire it, We but say to it Be! and it is.' The process is two-fold: first the 'wish' without the command, then the command 'Be!' moving it into being.

They, God be pleased with them, do not compete, nor are they competed with. The most that comes out from their tongues is, 'As God wills (mā shā' Allāh).' The clouds are subjugated to them, and they have the anchored stance in knowledge of the unseen. They have each night a spiritual ascension - in fact, during every sleep, whether during the night or day. They have the high vantage point overlooking the deep interiors of the world. And they see the kingdoms of the heavens and the Earth. God says, *Like this We showed Abraham the kingdoms of the heavens and the Earth so he would be among the sure ones.* And He said with regard to Messenger of God ﷺ, *Glory to Him who took His creature by night to ascend from the sacred mosque (in Makkah) to the farthest mosque (al-Aqṣā in Jerusalem), whose enclosure We have blessed, in order that We might show some of Our signs.* It is the heart of his Ascension, and 'The ones who know are the inheritors of the prophets.'

al-an'ām 6:75

al-isrā' 17:1

The states are concealment. If they were to be cut limb from limb, one would not learn what they have. And this is why Khaḍir said, *I did not do it from my command*; so concealment is part of their roots - unless they are commanded to propagate the good and notify the people.

al-kahf 18:82

al-aḥzāb 33:4

And God speaks the true,
and hu is the guide to the way.

(Written in the margin in the handwriting of Ibn al-'Arabī)
'The recitation completed to me by Ẓahīr Maḥmūd,
and written down by (me) Ibn al-'Arabī.'

CHAPTER 32

Overseeing Pivots

On ma'rifah of the Pivots who oversee - the people of the camels for riding (rikāb), of the second degree

In Chapter 30, the two degrees are described as (1) the swift, high-bred camels of internal energies and intentions (himam), and (2) the swift, high-bred camels of actions (a'māl).

Overseeing causes is a passion
for the one who does so;
thereby the names and the turns
of fortune are impassioned.

They decided against him, his ancestors who came
to an end,
concerning everything his being - the action - requires.

By him he arranged whatever is in existence: all
the wonders -
so each existence has in his knowledge
an appointed span.

لَقَيْتُ

I met one of these, of the (second) degree, in a group in Sevilla in the country of Andalusia. Among them was Abū Yaḥyā al-Ṣanhājī al-Ḍarīr, who settled in the Zubaydī mosque. I accompanied him until he died. He was buried on a high mountain with great winds at its peak. It was difficult for the people to ascend the mountain, because of its height and its great winds. But God stilled the wind, and she did not rage from the moment we laid him down on the mountain. The people began to dig his grave and cut his stone, until we had finished with him and had covered his garden over him and departed (a person is buried in one's jannat, because it is the link to one's ultimate felicity). And when we were departing, the wind rose up as was her custom, and the people were in wonder.

And among them also was Ṣāliḥ al-Barbarī, and Abū 'Abd-Allāh al-Sharafī, and Abū'l-Ḥajjāj Yūsuf al-Shurburbalī. As for Ṣāliḥ, he roamed for forty years and took, in Sevilla, to the mosque of Al-Ruṭandālī for forty years, in the mode of deprivation, in the state he had during his travels. And as for Abū 'Abd-Allāh al-Sharafī, he was one of the ṣāḥib khaṭwat (person of strides; in Chapter 334, ṣāḥib khaṭwat maḥmūlan is someone who strides, is carried up to walk in the air). He continued for about fifty years to not light a lamp in his house. I saw his wonders. And as for Abū'l-Ḥajjāj al-Shurburbalī, from a town people spoke of as Shubarbal, overlooking Sevilla, he was one of the ones who walked on water, and the spirits were intimate with him. And every single one of these I lived with in affectionate and blended association, and in love from them to us. I cited them with our teachers in al-Durrat al-fākhirah (The Precious Pearl) when citing 'the ones I have benefited from on the path of the other world'.

These four were among the family of this station, and they are among the greatest of the malāmīyah-friends. Placed in their hands is knowledge of overseeing and separating out in order to explain in detail; so they have the name the Detailing Overseers. Their customary speech is *Overseeing the command, explaining in detail the*
al-ra'd 13:2 *verses (signs).* They m are the brides on the bridal throne, and they have the customary midday verses - and non-customary ones too. The world, all of it, according to them, is verses (signs), explained in detail. With the general people, the signs according to them are only the non-customary ones, and only these (they think) will alert them to the greatness of God.

God has made the customary verses for different kinds among His creatures. Among them are the verses for the intelligent, such as
al-baqarah 2:164 His word, *Indeed, in the creation of the heavens and the Earth and the differentiation of the night and the day, and the ships which course in the ocean, for the benefit of the people, and what God sent down from the heaven of water, and made alive through it the Earth after she had been dead, and scattering throughout every animal; and the alteration of the winds and the clouds subjugated (to them) between the heaven and the Earth - signs (verses) for a people who think intelligently.* There are more verses for the intelligent, all of them (considered) customary. And there are verses for the ones of certainty, and verses for the ones of the kernel, and verses for the ones of intellect, and verses for the hearers - they are the family who understand (directly) from God. And there are verses for the people (worlds, 'ālamīn), and verses for the ones who know ('ālimīn), and verses for the faithful, and verses for the ones who reflect, and verses for the family of remembrance.

These, all of them, are kinds God has blessed with different qualities and different verses, each one of them verses cited for our sake in the Qur'ān. If you study them and ponder them, you will learn that they are verses and indications of different matters, referring to a single entity. Most people neglect this study, and this is why there are numerous kinds (of verses).

On account of the above-mentioned customary verses, the people do not perceive their indications with regard to their being humans, *jinn*, and angels; and they are the verses by whose
i.e. 'ālamīn and not 'ālimīn perception the world - with the vowel a on the lām - is described. And among the verses there is something difficult to fathom, not perceived except by one who has sound reflection. And among the verses there is something whose indications are a precondition for the ones of the kernel - and they are the intelligent, the ones who

consider the kernel of the matters, not their husks; and they are the ones who fathom the meaning dimension, even though the (ones of the) kernels and the nuhā (preventers, because their intellects prevent them from ugly behaviors) are intelligent. But He did not stop with the word 'intelligence' in the place the verses were cited as being for the ones of the kernels, as not every intelligent one considers the kernel of the matters and their invisible insides. In fact, the people of literalism have their own intelligence, no doubt, but they are not ones of the kernels. And there is no doubt that the foolish (qiṣlah, people who have no control over themselves, foolish; qaṣal are husks used for fodder) have intellects, but they are not people of sharp intelligence. So their kinds are different, as each attribute provided to a (particular) kind, such as a 'knowledgeable kind' (or a foolish kind), does not reach any but the one whose state is this attribute - and God does not cite them thoughtlessly.

God has multiplied the citation of signs (āyāt, verses) in the majestic Qur'ān. In places, they are consecutive and one of them follows another, and He complements by succession an adjective the 'ārifīn recognize. And in places (in the Qur'ān), they (the verses) are prime (isolated, not in a successive grouping). An example of the following of one of them by another is the procession in the sūrah (chapter) Rūm, as He continues to say, *And among His signs* is that He created you from earth, *And among His signs* is that He created for *al-Rūm 30:20* you pairs among yourselves, *And among His signs* is that He created *al-Rūm 30:21* the heavens and the Earth. All people will recite them successively, *al-Rūm 30:22* but only the specific kinds of people (e.g. *those who reflect, and those who know, and those who hearken* ۞ al-Rūm 30:21,22,23) are alerted by these verses, the ones cited in each verse specifically. It is as if these verses were sent down to these people as signs; but for others, they are there (not as signs but) to detach and separate the recitation, so they would be slowed down in their reciting.

Once when I was reciting this sūrah while I was at the station of this second degree and I reached His statement, *And among His signs is your sleep in the night and the day, and your seeking out His bounty* - I *al-Rūm 30:23* was utterly astounded with the fine, ordered arrangement of the Qur'ān and its consolidation, and why there preceded exactly what was appropriate, from an intellectual perspective, in the literal matter, lest there should be other than this arrangement. So the day is for seeking His bounty and the night is for sleeping, as He said in sūrah qaṣaṣ,

> Wa min raḥmatihi ja'ala lakum al-layla wa al-nahāra li-taskunū fīhi wa li-tabtaghū min faḍli-hi. Ibn al-'Arabī is explaining the hidden 'pronominal' referents to be as follows: the night, and the day, to rest in, and the day to seek out His bounty.

From His kindness, He made for you the night, and the day, to rest in. Thus *al-qaṣaṣ 28:73*

the ḍamīr (the grammatically hidden pronominal referent) refers
al-qaṣaṣ 28:73 to the night, and *so you would seek out His bounty* means in the day; so it is the hidden pronoun. If the two hidden pronouns both referred to the intended meaning, the Designer would have used bi'l-layli (in the night); and one may buy and trade in the night, just as one may sleep also in the day; but for most situations, the expression is seeking out bounty in the day and sleeping in the night.

There glimmered to me something from behind the veil of this verse, and the fine beauty of the expression lifting her veil - and it
al-Rūm 30:23 - is His word, *Your sleep in the night and the day* - an additional matter, beyond what one understands from her generally in context, about seeking out bounty as belonging to the day and about sleeping as belonging to the night, as we had mentioned.

And this is where God alerts us with these verses that the configuration of the next world is physical, but not similar to this configuration in this world - and that the one is not exactly the other; rather, it is another composition and another blend, just as was said in the revealed Laws and the prophetic knowledge about the blend of this other abode. Even though these intrinsic natures are exactly themselves, no doubt - and they are the ones that will be scattered in the graves and will be resurrected - yet the compositions and blends will differ, by happenstances and attributes appropriate to the other abode, not appropriate to this abode. And even though the image (form) is single to the eye, the ear, the nose, the mouth, the two hands, and the two feet, in the complete configuration - in fact, the difference is clear. Some of it is perceived and sensed, and some of it is not perceived. As the image becoming configured in the other abode is based on the image of this configuration, one may not be aware of what we are hinting at. As the determinative property is different, we recognize that the blend is different. This is the separating difference between the allotment of the senses and the intellect.

Ibn al-'Arabī develops these ideas throughout; just as with the mirror (the image is you; it is not you; it is not not you), your individual self is constant, while your form and aspect and look change - or viewers see you differently according to their perspectives. And different dreamers may agree they saw one individual, but each may have seen different forms (he was young, old, a man, a woman).

He *exalted* said, *And among His signs is your sleep in the night and the*
al-Rūm 30:23 *day* - and He did not mention waking, while it is one of the entirety of the signs. He mentioned sleeping but not waking, in the state of this world. This indicates that waking is not something that happens until death, and that the human being is asleep always, as long as one is not dead. So He mentioned that one is in sleep in the night; and the day is one's waking and sleeping - both. And in the report,

'The people are asleep; when they die, they awake' (become alert, aware of themselves, of the Divine Presence).

Do you see that the bā' (in) is not brought out in His word, *wa an-nahār (and the day)*? It has all it needs from the bā' of 'night', so one may verify for oneself this partnership - that He means the sleep during the state of customary waking. And its syncopation (being clipped off grammatically) is something which strengthens the perspective which we are bringing out for this verse. *al-Rūm 30:23*

So 'sleep' is what the sleeper is in during the state of one's sleep; and when one wakes, one says, 'I saw such-and-such,' indicating that the human being is asleep as long as one is in this configuration in this world - until one dies. The True does not express the customary waking, according to us, generally; rather, He takes the human being as being asleep in one's sleep and in one's being awake, just as was related in the prophetic report - that is, his ﷺ word, 'The people are asleep; when they die, they awake'; so he described them as sleeping during the life of this world.

The general population do not recognize sleep customarily as being anything but what happens typically, which they call sleep. But the Prophet ﷺ alerted us; no, he made it quite clear that the human being is asleep as long as one is in the life of this world, until one wakes up alert and aware in the next world. Death is the first of the experiences of the other world. So he confirmed what God had sent in His word, *And among His signs is your sleep in the night* - and it is the typical sleep - *and the day* - and it is this sleep which was made quite clear by Messenger of God ﷺ.

This is why we take this world to be a traverse, a bridge to be crossed - that is, one traverses across this world just as the dream *f* which the human being sees traverses across one's sleep. Then, just as what the dreamer sees in the state of one's sleep has no meaning in itself - rather, it has meaning for another - so one brings across ('abara, interprets) from this image dreamed of in the state of sleep to her meaning dimension what was meant by her in the awake world, when one awakes from one's sleep. (What the souls that He takes 'during their sleep' see is brought across to this world upon awaking ۞ al-zumar 39:42.)

In the middle of a dream, one is not 'interpreting' the dream - one is living it. Only upon awaking does the dream mean something, and only after awaking does one interpret its meaning. In the same way, Ibn al-'Arabī is saying, the events of this world do not 'mean' anything until we die; then they are interpreted and mean something - and they are, for instance, rewarded and shown to be good.

Similarly, the state of the human being in this world is not what is really meant in this world; but everything one sees, such as state, word, deed, in this world is rather something really meant for (and meaningful in) the other world. So there, you interpret (traverse), and there appears to you what you saw in this world - just as there appears to you in this world when you awake what you saw in the dream. Thus, this world is a bridge to be traversed, not settled in and populated! - just as it is with you, the human being, at the time you see something in your dream: you traverse; you interpret; you do not settle into a life populated there in the dream, because when you wake up, you will not find anything you saw in your dream, whether you saw something good or something bad - not houses, buildings, or tables - and no fine experiences or vile ones. But certainly the one who knows may interpret (traverse) for you metaphorically what you saw and will say to you, 'Your dream indicates such-and-such.'

Similarly, the life of this world is one of being asleep. When you pass on to the next world by dying, nothing transfers with you - that is, whatever was in your hand physically here, such as a house and a family and wealth. It is just as when you awake from sleep: you do not find anything in your hand now which had reached you in your dream when you were sleeping. This is why He said we are indeed asleep in the night and the day; and in the other world will be the awakening, and there the 'dream' will be interpreted and crossed over.

Ibn al-ʿArabī earlier told us about people who are fortunate because their 'meaning' is known before they die; others are sorted out at the Scale, and others are sorted out in the Fire.

So, for whomever God has enlightened his insight and interpreted his dream here, before death: such a person is blessed and successful. He will be like someone who saw a dream and then saw in his dream that he was awake; so he tells what he saw, while he is still asleep in his state, to some people whom he sees in his sleep. He says, 'I saw such-and-such' - and they interpret and cross her over for him, this person dreaming, based on what he sees (understands) from his learning about these things. Thus, when he awakes, at that moment there appears to him that he is still asleep, in the state of the dream, and in the state of crossing over her - and this is the most authentic crossover.

And, similarly, the one who understands the kernel in this abode, despite being asleep, sees that one is awake; so you interpret your dream in your sleep so as to become alert and awake and restrained by a chiding cry, and to travel the road of right tendency. Then, when you are awakened by death, you praise your dream and you are delighted in your having been asleep (all along). Your dream produced good fruit. And because of this truth, God does not cite in this verse awaking, but cites being asleep and attaches it to us in the night and the day; and seeking out bounty is the day, with regard to the one who sees in the dream that one is awake in one's sleep - so you interpret your dream, and this is the state of this world. God inspire us with the good guidance of our selves!

Chapter 32

This is part of His word, *Overseeing the command, explaining in detail the verses (signs)* - so this tafṣīl (explaining by separating in detail) is of the verses of sleeping in the night and the day, and seeking out bounty. And the verses (signs) are made for a people who hear - that is, understand; just as He said, *Nor be like the ones who say, We hear, but they do not hear* - meaning, (do not) understand God. And He said about them, Deaf, despite their hearing; dumb, despite their speaking; blind, despite their seeing - *so they do not think*. I have alerted you here to what is meant by hearing, speaking, and seeing. al-ra'd 13:2 al-anfāl 8:21 al-baqarah 2:171

So these second-degree riding mounts take as their source the things according to this definition which we have mentioned for these verses. In fact, we mentioned this source in order to inform you about their path - so clarified for you is their position compared with others. Their subtle essences in the fixed verses, the customary and the non-customary, are a stable view to the souls of the world - a view to the facets desired which they turn to face, by reason of their desires. It is a view to the Divine definitions (ḥudūd, e.g. punishments) which they are facing; they are not distracted from viewing this for a blink of the eye. Their distraction which their natures require, as with all human beings, is rather connected on their part as a distraction from what belongs to them. So they are awake to what is sought from them, distracted from what belongs to them - such that they do not exit the ruling force of distraction, because it is part of human nature.

For other than this group, heedless distraction turns them away from what is wanted of them. Even if that to which the attending occurs is an obedience, they still look for the intricacies which come to the fore; and they look at the Divine command which is related to the verse, and the Divine name which has dominion over her. Thus, the verse which they are seeking is separated out for them by Divine command. If the verse is customary - for example, the difference between the night and the day, and the subjugation of the clouds, and others, based on the customary verses which the general population of souls have no information about their being signs, until they lose them - then when they lose them and miss out (on the knowledge they convey), at that moment they retreat to the acequia (al-isʿtasqā'i, Spanish acequia: irrigation canal for water). And they recognize, at that moment, the context of the verses' evidence and their measure, and that they were involved in the verse, but were not aware. So when the signs come, and the clouds drop rain, they return to their neglectfulness.

This is a state of the general population, rushing about in this

Yūnus 10:22 abode - just as God said about them: *He is the One who makes you travel through the land and sea, so that you are on the ship and course with them with the fresh wind and delight because of it; there comes a storming wind and the waves come to them from every place, and they imagine they are being engulfed in them; they call on God, giving the dīn (religion) over to Him purely, yes. 'If you save us from this, we will be among the thank-*
al-'ankabūt 29:65 *ful ones.'* ❁ *But when He has delivered them safely to the land, behold, they associate* (gods with God, shirk), and *behold, they are arrogant on the*
Yūnus 10:23 *Earth with no right*. God says to them, *O you people, your arrogance is on yourselves; enjoyment of this worldly life*. And like this they are saying
Yūnus 10:23 in the Fire, '*If only we could return!* then we would not reject the signs
al-an'ām 6:27 of our Lord but would be among the faithful.' He exalted says, *But if*
al-an'ām 6:28 *they returned, they would go back to what had been forbidden* - just as the people of the ship went back to their shirk and their arrogance after having dedicated themselves purely to God.

Now when the Tribe observe these signs, they send them with their Divine imperative wherever it calls them to. If the verse *f* is non-customary, they consider and observe which Divine name is asking for her. If it is (the name) the Coercer and his brothers asking for her, then she is a verse of fright and chiding and threatening; they send her to their souls (to warn them). And if the name the Gentle and his brothers seek her - I mean this verse - then she is a verse of wishing; they send her to the spirits (to encourage them). Then, because of them, light rays radiate to the souls, and the souls thereby incline affectionately to their Creator; and they are sustained with success and guidance, and they are given pleasure by doing good deeds, and enthusiasm and eagerness stand strong in them. And in them, confusion and apathy are stripped away, and living with false people and associating with unmindful people dismissive of dhikr of God become hateful to them; and they begin to detest crowds and displays (jalwah), and they begin to prefer being alone and secluded (khalwah).

Belonging to this second degree is a truth of the Night of Power, and her kashf, her secret, and her meaning. With her, the second degree (people) have a Divine force they are distinguished by, and it is their allotment of time. Consider the high vantage point of their station, that God grants them time at its highest point - because the
al-qadr 97:3 *laylatu'l-qadr is better than 1,000 months*. In there is a time period of Ramaḍān, the day of jum'ah, the day of 'Āshūrā', the day of 'Arafat, and the laylatu'l-qadr herself. So it is as if He said, 'Multiply her goodness (khayr, khayr min, better than) 83 and 1/3 times (1,000 months / 12 = 83 1/3 years), because she is 83 years and 4 months (one-

third of a year).' And it may be that the four months are one of the ones in which is the laylatu'l-qadr, so the multiplication for each laylatu'l-qadr will be 84 times (84 x 4 = 336; 336/12 = 28, the number of days in a lunar month). Consider what goodness there is in this time period, and the time period distinguishing this group!

And God speaks the true,
and Hu is the guide to the way. al-aḥzāb 33:4

The 18th manuscript ends.
And all praise belongs to God!
Followed by the 19th

وَٱلْحَمْدُ لِلَّهِ

Chapter 33

Pivots of Purpo-sers

On ma'rifah of the Pivots of intentionality and their mysteries, and the mechanics of their origins. And one calls them the journeys' purposers.

Background: al-a'māl bi'n-niyyat is a widely known phrase among Muslims, which connects one's actions and behaviors (a'māl) with one's intentions. The non-Arabic Muslim usage is often in the sense of 'making an intention'. An example is the making of intention before the prayer, or before the ritual washing of ghusl. If one trips and falls, this does not constitute ghusl; one has to intend an action for it to be genuine. Niyyat includes the place one intends to visit or travel to.

Spirit belongs to organic body, and
intentions (niyyāt) belong to actions -
enlivened by them just as the
Earth is enlivened by rain.

And you see the flowers and the bushes
protruding with
everything coming out of the bushes,
such as ripened fruit.

In this way, images (seen in the grave) emerge
from actions,
having spirits: some putrid because they were built
from wrongful actions, and some sweet attar.

If not for the sharī'ah, the musk would be
ashamed of
her scents; in this way, my viewpoint requires it.

If the existential supports are combined for you,
there will be no difference between benefit and harm.

Cleave to his Law ﷺ; delighting in her as images,
you decompose as an image, blossoming
tall over eminent signs -

Like the kings you see on their thrones,
or like the brides, loved passionately by the sight.

رُوِينَا

We report a ḥadīth of Messenger of God ﷺ where he said, 'Indeed, actions are through intentions, and belonging to the doer is what one intended; so the one whose emigration (hijrah, from Makkah to Madīnah) is to God and His Messenger, his emigration is to God and His Messenger; and the one whose emigration is for worldly fortune or a woman to marry, then his emigration is toward what he emigrated to' - related from 'Umar bin al-Khaṭṭāb, God be pleased with him.

Learn that the shepherds of intentions (and the destinations one strikes out for) are Men having a special state and a special quality. I shall mention them, if God so wills, and I shall mention their states. Making intention for all movements and stillnesses (doing and not doing), of the one tasked with actions, is like the rain as he awakens the Earth. The intention *f* with regard to her dhát is single, differing in the connection to the intended - so the end result is commensurate with the connection to the intended, not commensurate with herself. The good share of intention is actually to get one to do or not do. Whether the doing is fine or ugly, good or bad, it is not the result of the intention, rather it is from some happenstance which happens - differentiated by the Law and designated for the one tasked. The intention has no effect at all from this particular perspective.

It is like water: his place-level is that he descends to or travels in the earth. And if the earth is dead, she is enlivened by the water - or he pulls down the house of a poor old man with his downpour. This is not on the water. A flower produces a good scent and a vile one, and a fruit a good and a disgusting one - from a badness in the mixture of the soil patch, or its goodness, or from the badness of the seed, or its goodness. He *exalted* said, *watered by a single water; We made some more excellent than others to eat*; then He said, *Indeed, in this are signs for the people who understand* (al-ra'd 13:4. Ibn al-'Arabī uses here the Warsh recitation tusqā where Hafṣ is yusqā.)

The intention with regard to this has additional aid, as He said (in answer to 'What does God mean by this parable?'), *By it He causes*
al-baqarah 2:26 *many to be misguided, and by it He causes many to be rightly guided* - that is, by the parable in the Qur'ān, meaning, on account of it, while it is part of the Qur'ān. So just as the water is a reason for the emergence of these different odors and different tastes, the intentions are a reason for actions, wholesome and not wholesome.

It is well known that the Qur'ān is a right-guidance, all of him, but - after interpretation of the parable put forth - misguides the one who will be misguided and rightly guides the one who will be rightly guided. It is because of his being a parable that his truth of being a right-guidance is not altered, because in fact the fault occurs in one's understanding itself. Similarly, the intention *f* provides her truth - and it is her connection to the one who intends; and the fact that what is intended is fine or ugly is not on her, rather this is on the person who decides to do good or bad. He *exalted* said, *We guided one on the way* - that is, 'We clarified the way of happiness and wretchedness'; then He said, *one may be grateful and one may be*
al-insān 76:3 *ungrateful*. This refers to the one tasked. If one intends the good, the fruit is good; and if one intends the bad, the fruit is bad. It comes to you only in the proper place - that is, good or bad.

al-nahl 16:9 And God says, *On God is the leading to the way* - that is, this He has obligated on Himself. It is as if God is saying, 'What is required of you from the Side of the True is that He clarify for you the way that connects you to your felicity - and I have indeed done so; and you would not know the way except through My signposts for you, and My clarification.'

The reason for this is that knowledge has gone before that the path of felicity for the creatures is for a particular reason, and the reason for their wretchedness also is along a particular path - which is nothing but a swerving off from the path of felicity, which is faith in God and in what was sent from God, which we are required to have faith in. As the world is in a state of ignorance of what is in God's (fore) knowledge - that is, the designation of this path - the signposts are designated by means of the adjective (attribute) of speech, and certainly the speaking that comes from the messenger. God said, *Nor do We send punishment until We have sent a messenger.* *al-isrā' 17:15*
We do not oblige God with anything but what He obliged Himself *al-Rūm 30:47*
with; and He has obliged Himself to notify us, by His word, *On God* *al-naḥl 16:9*
is the leading to the way - just like His word, *It is incumbent on Us to help the faithful*, and His word, *Your Lord has prescribed on Himself kindness.* *al-an'ām 6:54*

In the true dimension, He has obligated this on a relation, not actually on Himself - because He is too exalted that there be obligated on Him something on account of a defined legal obligation. It is as if it is this way: He connected Divine knowledge in timelessness to the designation of the path on which would be our felicity, but there was not with the (fore) knowledge, as knowledge, a format for conveying (knowledge of the path of felicity); and the conveying would be based on the adjective of 'speaking' - the conveying is designated in relation to Him being a Speaker informing us about the path on which is the felicity of the creatures whom foreknowledge so designated. Thus, with its translation from knowledge, Divine speech explained what was designated. The obligation is on the relation of the Divine to speech (i.e. the obligation is that there be a 'speaking related to the Speaker' of this conveyance of knowledge about felicity), because there are different relations. And it is like this for all the Divine relations, such as Desiring, Powering, and others.

We have already clarified the Presence of the Divine names, and their disputes, and their places in the race arena as they bring out this world - which is an expression for everything other than God - in the book 'Anqā' al-mughrib (The Wondrous Griffin), in which we wrote a chapter called 'The Timeless Presence for the Eternal Configuration'. And we wrote similarly in our book Inshā' al-jadāwal wa'l-dawā'ir (The Genesis of the Spirals and the Tables).

You have learned, if you understand clearly the learning of relations, how the Divine obligation is connected to the Divine Presence. About this was brought out His word, *On the day We shall*

Maryam 19:47 *gather the righteous to al-Raḥmān as a delegation*. But how will one be gathered to Him who is sitting with Him and is in His grasp? Abū Yazīd al-Basṭāmī heard the reciter reciting this verse, *On the day We* Maryam 19:47 *shall gather the righteous to al-Raḥmān as a delegation*, and he wept - so much so that the tears struck the minbar; in fact, it was related that the tears flew from his eyes so much so that they hit the minbar and cried out. Then he said, 'How strange! How can one gather to Him who is already sitting with Him?'

When our time period came, we were asked about this statement. I said, 'The only thing strange is the statement of Abū Yazīd!' You should learn that it was so because the muttaqī (above, 'righteous' - the ones who have taqwá, who do things mindful that God is going to hold them to account, thereby guarding themselves from wrath) were sitting with al-jabbār, so they were guarding themselves from His attacking; but the name *m* the al-Raḥmān (Supremely Compassionate) has no attacking, given His being kind and compassionate. Indeed, al-Raḥmān provides ease and gentleness, overlooking of faults and forgiving of them. And this is why one gathers to Him after the name al-jabbār, who provides attack and dread. It is the name al-jabbār whom the muttaqī sit with in this world, because they are muttaqī (fearfully guarding themselves with taqwá, mindful of Him).

According to this procedure, one takes the Divine names, all of them, and in this way one finds them as they were related in the languages of the prophets. If you seek the truth of a name and differentiate him from another, there will be two indications: an indication based on what is named, and an indication based on his feature by which he is differentiated from another name - so understand.

Learn that concerning these great ones, their occupation with knowing the intention is because of their looking at the language and into it. They know that the letters of the language are not composed and combined except to bring out a standing configuration, pointing to the meaning which is combined in colloquial usage. When the speaker utters the letters, the listener's internal energy is for understanding the meaning which comes forth - because by this process the benefit (of the sentence) occurs, and for this it is found in that language according to this particular set usage.

The universal audition gives meaning and does not make one dance or move.

This is why these great ones do not speak of the audition (samā') as conventionally defined - that is, musical melodies - because of their elevated internal (stirring) energies. They speak of the universal audition, because the general audition has no effect on them except understanding the meaning. It is a Divine, spiritual audition, and it is the greater audition. The conventionally defined audition with music produces an effect of melody on its people, and it is a natural audition. One claims, who claims, that he heard in the conventionally defined audition by means of the tune some meaning; and he says, 'If not for the meaning, I would not have moved (danced).' He claims that he was outside of the force of Nature (and the natural impulse to move) for this - I mean, the reason he was moving is external to the force of Nature, based (instead) on a meaning he understood. And we have seen one who claims this, among the fake shaykhs who are uninvited to the path. With the one of this claim, if he is not truthful, he will quickly be exposed as a fraud.

al-mutaṭaffalūn, intruders uninvited to the feast; al-mutashayyakhūn, ones who feign 'venerable old age' or being a shaykh.

And concerning this, regarding this one who makes a claim: when he sits in the audition, turn your attention to him. When the qawwāl (singer) of a phrase (qawl) with these tones incites movement by Nature to the constitutional mix which accepts it, too, and the states begin to flow through the animal-spirits,

The Latin is animalis, from living (anima), the feminine of breath, soul (animus). We could also say the 'animal' is the parasympathetic nervous system regulating the body, with the other part being the voluntary actions. The music animates someone.

and the incited skeletal movement is a circular movement, based on the principle of orbiting spheres - it is, I mean the circling, part of what indicates to you that the audition is natural, because the subtle part of human beings is not based on an orbiting sphere; rather, it is based on a spirit in-breathed, and it is not space-like (mutaḥayyazah). It is above the orbiting sphere, so it makes no circular movements in the body, or non-circular ones. This rather belongs to the animal spirit which is under Nature and the orbit. So, do not be unaware of your configuration, nor of what is moving you.

mutaḥayyazah, res extensa, occupying or extending into space

When this claimer is incited to move, and he is seized by the trance (al-ḥāl) and starts to whirl or jumps in a vertical direction without circling, and he disappears from and loses his sensation of himself and of the ones seated who are there - then when he has finished with his trance and his senses return to him, ask him: 'What is it that moved you?' He might say, 'The qawwāl said such-and-such, and I understood from it the meaning of such-and-such, and this meaning moved me.' Then tell him, 'What moved you was nothing but the fine tune, and the understanding in fact occurred to you according to sequence, as Nature rules over your animal-soul - so there is no difference between you and the camel with regard to the effect of music on you.' I am sorry that a discussion like this will be hard on him and weigh him down.

e.g. the sequence of music stirring the skeletal nature and causing an orbiting

He may say to you, 'What do you know about me, and what do you know about what moved me?' At that moment, say nothing to him, because someone with this claim may have been overcome with heedlessness. Then start with him on what phrase provided this meaning. Say to him, 'How fine the word of God when He says' - and then recite to him a verse from the Book of God that contains this meaning which incited him to movement by the sound of that musician, and verify it with him until he verifies it for himself; take it up with him and speak of it. He may not be seized by a trance, or movement, or annihilation, but it agrees with him; and he may say, 'This verse contains the sublime meaning, a knowledge of God.' There is nothing more harsh in exposing him in his claim (than this).

Say to him, 'My brother, this meaning is the same one you mentioned to me moving you during the samā' yesterday, when the qawwāl brought it out in his poetry and his beautiful singing; so whatever meaning penetrated you in yesterday's trance, this meaning is present in what I just formulated for you and conveyed to you in the word of the True - which is higher and more true - and I did not see you start trembling with appreciation and reaching understanding. Yesterday you were felled by Satan and "touched", possessed - as God said - and the natural audition veiled you from the eye of understanding. All that you achieved in your samā' was unawareness of yourself. And one who does not differentiate between his understanding and his movement, how will he hope for his success?'

e.g. 'The ones who have taqwā - when urges touch them from Satan, they remember (God), and suddenly they see (correctly)' al-a'rāf 7:201.

The samā' of the eye of understanding is the Divine samā'; and when it comes to its audience and is strong, as one wants from it some summation, the most it does in the body is to lay it down, nothing else, and to remove it from its senses - but no movement will originate there at all, from any perspective, whether they are among the greatest of Men or the least. This is the force of the Divine incoming power. It is the difference between it and the force of the natural incoming, because the natural incoming, as we have said, moves one in a circular movement; and stumbling about, and convulsing - these are the acts of the mad man (the majnūn).

The Divine incoming lays the body down, for the reason I mentioned to you, and that is where the human configuration is based on creation from earth. He *exalted* said, *From her We created you, and to her We will return you, and from her We will bring you out another time.* The human being: even though in you is the whole of the elements, yet the element which is greatest is earth. He also said, *Lo, the like of Jesus with God is the like of Adam; He created him from earth*; and human beings in their sitting and standing are far distant from their greatest root, the one from which they were configured originally, from most perspectives - because one's sitting, one's standing, one's rukū' (bowing in prayer) are branches of the earthly root (which is to lie flat, as the sick person does).

ṭā-hā 20:55

Āl-i-'Imrān 3:59

When the Divine incoming comes to one - and to the Divine incoming belongs an attribute of Self-Standing - it is a chance property for the human being, in relation to one's body; and your over-

The human being may or may not be able to stand up - it is by chance, not 'necessary being'.

seeing spirit is the one which stands you up and sits you down. When the human overseeing spirit is preoccupied and distracted from its overseeing, by what was received from the Divine incoming - such as Divine knowledge - there remains for the body no one to supervise your standing or your sitting; so the body goes back to its root - and this is its clinging to the earth, expressed as lying down on the ground. If you are on a bed, then the bed is actually an obstacle between yourself and your root in (atop) the earth. When your spirit is finished with this reception, and the incoming then issues back to its Lord, the spirit returns to overseeing its body and raises it up from its prostration. This is the reason for the 'lying down on the ground' of the prophets on their backs, when the revelation descends upon them.

See Ibn al-'Arabī's poem on the letter ṣād in Chapter 2.

We have not heard at all from a prophet that he was convulsed with the descent of the revelation; this (is the case) with the presence of the intermediary during the revelation - he is the angel (e.g. Gabriel) - so how much more so when the incoming is with intermediaries removed? It is not correct at all that they should have any loss of their senses, nor be altered from the state they are in. The Divine incoming with removed spiritual intermediaries flows throughout the entirety of the human being and seizes each limb; in fact, every single quantum in you has an allotment from this Divine incoming, including the fine and the coarse. One sitting with you does not realize this (when it is happening), and there is no alteration in you at all of the state you are in with regard to the one sitting with you. If one is eating, one continues to eat during this moment, or to drink, or to converse with whomever one is conversing with. This incoming generalizes, universally - and it is His word, *He is with you wherever you are*. Thus, one who is wherever he is at that moment - in the state of eating, drinking, conversing, or playing, or whatever it is - stays in one's state.

al-ḥadīd 57:4

When this exalted group see this difference between the natural and the spiritual incomings, and they see that confusion arises in the one who presumes that he is one of the Men of God, they scorn that they should be described with ignorance and insanity - because such is the site of natural existence; so they increase their internal energies to full attention toward intentions - as God has said to them, *They were not commanded except to worship God, handing over purely to hu*. And ikhlāṣ (sincerely handing over) is intention, and this is why intention is bound and tied, in His word, *to hu* (lahu); and He did not say just 'handing over purely' (mukhliṣīna).

al-bayyinah 98:5 - mukhliṣīna la-hu. The reading also sounds like, 'to hu'.

It is part of extracting out purely, because the human being may dedicate purely his intention to Satan, and he would be called 'purely dedicated' - but there would not be in his action anything belonging to God (nothing lahu, belonging to hu). And one may

dedicate purely to an idol. And one may 'hand over purely to God'; and this is why He said, *mukhliṣīna la-hu al-dīn (handing over purely to hu the religion)* - not to another, and not to the property of associa-
al-bayyinah 98:5
tion (with other gods).

They occupy themselves with the root in receiving actions and obtaining felicitous things, and having equanimity with what the Divine seeks with them - in what He addresses them to do, such as actions that are dedicated purely to Him. It is expressed by the intention, so they relate her to the majority of what they are occupied with, and they verify for themselves that the actions have no intended meaning in themselves; rather, their meaning is what is sought by means of them. It is the intention in the action, just as meaning is to the speech (i.e. the reason it is done) - because speech is not sought out for itself, rather it is sought out for what is included in it.

huwa al-niyyat fī al-'amal

Then consider, my friend, how delicate is the view of these great ones. This is expressed in the path as self-accounting; and Messenger of God ﷺ has said, 'Hold yourselves to account before you are held to account.' I met two of these great ones in Sevilla: Abū 'Abd-Allāh bin al-Muhājir and Abū 'Abd-Allāh bin Qassūm. This was their station, and they were among the Pivots of the great ones, the journeys' purposers (niyyātiyyīn).

Now when we entered this station to emulate the two and the people of this station - in order to comply with a command of Messenger of God ﷺ, the one whose command is obligatory to be obeyed, to 'hold yourselves to account' - our teachers were holding themselves to account for what they were saying and what they were doing, and they would write it all down in a notebook. If it was after the ṣalāt al-'ishā' (in the late evening) and they were secluded in their houses, they would take a reckoning and get their notebooks; and they would observe what had come out of them, during their day - each speech and deed. They would compare each deed with what was appropriately merited: if the action merited repentance, they would turn in repentance; and if gratefulness was merited, they would give thanks, until they had finished with everything concerning them during that day. After this, they would sleep.

Now, we exceeded them in this context by writing down the incoming thoughts as well; and I used to write down what they told my self and what they were about, in addition to my speaking and my doing. I used to hold my soul *f* to account just like them at that time, and I would get out the notebook and demand of her everything that had come in to her and what she had spoken to herself about, and what had emerged visibly in word and deed - and whatever she intended with that incoming thought and self-talk. The incoming and the less-than-excellent thoughts became few, except those concerned with what was disquieting me. This is the extra benefit of this chapter and topic, and the extra benefit is the full occupation with intention. There is nothing on the path which is more neglected than this topic, because this goes back to the shepherding of the breaths - and this is rare indeed.

And after having informed you of the roots of this Tribe - and the reason for their full occupation with it, and that they have a Law command, and what they have of it, such as mysteries and knowings - then learn also their station and what they have. This Tribe is 'upon the heart' of Jonah عليه السلام. *When he departed angry* and thought *al-anbiyā' 21:87*
it was God who was constricting him with regard to what He had promised him, such as the vast kindness of God; and he observed this Divine vast kindness with regard to others, as his community received this Divine vast kindness; and it constricted his self - and anger is the light-blocking darkness of the heart - so it affected his outwardly high position. And he lived in the light-blocking interior of the whale, as God wished, so God would alert him to his state. When he was a fetus in the interior of his mother, who was overseeing him there? And in that place would he have imagined that he would be angry or he would become angry? No, he was in the sheltered fold of God, not recognizing any but his Cherisher. Therefore, he was returned to this state - in the interior of the whale - to teach him by action, not by words.

So he called out in the light-blockings, There is no god but You, since *al-anbiyā' 21:87*
forgiveness for his community is in this tawḥīd (declaration of Divine unity) - that is, 'Do as You like; Your kindness spreads over whomever You wish'; *Glory to You! I am one of the wrong-doers*, where *al-anbiyā' 21:87*
ẓālimīna (wrong-doers) is derived from ẓulmah (light-blocking). That is, my light-blocking (in my heart, from anger) has returned to me; it is not You who have light-blocked (wronged) me; in fact, what was inside me coursed to my outsides, and the light passed to my insides and it illumined; and the light-blocking of anger was erased, and there shone there a light of tawḥīd (there is no god but You); and the kind compassion spread all over, and the light suffused all over into his outwardness - as the light-blocking of anger had coursed out.

Then his Cherisher answered him and saved him from sadness, and the whale flung him out of his insides, an infant flush upon sound fiṭrah (the innate, natural, 'primitive' state; dīn al-fiṭrah, the innate, natural, correct 'religion' or 'way' of life). No one from the children born of Adam is born twice, except Jonah عليه السلام. He emerged weak, like an infant - as He said, *He was sickly*. He was cher- *al-ṣāffāt 37:145*
ished (raised; cf. rabb, cherisher) by a gourd plant that spreads across the ground, with no vertical stems, because her leaves are soft; and animals would not descend on him, as because of his weakness the

infant is not able to repel the animals from himself. So he was enveloped by the bush, distinguished by the animals not approaching her despite her soft leaves, because the leaves of the gourd (yaqṭīn) are like al-quṭun (cotton, algodon) in softness - contrary to the rest of the bushes' leaves, all of them, because in them there is roughness. So God created him into another creation twice-born.

i.e. defense against seed predators

When this group saw that Jonah ﷺ obtained only what came to him from his interior - that is, the description (infant) that he was raised from, and his aspiration - they occupied themselves with examining and testing the intentions and the true aspiration for their movements, all of them, so that they would intend only what God had commanded them that they should intend and aspire to; and this is the utmost of what they master, the Men of God.

This Tribe among the Men are very few, because it is a severely straitened station, requiring of its resident to be continuously Present. The greatest who was there was Abū Bakr al-Ṣaddīq ﷺ; and for this, 'Umar bin al-Khaṭṭāb ﷺ said about him during the battle of Yamāmah,

> *'Umar asked Abū Bakr why he would fight this battle against apostates after the death of the Prophet ﷺ, since they had not stopped testifying that 'there is no god but God.' They had stopped, however, paying zakāt (the fixed minimum amount given to the poor and other categories of recipients). Abū Bakr said: 'I will fight whoever separates prayer and zakāt, because zakāt is a responsibility of the wealthy. By God, they have even withheld from me the 'iqāl (there is a historical disagreement whether this is a term for 'general zakāt' or the hobble cord of a camel) they used to give (as payment) to Messenger of God ﷺ.' Then 'Umar responded as Ibn al-'Arabī cites:*

'And right then, I saw that God had opened the heart of Abū Bakr to accept that he should fight, and I recognized that he was right' - with 'Umar's understanding the resolve of Abū Bakr in his inside.

When there originates from you a movement in your outwardness, it originates only from illatun (something sacred, a revelation) - and it is rare. This is why the one who understood the stations among the earlier generations among the people of the Book, when they heard, or it was said to them, 'Messenger of God ﷺ said such-and-such,' they would say, 'This word did not come out from anywhere but the sacred' - that is, it is a Divine word, not a word from a created being. Consider how fine the knowledge is, and in what station this Tribe is firmly stationed and to what pillar they adhere. God make us one of them! Their actions radiate in the interior. The abodes of the travelers among them are caves and caverns; and in the cities, they live in whatever others among the creatures of God *exalted* have already built, not laying one brick onto another brick or weaving one reed with another reed. And Messenger of

God ﷺ was this way until he passed away to his Lord: he built no abode for himself at all.

The reason for this is that they see this world as a bridge erected from planks over a great river; and they are traversing it, then departing from it. Do you see anyone building a house on a bridge of planks? No, by God, and especially not anyone who knows that the rains will fall, and the river will swell with the torrents feeding it, and the bridge will be broken. Anyone who builds on a bridge will surely be exposed to destruction.

If the builders of this world were given kashf from God, opening their sight so they could see this world as a bridge, they would see the river over which it was built - that it is extremely perilous; and they would not build what they build, such as lofty castles. But they do not have eyes to see that this world is a bridge of planks over a great, tremendous river, nor do they have ears to hear the statement of the Messenger, the one who knows what God reveals to him: 'This world is a bridge (inna al-dunyā qanṭarah).' They do not act based on faith, nor from a vision and kashf reaching them, so they are as God said about them, *They reckoned there would be no trial, so they became blind and deaf; then, God turned to them* at the moment *al-mā'idah*
of their hearing from the Messenger ﷺ when he said to them, *5:71*
'This world is a bridge' - and so on. Now do not occupy yourselves with building and being roused to rise up. And he had hardly finished with his ﷺ words when many of them turned back to their blindness and their deafness, even though they were Muslims, faithful. Therefore, God reported to His Prophet with His word, *yet again many of them became blind and deaf* - after having turned to God *al-mā'idah*
in repentance. One might ask, 'What is the use of speaking about *5:71*
them?' My friend! - if we assigned continuation to this world, would we not see our journey away from her, generation after generation? (Instead, the 'continuing world' is the next world, where we journey after death, generation after generation.)

Among the states of this group is their shepherding in their hearts their mysteries connected to God with regard to knowing themselves. One does not meet them in the daytime together with the distracted ones. Their movement is at night. Their view is to the unseen. The station of sadness

> *ḥuzn (sadness) is the tone of the Qur'ān, as if the beauties and mysteries described can never be fully appreciated; also heart softening compassion and empathy, and roughness, as in rough tracts of land (corresponding to English 'going through a rough patch'). This heart-polishing roughness, and ḥuzn, is necessary for us to maintain compassion and empathy for creation.*

overwhelms them - because sadness, if it is missing from the heart, the heart becomes ruined. So the one who recognizes (the 'ārif) eats sweets and honey; but the great one who verifies for oneself (the muḥaqqiq) eats bitter gourd, very perturbing, taking no pleasure at all in tasting it as long as one is in this abode, because of one's full occupation with what God addressed one with - that is, thankfulness for it. I met one of them in Dunaysīr (Kochisar, Turkey), 'Umar al-Firqawī, and another in the city of Fes, 'Abd-Allāh al-Sammād.

The 'ārifūn, viewed next to these, are like infants who do not think, enjoying and taking pleasure with their rattles. So what do you imagine compared with the aspirants (students, murīdīn), and what do you imagine compared with the general population? The ones who verify for themselves (the muḥaqqiq) have the anchored stance in tawḥīd; and they have the mushāfahat al-fahwānīyah,

mushāfahah, 'he spoke to him putting his lip near to his lip,' from the lexicon Tāj al-'arūs. The term al-fahwānīyah is in the iṣṭilāḥ (discussion of terminology, found in Chapter 73) - when the Divine addresses one in an encounter, a 'Divine address heard face to face in the intermediary world'.

making the refusal of stability (i.e. being fixated on an assumption) a priority, because being free from all (transcendence) is their pursuit - like the phrase, 'no god but God'. It is the best word brought by the messengers and the prophets. Their tawḥīd (no god but God) is an matter of intelligence. They do not act from the lower self in anything; they have the complete Presence, continuously, and in all actions. They are distinguished by knowledge of life and giving life, and they have the upper hand; and they learn from animals what no one but they know - and especially from every living being who moves on his stomach, because of his proximity to his source from which he was created.

Indeed, every animus (animal) is distant from his root, deficient in his understanding of his root commensurate with his distance therefrom. Do you see the sick person who cannot stand or sit up, but remains prostrate because of his weakness? It is his return to his roots. You see him utterly dependent on his Lord, impoverished, the picture of weakness and neediness, telling you so by circumstance (circumstantially, as the infant cries are communicative without being articulate) and by (articulated) words. This is when his root is
al-Rūm 30:54 ruling him, so he nears it. God says, *We created you to be weak*; and He
al-nisā' 4:28 said, *Humankind was created weak*; so when he rises up standing and becomes distant from his root, he becomes a pharaoh and acts arrogantly and presumes to have strength - and says, 'I'.

As with the English, the Arabic 'I' is arrogantly erect - أنا. Also, in classical Arabic, one tends not to use 'I', because the first person singular is already signaled in the verb's conjugation. In formal Dhivehi, 'I' is alhu-gandu, 'this slave thing'; and in the sub-continent, languages carry the idea of who we really are: one is a banda - someone tied, as a slave, to God.

The true Men are those who are with God in their standing and their (picture of) health as they are when lying down sick and weak; and they are rare indeed.

They engage in intense examination in viewing their actions and the actions of others with them, on account of the intentions with which they turn to face; and they correlate them from the intensity of their examination until the deeds belong purely to them, and they purely separate out the ones belonging to another. This is why it is said they are niyyātiyyūn (the people based on niyyāt, intentions and purposes), just as one is said to be malāmīyah (one based on blame) and ṣūfī (one based on wearing the wool of the devotee) - based on the particular states they have. They have knowledge of chiding, energizing, resolving, desiring, and aspiring. These, all of them, are prior states (prior to action), belonging to the intention (which comes first). The intention *f* is the one which comes from him upon a skin-to-skin contact with his actions: she is expressed in the Divine revelation. In her they dig deep, and she is the linkage point of ikhlāṣ (sincerity purely devoted).

Our ʿālim (teacher) Imām Sahl bin ʿAbd-Allāh was scrupulous in this pursuit, and he was the one who alerted me to scrutinizing the incoming thought. He used to say, 'The (pursuit of, *m*) intention *f*, he is that chiding, and he is the primary reason for the new creation of internal stirring energy, and resolving, and desiring (something to *Be!* and it is), and aspiring.' He leaned for support on him (the pursuit of intention) - and according to us this is valid.

And God speaks the true,
and Hu is the guide to the way. al-aḥzāb 33:4

وَاللَّهُ يَقُولُ الْحَقَّ وَهُوَ يَهْدِي السَّبِيلَ

Chapter 34

Verified by the Breaths

On ma'rifah of a person who verifies for oneself at the alighting place of the breaths; and specified by these breaths are matters I shall mention, if God so wills.

Verified by the Breaths

Chapter 34

The one made true, verified by the breaths,
is a supremely compassionate one -
and the (cosmic) Throne m *is in his*
truth, if he is a human being.

If this one turns to face the direction of the
(stabilized) entity f*,*
the Mist m *seeks her for himself, and a beautiful*
conduct - so he is beautiful, sincere.

His station is in the interior of the Heights, settling
therein -
helpers visiting him, and assistants.

helpers (anṣār) are the ones about whom was said, 'A breath of the Supremely Compassionate comes to me from Yemen' (the people originally from Yemen - many of the Anṣar in Madīnah).

He has of the night, if you verify for
yourself, its end (third) part,
just as he has, of the being of the
eye ('ayn), a pupil (insān).

If his visible aspect glimmers, you say, 'a Qur'ān' -
or if his invisible aspect glimmers,
you say, 'a Criterion'.

God has combined in him every generous behavior;
and this one is the universally
complete, with no deficiency.

generous behavior is manqabah, also a straight and narrow path, root naqaba, and pl. nuqabā' (the overseers, responsible for the people).

إعلم

Learn, may God assist you with a holy spirit, that the objects known are different in themselves and that the perceiving things, by which the objects known are perceived, are also different in themselves - just as the objects known are - but in the place of their selves and their beings, not in the place of their being perceiving things, even if this is an issue of disagreement according to the masters of examination.

Now, God has made for each truth which may be known a specific perceiving (instrument), conventionally though not in truth - I mean their site (e.g. ear, eye; and 'conventionally', because the objects known are perceptible by any and all perceiving instruments, as will be explained later); and He made the site perceiving these objects perceived, belonging to these sites of perception, to be a single entity ('ayn wāḥdat).

The sites and instruments of perception are six things: hearing, seeing, smelling, touching, tasting, and intellect. For all of them except the intellect, the perceiving belongs to the things (instruments), self-evidently. Now the things which the intellect links to and depends on customarily never err, ever. (The data the eye perceives is never wrong, but the intellect may interpret incorrectly.) About this the majority of the intellectuals are mistaken; they attribute the mistake to the sense (e.g. the eye), but it is not so; no, the mistake belongs to the judge (who incorrectly interprets the data).

As for the perception of the intellect of the intelligible things, it is in two divisions: there is something self-evident, as with the rest of the things perceived, and something not self-evident. In fact, the intellect depends for its information on six instruments: the five senses which we have mentioned, and the reflective faculty. A thing known will be known by a created being certainly and correctly, based on its being perceived by one of these perceptive faculties.

But we are actually saying here that the majority have erred about the perception of the senses, by attributing errors to them; and this is where they see (for example), when they are on a ship taking them along the shore, they see the shore coursing with the coursing of the ship. So the sight has provided them what is not true and what is not something known (to be true). You see, they are knowers with a self-evident knowledge that the shore is not moving from its place, but they cannot deny what they are witnessing - that it is moving.

But the matter according us is not so. The shortcoming and the mistake occurred in the judge, who is the intellect, not from the senses, because the senses perceived them as their truth provided them self-evidentially - just as the intellect, concerning what it perceives self-evidentially, does not err; but concerning what it perceives by means of the senses or by reflection (and not self-evidentially), it may err. Therefore, the senses make no mistake at all - nor does whatever perceives self-evidentially.

There is no doubt that the senses saw movement - no doubt; and tasted bitterness - no doubt. So the sight perceives the movement essentially, and the taste perceives the bitterness essentially; and the intellect comes and judges that the shore is moving, and that the sugar is bitter. But another intellect comes and says, 'The bile mistake arose at the site of the tasting faculty, so it perceived bitterness; and this mistake intruded between the tasting faculty and the sugar. Therefore, the taste tasted only bile bitterness.' Now the two individual intellects agree that you perceived bitterness, no doubt. But the two intellects disagree about what was perceived at the site of the tasting (i.e. the sugar - was it bitter?). (The latter intellect) clarifies that the intellect erred, not the senses; so the attribution of the mistake, in the true dimension, must always be to the judge, not to you the direct experiencer.

With me, for this issue there is yet another matter contradicting what they allege, and it is that the sweetness which is in the sweet, and in other foods, is not actually in the food, because of a matter which, if you dig deep you will find the veracity of what we are arguing. It is this way for the judging factor of all the perceivers. If, in practice, there was above the intellect another perceiver, judging over the intellect, taking from it - just as the intellect judges over the senses - that perceiver too would be mistaken as a judge of what has been considered self-evident to the intellect; and it would say, 'The intellect is mistaken about what is self-evident to it.'

So when you confirm this, and you learn how God arranges the perceivers and the things perceived, and that the connection is a matter of convention (where we typically identify sweetness with sugar) - then learn that God has other creatures for whom the fabric of the conventional is torn with regard to their perception of the things known. Among them is one for whom is placed a perceiver who perceives by means of any of the faculties, perceiving intelligible and sensory things with the faculty of sight alone; and another (perceives everything intelligible and sensory) with the faculty of hearing (alone) - and so on, perceiving by means of the entirety of the faculties. (As soon as we confirm for ourselves that sweetness is not in the sugar, just the way pain is not in the amputated leg, we may consider a disengagement of tasting from object tasted; then we may experience a sweet taste by means of sight, or hearing, or any or all senses.) Thereafter, there is perceiving by happenstance matters different from (typical sensory) faculties, such as striking, and moving, and stilling, and so on. Messenger of God ﷺ said, 'God struck His Hand between my shoulder blades, and I found a coolness of His Fingers in the front of my chest; then I learned the knowledge of the firsts and the lasts.' Included in this knowledge is every thing known, intelligible and sensed, which the created being perceives. This is a knowledge arriving not from one of the faculties, either sensory or meaning (e.g. imagination, memory); this is why we say, There is then another means (sabab, rope) different from these faculties, which perceives the objects known.

We therefore state, The object known may be perceived by

other than the conventional faculties. Thus, we judge these perceived things belonging to their conventional sites of perception, conventionally. For example, the intuitive: the person with intuition observes an individual, and he knows what is coming from him, or what he is thinking inside, or what he did. It is the same way with the diviner (zājir, e.g. who stirs up birds and augurs the future, based on their flight) and people like him.

We in fact brought this out, all of it, as something to familiarize you with what we wish to relate to the family of God - the prophets and the friends - in what they perceive of knowings coming from the non-conventional path. When they perceive knowings, they relate them to this quality by which they perceive them - these things known. Thus, they say, so-and-so is someone of observation - that is, by observation, such a person perceives all the things known. I tasted this with Messenger of God ﷺ. And so-and-so is someone of hearing, and so-and-so is someone of tasting, and someone of breath, and breaths - meaning, smell - and someone of touch, and so-and-so is someone of meaning. This last is external to these; in fact, it is as one says among the general population: someone of sound reflection. And among the people there is one whose endeavor to understand is provided by another faculty, commensurate with what is provided; and you have a return to this other faculty when you become habituated to it, because this habitual return (ʿādat) is derived from reversion (ʿawd) - that is, this process reverts to you during every observation, or in every smell. There is nothing other than this.

And in this way also, you may learn that the Divine names are like this; and even though each name provides a particular truth, within its power is that every single Divine name provides what the entirety of the names provides. He *exalted* said, *Say: Call upon Allāh or call upon al-Raḥmān; whichever (name) you call, to* hu *belong the Most*
al-isrāʾ 17:110 *Beautiful names.* And in this way, if you recite every name *m*, you may say about him, 'Indeed, to hu belong the Most Beautiful names.' This is because of the Oneness of the Named - so understand this.

In Chapter 167, 'We therefore said Divine because of the citations of settling (on the Throne), and descending (in the third part of the night), and with (you wherever you are), and the multiplication of Divine names over the One named, (each Divine name) having different meanings.'

Among the people there are those for whom the name *m* Allāh is special, so his faces by which he is recognized are based on ilāh (in English: God, based on god). And among them are those for whom the name al-Raḥmān is special, so his faces by which he is recognized are based on raḥmānīyah (compassion). It is the same with the physical faculties, about which one may say, 'The faces by which this individual is recognized are based on observation.' And with regard to another, based on hearing. So one is part of the observing world, or the hearing world, or the breaths' world. In this way, the faces by which one is recognized based on Divine matters (ilāhīyāt) are related to the Divine (ilāhī) name which is opened up for him there; then enfolded therein are the truths of the names - all of them.

When you understand this also, then learn that of all the Divine names, the one singled out in this topic for this particular individual is the name al-Raḥmān, and that of all the faculties singled out is the one affiliated to the faculty of smell, and connected to her are the wafting scents - and they are the breaths. Thus, one is part of the world of the breaths, in a correlation of the faculties (i.e. smell) and founded on the compassion-based ones, in the step-levels of the names.

We state: this person who is designated in this chapter, whether he is Zayd or 'Amr, his recognizable face is based on compassion (raḥmānīyah). Every matter related to the name al-Raḥmān in the Book or the Sunnah is related to this individual. This name is mumidd (extended in space, like ink stringing from the inkwell onto the page) in aid for you; and no other Divine name has authority over you, except through the intermediary of this name al-Raḥmān - (over you) in whatever facet it may be.

This is why we state: God *glorified is He, and exalted* has hidden inside in different places His compassion in His torment, and His retribution - as with the sick person in whose torment of sickness He placed a compassion *f* by whom his offenses were covered over; so this is a compassion (overlooking sin) in retribution (the torment of sickness). And it is this way with the one against whom is established the ḥadd (punishment) avenging Him (because stealing, for example, is an offense against the right of God), by killing or beating. It is a present moment punishment in which is an invisible compassion. By her, what he is subject to prosecution for in the next abode is lifted from him. It is just the same as his good fortune in this world - coming from the name Giver of Good Fortune - has hidden inside His (later) retribution; so he is enjoying good fortune today by means of what will torment him - because of the torment hidden inside - in the next abode (e.g. ill-gotten gains, which will be paid for later in torment), or during the time period of repentance (in which turning - tawbah - will cancel retribution).

So, when the human being turns in repentance and observes (his action) and reflects on the forbidden acts which were giving him pleasure, these images summoned in the mind return to him now as torment - while before his turning in repentance, when he summoned them to his mind, he was enjoying them with the utmost of pleasure. Therefore, glory be to the One who hides His compassionate kindness inside His torment, and His torment inside His compassionate kindness, and His blessing in His retribution, and His retribution in His blessing. Thus, the site hidden in the belly (mabṭūn) is ever *hu*, a spirit of the visible entity - whatever thing it may be.

You see, with this individual, as his recognizable face is based on compassion and the name al-Raḥmān, settled on the Throne - He
ṭā-hā 20:5 *exalted* said, *al-Raḥmān, settled on the Throne* - so the stirring energy of this individual is Throne-based. Then, just as the Throne belongs to al-Raḥmān, the stirring energy belongs to this recognizable face as a site for her (cosmic) settling down. It is said then that one's stirring energy is Throne-based, and the station of this individual is a
cf. al-a'rāf 7:46f. hidden interior of the Heights - and they are the enclosing walls (suwar; cf. sūrah) between the people of felicity and the wretched. And belonging to the Heights are Men we will cite, and they are the ones who are not delimited by adjective - such as Abū Yazīd al-Basṭāmī (who, when asked how he was that morning, replied 'I have no morning and no evening') and others. His station was the interior of the Heights, because his recognizable face was compassion-based; and his stirring energy was Throne-based - because the Throne is the settling site of al-Raḥmān. And in the same way, in the interior of the Heights there is kind compassion, just as in its exterior there is torment.

This individual feels compassionate kindness toward all beings, every one of them, toward the disobedient and the ingrates, and toward others. He *exalted* said to the master of this station - he is Muḥammad ﷺ - when he called down curses against Ri'l, Dhakwān, and 'Uṣayyah to be tormented, and for revenge (for their treacherous killing of seventy Anṣār called the Reciters), saying, 'Against you this and that,' and he recited what they had done - God said to him, 'God has not sent you to vilify and curse; He sent you to be compassionate kindness.' So He forbade cursing them and vilifying them and hating; and God sent down to him, *We did not send*
al-anbiyā' 21:107 *you except as a compassionate kindness for the worlds.* So he spread out universally over the world - namely, to be compassionate toward all and to pray for them, not against them. He exchanged His word,
Muḥammad 47:23 *God cursed them*, for 'God turned to them and guided them' - just as he uttered when they wounded him (in the battle of Uḥud, against the Quraysh), 'O God, guide my people, because they do not know,' meaning, the one who called him a liar (because he does not know better) - someone not of the people of the Book, or the followers of the people of Book, or others (who should know his status with God). ('Guide them' was a frequent prayer of the Prophet ﷺ, often as a response referring to his followers when he was being asked to curse this or that person or tribe for wrong-doing.)

This is why we state with regard to this individual who has this station, 'He is most compassionate (raḥīm) to the disobedient and the ingrates.' If this person is a judge, he upholds the ḥadd (Law-defined punishment); or if he is one of the ones designated as a witness to uphold the ḥadd, he gives testimony or upholds it, but he upholds it only from the door of kind compassion, and from the name al-Raḥmān - with regard to the one receiving the ḥadd or being testified against - not from the door of retribution. And seeking to take out one's anger on someone: the station of this name does not involve doing so, nor does the state of this individual provide for this. He *exalted* said in a story about Abraham (that he said to his father), *I fear that punishment may afflict you from al-Raḥmān.* *Maryam 19:45*

Whoever has this as one's station and recognizable face, and this name al-Raḥmān looks out for you, you are appointed mysteries tasted: between the correlation of settling on the Throne, and between the correlation of the where (was our Cherisher before He created the creation?) to the Mist. The question is whether the two correlations have a single or multiple definition. You will learn what the True has in the description of Sublime Majesty and Gentle Goodness simultaneously, between the Mist and the settling (on the Throne). You see, He was in the Mist while there was no Throne, so He is described as settling there; thereafter, He created the Throne and settled there with the name al-Raḥmān. The Throne has a definition distinguishing him from the Mist, who belongs to the name al-rabb (the Cherisher, who was in the Mist, no wind above and no wind below); and the Mist has a definition distinguishing him from the Throne - so, inescapably, there is a shifting from adjective to adjective.

The characterization of *hu exalted* lies not between the Mist and the Throne, or in whatever correlation comes out between the two, as each one has been distinguished from the other by his defining boundary and his truth - just as the Mist is distinguished which was wind above and wind below: it is the radiating, foliating cloud which carries the wind which is under it and above it - based on the Mist, above which is no wind and below which is no wind; it is a mist not carried (by wind).

The listener learns that the Mist which was made to belong to the Cherisher has where-ness. It is a mist not carried. Then came His word, *Will they wait until God comes to them in shadows of clouds?* Is this 'clouds' the referent of this Mist? Then the Mist would be a bearer for the Throne, and the Throne the settled place of al-Raḥmān; so the Day of Arising would combine the Mist and the Throne. Or is this cloud the conventional cloud above which is wind and below it is wind? The one with this station is provided with knowledge of this - all of it. *al-baqarah 2:210*

Then the one of this station is provided also with Divine knowings of this category of the name al-Raḥmān: the descent of the Cherisher to the sky of this world from the Throne. Is this descent from the Throne or from the Mist? You see, the Mist is cited when the questioner asked about the name the Cherisher. He was asked, 'Where was our Cherisher before He created the creation?' He answered, 'He was in the Mist, above it no wind and below it no wind.' Thus, hidden in the pronoun 'He was' is 'Our Cherisher'. And he said, 'Our Cherisher descends to the sky (of this world, in the third part of the night)' - so this shows you that His descent to the sky of this world is from that Mist, just as His settling on the Throne is from this Mist.

His (spatial) relation to the sky of this world is like His relation to the Throne - no different - and He does not become separate from the Throne in His descent to the sky of this world; and He does not separate from the Mist in His descent to the Throne, nor to the sky of this world. As the Prophet ﷺ reported that God says about the descent to the sky of this world, 'Is there someone turning for forgiveness, so that I may turn to him? Is there someone seeking forgiveness, so that I may forgive him? Is there someone asking, so that I may provide to him? Is there someone calling, so that I may answer him?' - This, all of it, is therefore part of the context of His kind compassion and His gentleness, and this is the truth of the name al-Raḥmān, who settled on the Throne. This attribute descended with the name the Cherisher to the sky of this world. It is what we have taught you: indeed, each Divine name includes and embraces the determinative property of the entirety of the Divine names, in the place where the One named is One (wāḥid, single).

The possessor of this station learns from this Cherisher-based descent to the sky what is singled out by the name al-Raḥmān therein, the One who says, 'Is there someone turning for forgiveness; is there someone seeking forgiveness', because al-Raḥmān is sought by this word (e.g. Forgive me!) - no doubt. This is an allotment the possessor of this station learns, based on this descent (to this world) with no intermediary (responding to these requests of the people awake at night pleading). And one learns the descent of the Cherisher from the Mist to the sky of this world through the intermediation of the name al-Raḥmān. You see, the name the Cherisher has no dominion over the possessors of this station, belonging instead, as we said, to the name al-Raḥmān. And they do not learn anything based on the name the Cherisher or any of the other names - just from the name al-Raḥmān. They learn matters by means of the teaching of them by al-Raḥmān - what the True desires by descending from the Mist to this sky. Your face by which you are recognized is according to this aspect.

Then, some of what singles out the possessor of this station - by means of an intermediation of the name al-Raḥmān - is understanding the statement of God: 'Not vastly spacious enough for Me are My heavens and My Earth, but vastly spacious enough for Me is the heart of My faithful slave' - brought out with the yā' (signaling the first person possessive) attaching the noun to 'Me', for spacious (spacious enough for Me) and for 'ubūdīyah (My slave).

The mu'min is the one who has faith and the one who is grateful.

The 'abd is the creature and the slave; 'ibādah is worship; 'ibād is creatures; and 'ubūdīyah is the state of slavery to the Divine. To be a creature of the Creator is to worship, knowingly or unknowingly, and to submit to the All-Powerful, voluntarily or involuntarily.

You take from God only the amount the yā' alone provides you (and that is you as spacious enough for Me and you as My slave; the question then becomes: who is the referent of Me and My?). Embraced here are two knowings: a knowing of the grace in here for the slave of *hu* who is faithful, so you take this from the name *m* al-Raḥmān himself; and a knowing of a concealed secret in here annexed to the letter yā', so you take this from God by means of the interpreting dragoman - the name al-Raḥmān. Then you learn that the spacious here - the meaning of it - is the image which the human being was created in (as 'Adam was created flush against the image of al-Raḥmān').

It is as if He is saying, 'My names emerge visibly - all of them - only in the configuration based on the human being.' He *exalted* said, *And He taught Adam the names, all of them* - that is, the Divine names from which the beings come into being, all of them; and they were not provided to the angels. He ﷺ said, 'God created Adam flush against the image of *hu*'; and the pronominal referent of *hu* (His/his/Hers/its), according to us, is multi-faceted: it may refer to Adam (God created Adam in Adam's own image), so then there would be a refutation against some of the philosophers among the people of reflection; and there is a facet that would refer to God, so that Adam takes on as characteristics (takhallaqa) the entirety of the Divine names (so God created Adam flush against His own image - where the 'His' includes all His names). *al-baqarah 2:31*

So now, learn about this vastness that, in fact, she accepts (spaciously) the faithful slave, given one is 'flush against the image' *f*, just as the mirror accepts the image of the gazer, but not non-mirrors - things neither polished nor clear (on the surface). This does not pertain to the sky, given her being translucent (and non-reflective), nor to the Earth, given her being non-polished. Therefore, you are pointed to the fact that in the creation of the human being, even if it is based on orbital movements, she (the sky) is the human being's father; and (even if it is) based on receptive elements, she (the Earth) is the human being's mother. Indeed, you have from the Side of

the True some matter which is not there in your fathers or in your mothers; based on this matter, the sublime majesty of God is vastly encompassed. You see, if this were in the capacity of your father, who is the sky, or your mother, who is the Earth - or from both of them - then the sky and the Earth would be more deserving of being spacious enough for the True, compared with you who were born from them both; and this is especially true since God is saying, *In fact, the creation of the heavens and the Earth is greater than the creation*
ghāfir 40:57 *of the people, but most people do not know* - meaning, greater in significance, not in mass. But despite this, the human being is not distinguished by some matter giving one this adequate spaciousness which the sky and the Earth are too constricted to provide. So one does not have this spaciousness except with regard to some other matter from God by which one is made to be more excellent, compared with the sky and the Earth.

Every single one in the world is exceeding, exceeded (mafḍūl, lacking, less excellent). Every single one is exceeding in the world with its excess, through the wisdom placed in neediness and deficiency - which every one other than God has. When the human being gloats in this vastness and boasts himself high over the Earth and the sky, His word comes: *The creation of the heavens and the Earth*
ghāfir 40:57 *is greater than the creation of the people.* And when the sky and the Earth gloat with this verse over humankind, there comes His word: 'Not vastly spacious enough for Me are My heavens and My Earth, but vastly spacious enough for Me is the heart of My faithful slave.' Knowing this makes it disappear, this gloating and pride, from both of them; thus, all depend on their Lord and all are veiled from gloating - and from their (lower) selves.

ghāfir 40:57 His word, *But most people do not know*, indicates that some people do know this; one knows this who knows it among us, based on the name al-Raḥmān, which one has and by whom one is verified; thus, one accomplishes this matter fully informed. You are compassionately provided (this answer) at the moment of gloating, by means of learning what makes you more excellent than the sky and the Earth; and you learn from this that you obtained from the name al-Raḥmān only the measure of what was disclosed in kashf to you from that in which is your medicine. Indeed, this matter by which this creature exceeds the sky and the Earth is, again, based on the name al-Raḥmān - but the name did not flow abundantly over this creature.

And do not say: 'This is a defamation, given the fact that humankind is a nuskhah (transcript, copy) of the world.' No, in fact he is in truth a copy of the entirety by expressing the metaphor that one has something from the sky in some facet, and something from the Earth in some facet, and something from everything in some facet

- but not from every facet, because the human being in truth is the entirety of the created beings. One does not say about him, 'He is a sky but not an Earth and not a (cosmic) Throne'; but one says about him, 'He resembles the sky from such-and-such a facet; and the Earth from such-and-such a facet; and the Throne from such-and-such a facet; and the element fire from such-and-such a facet; and the element air from such-and-such a facet; and water and earth and everything in the world.' With this metaphoric expression, he is a transcript, and he has the name human being - just as the sky has the name sky.

Part of the knowings of the possessor of this station is the descent of the Qur'ān as a furqān (a Criterion). If one knows it as a Qur'ān, then it is not from the name al-Raḥmān, because the name al-Raḥmān is a translation of another Divine name who includes the name *m* al-Raḥmān. Indeed, *hu* comes down during the Blessed Night - she is the laylatu'l-qadr - and *hu* teaches with a descent of *hu* the measures of the things and their weights; and *hu* teaches the measure and power (qadr) of *hu* during this night - just as the Cherisher does in the last remaining third of the night.

e.g. 'Blessed is He who sent down the Criterion to His creature so it would be an admonition to the worlds' al-furqān 25:1. And refer to this chapter's poem.

The night is a site of descent in time for the True and His adjective - she is the Qur'ān. And the third remaining part of the night, during the descent of the Cherisher, is the unseen Muḥammad ﷺ, and the unseen of this kind of humanity - because the unseen is a veil, and the night is a veil; and this remaining part of the night is called the third because this human configuration has perpetual remaining, forever, in the everlasting abode. (The first third is the time of the alastu; the second third is the time in this world; the last third is perpetual existence in the other world.) Indeed, the first two thirds depart with the presence of the one third remaining part - or the last part of the night - in which the True descends; so, again, this part must remain.

Hu is a night not followed by a dawn, ever; nor does *hu* vanish, but (hu) transfers from passing state to passing state and from abode to abode - just as the night *m* transfers from place to place in front of the Sun *f*. He runs ahead in front of her lest his entity vanish. You see, light negates the light-blocker, and light-blocking negates light; however, the dominion of light is stronger, so the light chases away the light-blocker, while light-blocking does not chase away the light. It is the light transferring, so light-blocking emerges in the site which the light has no entity existence in. So do you see? The True is called Light but is not called light-blocking. Light is a found, existent thing; and light-blocking is non-existent. As light does not get dominated by light-blocking, rather the light dominates, in this way the True does not get dominated by creation; no, the True dominates - so He calls Himself Light.

Then the sky *f* vanishes - this is the first third of the night; and the Earth *f* vanishes - this is the second third of the night; and the human being remains in the other abode, for ever and ever, until no endpoint - and this is the third third of the night. And he is the child coming from these two parents: the sky and the Earth. Then the Qur'ān is descended during the Blessèd Night *f*, in the last third of her; and this (three-thirds being) is the universal, complete human.
al-dukhān 44:4 In him is separated and differentiated *every matter, in wisdom* (fī-hā, in her - the Night - yufraqu kullu amrin ḥakīm). He is distinguished
al-shu'arā' 26:193,4 from his parents by the remaining: *the peaceful spirit descended with him (the Qur'ān) onto your heart* - he is Muḥammad ﷺ.

نَزَلَ بِهِ ٱلرُّوحُ ٱلْأَمِينُ
عَلَىٰ قَلْبِكَ

Do you see how the Lawgiver speaks of the child of adultery? 'He is the third bad thing' - and in this way the child of lawful marriage is a third good, from this particular perspective. Thus, the fluid from which the child is born from the man and the woman wants to exit, and it is the fluid from which the child comes into being - it is the third matter. The two parents move sexually, when it wants to exit, in order to bring it out; so its putting them into movement, in regard to the two, is without any consideration of what the Law is pleased with - it is called copulation. One says about it, 'it is the third bad thing' - meaning, it is the reason for the movement by which the word bad is applied to all three of them. He makes it three thirds: the parents are two thirds, and the child is one third.

In this way, the night is divided into three thirds. Two thirds vanish - they are the sky and the Earth; and the third remains - he is the human being. In him there emerges visibly the image of al-Raḥmān, and in him descends the Qur'ān. In fact, the sky and the Earth are called night because light-blocking belongs to them, essentially; and the illumination in them comes from others, such as the masses which illuminate - the Sun and others. Thus, when the Sun disappears, the sky and the Earth are darkened.

With this, my friend, you have been abundantly informed of knowings not recognized before this. They are knowings of this individual who is verified and authenticated by the alighting place of the breaths; and everything this individual perceives, he in fact perceives from the wafting scents by the faculty of smell, nothing else. We met of them a congregation in Sevilla, and in Makkah, and in the Holy House (in Jerusalem); and we conferred with them about all this with a circumstantial conference (conferring by seeing and showing), not by an articulate conference. It was just as I conferred with another group, who were ones of visual observation - by sight; I asked them questions, and they responded; we were asked and we were responded to, with bare sight (and no other sensory faculties employed). Among us there was no usual discourse and no conventional visible (e.g. hand) signals (exchanged) at all. Yet, when I looked at one, I knew the entirety of what he wanted of me; and when he looked at me, he knew the entirety of what I wanted from him. His look at me was a question or an answer, and my look at him was the same. We were given to reach comprehensive knowings among us, with no talking.

This amount is enough, with some knowledge of this individual. His knowings are many, which we encompassed; so whoever wants to learn some of what we mentioned, learn the difference between 'in' in His word, 'He was in a Mist', and 'settled' in His word,

al-Raḥmān, settled on the Throne — *ṭā-hā 20:5*

- and do not say 'in' in the way He said,

in the sky ۞ — *Āl-i-'Imrān 3:5*

and in the night. — *Āl-i-'Imrān 3:27*

In everything we have cited is clarified for you a station of the jam' al-jam' (the collection of the collection: the collection of maps, cf. suwar, of the Qur'ān like an atlas, which is the manzil al-manāzil - the alighting place of the alighting places, introduced in Chapter 22 and then discussed in all of the fourth section of the Futūḥāt al-Makkīyah), and a station of the jam' (the Qur'ān), and a station of the differentiation (furqān, the Criterion), and a station distinguishing the step-levels.

And God speaks the true, and Hu is the guide to the way. — *al-aḥzāb 33:4*

The 19th manuscript ends, followed by the 20th.

Chapter 35

A Manzil of the Breaths

On ma'rifah of this person who is verified in the alighting place of the breaths and his mysteries after his death, God be pleased with him.

A Manzil of the Breaths

Chapter 35

The ʿabd (slave) is the one who is in
the passing state of his life,
like his state after death, in body and spirit.

And the ʿabd is the one who in the state of being
veiled is a light,
like a lighting of the Earth from Yūḥ (the Sun).

The state of death: no claim accompanies it -
just as life has the clear claim.

Against a people, and about a people, there is
with them
this claim, by a gesture of the head, or the hand.

If you understand what we are saying, you will
rise -
weighty, transcendent above
diminishment and preponderance -

And you will be one of those who purify
their truths;
and there is no access point to
calumny and defamation.

And if you are unaware of what we are saying,
go to the abode of accounting, by means
of a chest laid open (masrūḥ).

mashrūḥ, as in a-lam nashraḥ laka ṣadrak, Did We not open your chest for you? ۞ al-sharḥ 94:1

إعلم

Learn, may God assist you with a holy spirit, that this person who is verified in a manzil (alighting place) of the breaths, whatever person it may be: one's state after one's death is different from all the other states of death. Let us first cite the enclosure of the source of the family of God for their receiving knowings from God - just as we established in the chapter before this - and let us discuss their final outcome and the consequences of this source in themselves.

Thus we state: My friend, knowledge of the family of God taken from kashf is in the same format as faith, so everything faith accepts is given in kashf to the family of God - because it is true, all of it; and the reporter of it - he is the Prophet ﷺ - reports it from authentic kashf. The selves of the knowers of God *exalted* are according to the adjective of the thing from which they drew out knowledge of God, whatever it may be.

Learn that the adjectives (attributes) are of two kinds: personal adjectives and meaning (idea) adjectives. The adjectives based on meaning with regard to the thing described are those which - when removed from the dhát described - do not remove the dhát which was their object of description (e.g. the idea of generosity is not removed when the person who was generous is gone). And the personal attributes are the ones for which - when you remove them from the one described by them - the one described is removed thereby, and there remains no being based on the entity, nor a being based on the intellect, whence it was removed. There is then no personal adjective belonging to the one described which is not a thing additional over her dhát (e.g. Zayd is additional to 'human being'), unless she has a personal adjective by which she is distinguished from another. It may be a dhát described, composed of two personal attributes, and more above this - and they are the dhát-based definitions.

Ibn al-'Arabī is leading the audience to consider the relationship of the adjective to the noun (the ṣifat to the dhát). He opposes the idea that the dhát of God is divisible or composite; therefore, the Living is not separable from the Knowing, nor are the adjectives additive, leading to a sum making up the dhát of God.

And here, the door is locked. If we open it up, there may appear something that makes the intellects vanish and makes confidence in the things known disappear. And perhaps the matter may go back with this to where the first cause for the adjectives is the enabled beings themselves. Just as if you were to take the reason as a condition in the existence of the thing conditioned, and you removed the condition - the thing conditioned would be removed, no doubt; but the reverse is not necessarily so. This flows forward continuously but not in reverse, so we will leave the door bolted for the one who would find its key and open it.

E.g. a ball rolling down the hill because of the condition of gravity. Take away gravity, and you take away a ball rolling down the hill; but taking away the ball rolling down the hill does not take away gravity. Ibn al-'Arabī is leading us to consider our entities - enabled to be by Being, and described as objects of being - if we were not to be: meaning, if we had no stand-alone personal adjectives. Then, continuing this example, there is still gravity, as well as the personal adjectives of laughing, and settling, and descending, and being cheered by. But the dhát has, not multiple personal adjectives, but one - 'one' (waḥdat). And so, 'hu is the First, and the Last, and the Outward, and the Inward' ⊛ al-ḥadīd 57:3.

Since the matter with us and with every intelligent person is of this vantage point, you have learned that the adjectives are meanings that do not stand up by themselves (have no independent existence); and they do not come out except in the described thing itself. The personal adjectives are ideas (meanings), and they are the thing described itself. The meanings do not stand up by themselves, so how can they be the thing described itself - nothing else? The thing is described by itself, and it starts to stand by itself, the one whose truth it is. Will it not stand by itself? Every described thing is the totality of its personal adjectives, and the attributes and adjectives do not stand by themselves; and there is after all no dhát but Her, gathering the adjectives together and emerging visibly.

I have alerted you to a tremendous matter so you would understand where the intellectuals' knowledge returns with regard to their reflections. And I have explained to you that authentic knowledge is not provided by reflection, nor by what the intellectuals confirm with regard to their reflections; and that authentic knowledge is rather what God casts onto the heart of the learner; and it is a Divine light by which whoever He wishes is singled out among His creatures - that is, angel, messenger, prophet, friend, faithful one. Who has no kashf has no knowledge.

This is why there come the messengers and the Divine notifications about what the intellects consider impossible; then they feel compelled to interpret some of it in order to accept it; and they feel compelled to concede; and they feel incapacitated before things that do not accept interpretation at all. And the utmost is that they say, 'It has a facet only known by God which our intellects do not reach.' This, all of it, is a consolation for the soul - not knowledge - so that they will not reject anything brought prophetically. This is the state of the believing intellectual. As for other than the believer, he does not accept any of it.

There have come many reports which the intellects consider impossible - some of them about the elevated Side, and some of them about the truths and alterations in the entities. As for the ones from the elevated Side, the True describes Himself in His Book and on the tongue of His messengers only with something that obligates faith in it; and the intellect does not accept it with its evidence literally, unless they interpret it with a far-fetched interpretation. His faith then is in his interpretation, not in the report; and he does not have kashf, as there was with the Prophet - thus, he (ﷺ) knew the meaning of the True in this report; and He described Himself with the grammatical vessels of time and space (e.g. 'God was (temporal) in (spatial) the Mist, and nothing is with *hu*'), and with this His Messenger ﷺ described Him, and all the messengers; and all of them are with a single tongue about this, because they speak from a single, sacred origin.

Origin here is illun, the sacred, the revelation, the 'el' in Gabriel and other Hebrew names.

The intellectuals are people of afkār (mental examinations, thinking-thinking). Their statements about God differ commensurate with their observation. Then the god which is worshiped with the intellect is stripped of faith; it is as if it were - rather, it is - a god established according to what that intellect's observation provides. Its truth differs according to the view of every intellect - and the intellects are oppositional and contradictory. Each group among the people of intellect calls the other ignorant of God; even if they are among the islāmīyīn ('Islamic') interpretive intellects, each group calls the other kāfir (disbeliever).

But with the messengers, God's blessings on all of them, from Adam عليه السلام to Muḥammad ﷺ, there is no disagreement transmitted from them concerning the qualities and adjectives they relate to God. In fact, all of them are of a single tongue about this. The books they brought, all of them, articulate about God with a single tongue. Not two among them disagree; they affirm each other, one of them the other - despite the long time periods (separating them) and not having met. And despite the sectarianisms contending among the intellectuals, the messengers' ordered arrangement has not been disordered.

It is like this with the believers in them, who are upon insight: the Muslims who submit safely, the ones who do not get themselves involved with interpretation. They are one of two (types of) men: either a man who has faith and hands (the religion) safely over (without intellectual interpretation), and you hold the knowledge of this to yourself until you die - this is the muqallid (who binds oneself to the tradition); or you are a man who practices what you know of the branches of the legal principles, and you bind belief to what the messengers and the Books come with, so God gives kashf to your insight and you become full of insight in your affair - just as did His Prophet and His Messenger ﷺ, and the people of His grace. He had kashf and insight and invited the people to God upon insight - just as He said with regard to His Prophet ﷺ, reporting about
Yūsuf 12:108 him, *I call (invite) people to God upon insight, I and whoever follows me.* And these (the second type of men) are the knowers of God, the ones who really know. And even though they are not messengers or prophets, they are upon a clear explanation from their Lord in their knowledge of Him and in what was brought from Him.

And in this way He described Himself with many of the adjectives of the created beings, such as arriving, coming, manifesting to things, and definitions, and veils and face, and eye and eyes, and hands, and being satisfied, and disliking, and wrath and rejoicing, and being cheered - and every authentic report coming in the Book and Sunnah.

Examples of these authentic reports: God 'arriving in the heaven of this world in the third part of the night';

coming - idhā atānī yamshīya ataytuhu harwalatan ('when he comes to Me walking, I come to him rushing');

manifesting - falammā tajallā rabbuhu li'l-jabali (When his Lord radiated - and manifested - to the mountain ۞ al-a'raf 7:143);

definitions (hudūd) are spatial limitations, such as the five places (kā'ināt) where God is - ('in the Mist', settled 'on the Throne', descending to the sky of our world in the third part of the night, 'and He is with you wherever you are' ۞ al-ḥadīd 57:4, 'and He is God in the heavens and the Earth' ۞ al-an'ām 6:3);

veils - 'Between God and creation are 70,000 veils'

the Face of God (wajh-Allāh: wherever you turn, there is the Face of God ۞ al-baqarah 2:115)

eye -'alā 'aynī (under My Eye ۞ ṭā-hā 20:39);

eyes - fa-innaka bi' a'yuninā (you are in Our Eyes ۞ Hūd 11:37),

hands - bi-yaddayya (by His Hands ۞ ṣād 38:75);

satisfied - fa-raḍīnā 'anka wa raḍīta 'annā ('We are satisfied with you, and you are satisfied with Us');

disliking - karihtu liqā'ahu ('I dislike meeting him');

wrath - rabbī ghaḍiba al-yawm ghaḍaban lam yaghḍab ('My Lord will be wrathful on that Day with a wrath He had not had before');

rejoicing - lillāhu ashaddu farahān bi-tawbati 'abdihi ('God is more intensely joyful with the repentance of His creature');

cheered - tabashbasha allāhu lahu ('God is cheered by him').

The reports are more than can be counted, including what is not accepted except by the one with faith in them without interpretation, or some of the masters of observation among the believers with the interpretation one's faith compels one to make.

So consider the step-level *f* of the faithful, how honored she is, and the level of the people of kashf, how great she is, where her people catch up to the messengers and the prophets, peace be upon them, with the Divine knowing they are distinguished by - because the ones who know are the inheritors of the prophets; and they do not inherit dīnārs or dirhams - they inherit knowledge. He ﷺ said, 'I am in the company of the prophets; we do not leave inheritances, nor do we leave something for charity.' If you own something of this world, better to leave it as a waqf (an irrevocable gift), as a charity, as you see fit to one of the family of the nearest to God - that is the true relationship (being near to God); or abstain from your wealth. You leave nothing for inheritance if you want to catch up to them, nor do you inherit from anyone. And all praise belongs to God, who gave me an abundant allotment from this station! This is one of the descriptions which were received by me from God *majestic, sublime* about God *exalted*.

Now, concerning the heart of the truths, all agree among the intelligent ones that there is no disagreement. The evidence (in this regard) indicates (that we are here discussing) the limited intellect, from the direction of its thinking and its observation, not from the direction of its faith and its receptivity (to revealed texts). You see, there is no one more intelligent than the messengers and the family of God, knowing as they do that the entities do not undergo alteration of their truth in themselves, and that the qualities and the happenstance events - in the school of one who argues that these entities are concrete entities - do not stand by themselves; no, necessarily they will have a location (which is either) standing up by itself or not standing up by itself (i.e. self-standing, independently existent) - but it will be in a 'standing up by itself', necessarily. An example of the first is black, for instance, or whatever color it may be. You see, it does not stand up except in the place about which one may say, 'Blackness has stood up here; it is black.' And an example of the second is like the black-brightening place, for instance (where the Sun rises to dispel darkness). Then the blackness is the brightening place, because it is a characteristic the brightening place has (inseparably). This is the meaning of my saying, 'or not standing up by itself - but it will be in a "standing up by itself"'.

This issue is one of khilāf (where one argues one way one time and another way another time) among the observers (the natural scientists), whether the meaning (idea) stands by means of meaning (i.e. if the black of the black-brightening place is removed, is there still the idea of the black-brightening place?). There is one who says it does and one who says it does not. It has been established that actions, all of them, are incidental (happenstance); and that they vanish and do not remain permanently; and that they do not have a concrete entity after their vanishing departure; and that they are not characterized as shifting (concretely from one place to another); and that death is either a happenstance that happens to the dead - in the argument of some of the observers - or it is a correlation of separation after having been together (i.e. life plus body). And then it is the same way for the entirety of beings - in the argument of some observers - and this is correct according to what the evidence requires. In every state, death does not stand up by itself. (Therefore, death is a shifting correlation, and life separates from the body; and the body returns to a mineral state, where it is alive and celebrating God with His praise.)

And the prophetic reports come with something that opposes this, all of it, despite the fact that we agree that the actions are incidental or relational. The Lawgiver says - and he is truthful, having authentic knowledge and clear kashf: 'Death will come on the Day of Arising in the image of a salt-colored ram, which the people will recognize and no one will deny, and he will be immolated between the Garden and the Fire.' It is narrated that John the Baptist (Yaḥyā) عليه السلام will lay him down and slaughter him with a knife he has in his hand, and the people will be watching him. And it is also narrated in a report that a deed of the human being will come to him in his grave as an image, handsome or ugly, and he will ask him (the image) who he is; and he will say, 'I am your deed.' And here, the one who holds back from paying zakāt (required charity) - his wealth will come to him as a serpent with two foamy dots on its head. And statements like this in the revelation are too many to count.

As for the faithful, they believe in this, all of it, without interpretation. As for the people of observation among the people of faith, and others, they say, 'Carrying this over in its literal sense is impossible intellectually, so there must be an interpretation.' So they carry it back interpretatively, commensurate with what their examinations provide them. Then, they - the people of faith among them - say, following their interpretation, 'But God knows best' (wa Allāhu a'lam) - meaning, about this interpretation specifically, which they argued for: was it what God meant or not? As for carrying it over in its literal sense, it is impossible, according to them, in aggregate; but the act of faith instead connects to the phrase the Lawgiver used specifically. This is the belief system ('aqīdah) of the people of afkār (mental examinations, sg. fikr - arranging things in the mind).

Now after we have explained to you these matters and the levels of the people in them - because they are part of this chapter we are in the midst of - learn that there is nothing further except beings God created, as an excellence from Him for them, standing by themselves; and everything described is relations and affiliations between them and the True, in the place they are described. Then, when the One who brings into being brings into being, one says about this: '*hu* is powerfully able to bring into being. If not for this power, He would not bring into being.' And when the enabled is distinguished by an imperative from another - who could also be made to stand - about this, one says, 'murīd (the One who desires)'. If not for this, the enabled being would not be distinguished from another. The rope (sabab, motive, cause) of all of this is provided by a truth of the enabled being; thus, the enabled beings provide these correlations (of Able to enabled, Desiring to desired) - so understand, if you are one of the kernel and of ilāhī (God-based) vision and Raḥmānī (al-Raḥmān-based) kashf.

We have established in the chapter before this that the source from whence the things known are taken is based on different paths: they are hearing, seeing, smelling, touching, tasting, and intellect. We mean the intellect in the place of its self-evident data: it is what the intellect perceives by itself, without taking from any other faculty and also in the place of its sound reflection - that is, data referred through the paths of the senses, or self-evident data, or badīhīyāt (suddenly formed intuition, without premeditation, bypassing the judge who is the source of erroneous interpretations of sensory data); nothing else. This is called knowledge.

And the unexpected, happenstance ('āriḍah, clouds collecting and suddenly coming toward one) events - from which the object of the known arrives - again revert to the referral of these roots, not disengaged from them. In fact, they are called unexpected events because the expected convention concerning perception of colors is that touch will not perceive them; no, the sight will perceive them. Therefore, when the blind person perceives colors by touch - and we have seen this - he has unexpectedly turned toward the sense of touch what is not usually part of its truth to perceive. It is this way with the rest of the paths: when turned unexpectedly toward them, they perceive what is not part of their usual pursuit to perceive. You then say about this, 'One turned unexpectedly toward them.'

Ibn al-'Arabī is focusing our attention on the primordial process of creation. The stabilized entities, waiting in the void, are first desired (When We desire a thing, We but say to it Be! *and it is ۞ al-naḥl 16:40); then al-qādir acts, the One who is powerfully able, to enable the thing to become. Then iqtidār is the readying of something, a powering cast flush against something, providing qudrah (power, capacity). This powering is what Dhū'l-Nūn says he heard always, everywhere, because he heard the primordial alastu (Am I not your Cherisher? ۞ al-a'rāf 7:172) always. And in the atemporal configuration of creation, each entity is being turned on and off every quantum time period (Every day hu is upon a radiant brilliance ۞ al-Raḥmān 55:29); therefore, the iqtidār powering it on is (theoretically) perceptible at every moment.*

God has made this as an alert for us: that there is then no truth that Divine powerful ability (iqtidār *f*) does not penetrate into, contrary to what the people of observation presume. In fact, this truth is God's setting of her into this image, and she is not actually perceived (only) by the things (sensing instruments) linked to their perception of her - for example, 'seen' by sight and not by something else. God is saying, 'No, it is by Our setting her so' - thus, one perceives the entirety of the known objects, all of them, by means of a single truth, based on these truths, when the True so wishes. This is why we stated, 'A perceiving turns unexpectedly to that which typically is not the one to perceive' (as the blind person perceiving color through touch). And we know certainly that *hu* may be One who turns unexpectedly to this, where you know and you see based on *There is nothing like hu* - even though the perceiving instruments do not perceive anything at all, except when many things, from the entire set of objects perceived, are like it. *al-shūrā 42:11*

Ibn al-'Arabī is considering two means of perception. The first is where we see a tree, and our perception of the tree is processed by matching this new data to our memories and conceptions of trees. But what happens when something 'nothing is like it' (laysa ka-mithlihi shay'un) appears suddenly before us?

And glory be to *hu* beyond! *hu* is not negated from being perceived by any one of the perceiving faculties which He created, except the sight. He said, *Sights do not perceive hu* - and this is forbidden by Law. But He did not say *hu* is not perceived by hearing, or intelligence, or by any other of the faculties the human being is described as having - just as He did not say, either, 'Indeed, other than the sight perceives Me.' No, He left the matter in ambiguity. The unexpected matters emerge, which turn themselves in display to these faculties, in an occasion for alerting us that perhaps He placed this into our view, based on *There is nothing like hu* - in the same way as we see something for the first time, or hear something for the first time, or smell something for the first time, or taste something for the first time, or touch something for the first time, or understand with the intellect something for the first time; these are firsts which have no previous template (mithal, example, likeness) in us, even if what is a first (for us) is like something else, as the matter truly is. *al-an'ām 6:103* *al-shūrā 42:11*

But in the 'first time perceived' there is a strange mystery negating likeness to it. The perceiver has perceived someone who has no likeness, according to him, so he correlates analogically (the one I perceived for the first time is like this other one). Now, given the fact that this object perceived accepts essentially a likeness, or does not accept a likeness, this is another matter, additional to its being an object perceived; (and it is a matter) not needed in order to be perceived - if you possess decisive understanding!

No, our statement is that the Divine infinite vastness requires that there is no likeness (mithal, similarity) in the entities which are sites of being. Similarity is an intelligible, imaginable idea - because if similarity were authentic and true, no thing would be distinguishable from another thing which could be called its like. (We can imagine that tree1 is like tree2, but if this were really true, we could not differentiate tree1 from tree2.) This by which one thing is differentiated from another thing is exactly the entity of the other thing; and that which cannot be differentiated from another is exactly a single entity.

If you say, 'We see this as bifurcations bifurcating, being separated, this from that, despite the fact that they are like each other in definition and in reality' - I reply, You are mistaken, because that by which a separation occurs is expressed by 'it is this entity'; and what does not make separation occur is the thing you are presuming is the likeness. This is one of the most recondite issues in this chapter and subject.

There is then no likeness at root, and yet it is not possible to deny the likenesses - but by definition, nothing else. This is why likeness is applied in the context of the total intelligible truth - not to the concrete thing. Therefore, the likenesses are intelligible, not concrete (mawjūdah). And we say about the human being, one is an articulate animal - no doubt. But Zayd is not the entity 'Amr, in the context of his image, but he is the entity 'Amr in the context of his humanity; he is not otherwise, basically. Now, as he is not other than him in his humanity, so he is not his like; no, he is he (bal, huwa hu). Indeed, the truth of humanity *f* is not divisible; no, humanity is in every human being herself (as an entity), not divided; so she has no likeness. (That is, Zayd's humanity is not like 'Amr's - humanity is humanity.) And it is this way for the entirety of the truths - all of them.

Likeness (mithalīyah *f*) is not correct if she is considered to be other than the entity of the resembling likeness. Thus, Zayd is not 'Amr in the place of his humanity; no, he is he. And Zayd is not like 'Amr in his image. Indeed, the criterion separating the two is obvious. If not for this distinguishing criterion, Zayd would be confused with 'Amr - and there would be no recognizable face in the things (distinguishing one from another). Therefore, the perceiving instrument perceives, whatever thing it perceives, based only on *there is nothing like* (third person singular pronoun) *it*. *al-shūrā 42:11*

This is because the root which we return to in (and for) our being is God *exalted*, who is *There is nothing like hu*. Therefore, whatever is brought into being from *hu* is only flush against a truth that there is nothing like it. You see, how could anything be created who was not given the quality and adjective of *hu*? And the truth of *hu* does not accept likeness; then, inescapably, every quantum (fard, single) jawhar in the universal will not accept likeness - if you possess decisive understanding and the kernel. Then, indeed, there is no truth in the Divine which accepts likeness. *al-shūrā 42:11*

If an acceptance of likeness were present in the world, it would have to lean for support for its being, from this facet, on a non-truth of the Divine; and there is, after all, no creating site but God; and there is no likeness He has - so there is, in being, nothing having a likeness. No, every site of being is differentiable from another, by means of a truth it is flush against in its dhát. This (conclusion) is what is provided by kashf and by true Divine knowing.

Then, if I apply likeness (semantically) to things, as has been established, learn that I am applying this according to conventional usage. He *exalted* said, *Communities like yours* - that is, as the word 'community' is applied to you. In the same way, the word 'community' is applied to each animal, and bird flying on the wing; and in the way every community and every entity in existence, other than the True, depend for their creation on the mawjid (the One who brought them into being). With this correlation we may speak of each one: that each one is like the other in depending on God. *al-an'ām 6:38*

From this it is certainly correct that God is *There is nothing like Him* - with the addition of the kāf, or by the likeness being assumed (so the ka is an emphatic particle, 'There is really nothing like Him'); then when you recognize that everything that comes out newly does not accept likeness, just as we established it for you - and the True is first in this quality - so there remains only the likeness that comes in the Qur'ān and elsewhere, concerning the dependence on God, the One who brought out the entities of the things.

al-shūrā 42:11 laysa ka-mithli-hi shay'un: laysa (not) kā (like) mithli-hi (His like) shay'un (a thing). 'There is not like His like a thing.'

Now we return, and I say, With every single one of the family of God, there will be a situation where God has made a knowledge for this individual of the things in the entirety of faculties, or in a specific faculty itself, as we have established: either in the smell, and one is a possessor of knowledge of the breaths; or in the sight, so one says one is a possessor of sight; or in the touch, and this is part of the subject of touching, along a special path - this is why we allude to this by the presence of 'cool fingers'. The possessor of this adjective, by which the object learned is obtained, is given an affiliation: you say, he is a possessor of this or that.

As we have established, the adjective (descriptor, e.g. a black painting) is the described object itself (the painting), in this topic and chapter - I mean, the personal adjective. Just as the meaning returns, about which one says, 'It (e.g. the color black) does not stand by itself' (and must be 'in' or descriptive of something else, e.g. a painting) - so, in this way, the image which is the 'thing by which it is known' returns to an idea. This is in order for you to verify for yourself the idea (meaning) and its cleaving together to the 'thing by which it is known' (e.g. the idea of black cleaving to the painting) - just as these ideas cleave together. Thus, there begins to be, based on their cleaving together, a dhát, standing up by herself (e.g. a black painting). You say about her: 'a body', 'a man', 'a horse', 'a plant' - so understand.

Then the possessor of knowledge of taste begins to taste, and the possessor of knowledge of smell to smell; and the meaning of this is that one does to something else what the taste does if one is a possessor of tasting, or what the smell does if one is a possessor of smelling. Thus, the something has been glued and adhered, virtually, to its meaning (idea); and it begins to become, in itself, a meaning by which the perceiver of the things perceives - just as the viewer looking at the mirror perceives things which are not perceived in this state, only in the mirror.

The teacher Abū Madyan had a small child from a black woman, and Abū Madyan was a possessor of sight. This child - he was a child of seven years - would look out and say, 'I see on the sea in such-and-such a place a boat, and such-and-such has happened there.' Then, after some days, this boat would arrive in Bajāyah, the city this child was in - the matter turning out to be just as the child had said. So they asked the child, 'How do you see?' He would say, 'With my eye.' Then he would say, 'No, rather I see with my heart.' Then he would say, 'No, rather I see by my father. When he is present, and I look at him, I see this which was reported to you; and when he is absent from me, I do not see any of it.'

It has come in a true report from God about the creature who approaches to God through nawāfil (extra devotions) until He loves it, that He says, 'And when I love it, I become the hearing which it hears by, and the sight by which it sees'; the ḥadīth continues. By Him, one hears and sees and speaks and strikes and runs. This is the meaning of our statement: The verified one returns to be like an ideational image of whatever one was verified (and validated) to be. Thus, you look at your parents in the same way as human beings look with their eyes into the mirror - so understand. (Their image is 'you' because you came from them, but they are not you; and in the mirror, it is you, it is not you, and it is not not you.) In this way is the possessor of one of the paths of these faculties. You combine the all into a single 1; and you see by means of every faculty, and you hear by means of every faculty, and you smell by means of every faculty - and this is the fullest, most complete collection gathered together.

As for their states after their death: to the extent they were in this world devoting themselves exclusively to some designated matter, or to different matters, and to the extent they verified and were validated as being exclusively so devoted - they are in the next world commensurate with their states in this world. The one who was a pure slave in this world is in the next world a pure sovereign. And the one who was in this world described with sovereignty, even if he was a sovereign only over his own limbs - he is deficient in sovereignty in the next world commensurate with what he received full measure of in this world. And if he established justice in this (area), and expended and discharged however God obligated him, according to Law, and he believed that he was a sovereign over this area (operating externally to the Law) on account of negligence coming forth in him - then the calamity that this is will revert to him and have consequences for him.

No one is more honored in the next world than the one who reached the utmost of humility in this world, at the Side of the True and the truth. And there is no one more humiliated in the next world than the one who reached in this world the utmost of honor and pride in himself - even if he was maṣfūʿan (slapped with the open hand) in this world. I do not mean by 'honored in this world' that he was in this world a king - only that he had the description in himself of being proud. And it is this way for humility. As for the one who was literally a king, or something else, we do not consider whichever station and whichever state the True set up His creature in literally; instead, it is the metaphoric expression for his (true internal) state (that we consider).

ʿAbd al-Karīm bin Hawāzan al-Qushayrī mentioned in one of his books, and others, a man among the people: that he had buried a man from among the integrated ones. When he was placed in his grave, his shroud slipped off his side and his side hit the earth, and the corpse opened its eyes and said to him, 'You, are you humbling me in front of the One who honors me?' This was astonishing, and he came out of the grave (he was digging). And I saw something like this with a slave of God, my friend al-Ḥabshī, in his grave. I saw him being washed (for burial), while the washer was afraid, in a long story

This is from Austin's Sufis of Andalusia (excerpting Ibn al-ʿArabī's Durrat al-fākhirah): Kamāl al-Dīn Muẓaffar heard a voice telling him to wash, and he kept replying, 'I do not need to wash myself.' Then he was told to be ready to wash someone else tomorrow. He was called in to wash al-Ḥabshī and he was thinking how unworthy he was to wash such a man, when (returning to the text):

- when he opened his eyes toward the washer and said to him, 'Wash me!'

One of their states after their death is that they are alive with the vital principle (nafsī, soul-based, spirit-based) of life, by her every thing celebrating God; and he who has himmat (internal energy) in his worship site stirring during the state of his worship / during his life, where he guarded her against anything which would enter therein so that the state (of hers) would not be altered, if he was someone of breath - then when he dies and someone after him enters his site of worship and would do there what was not appropriate for its (original) owner to do, who had lived there, there would appear a sign. And this we have seen in a story of Abū Yazīd al-Basṭāmī. He had a house in which he worshiped, called the Bayt al-Abrār (the House of the Devotees); and when Abū Yazīd died, the house remained guarded, protected, nothing happening there except what was appropriate for a mosque. It happened that a man came and urinated there. They say that while he was there, unclean, his clothes burst into flames - without the usual fire - and he fled the house. And anyone who entered and did there anything except what is appropriate saw some sign.

The trace of this person remains after his death, doing just what he would do in his life - the same. Some one of them said - he loved the prayer - 'O Lord! If you would grant to a single one that he pray the ṣalāt in his grave, make me that one!' He was seen once while he was praying in his grave. Messenger of God ﷺ passed the grave of Moses عليه السلام during the night of his Ascension and he saw him as he was praying the ṣalāt in his grave.

One of the states of this individual after his death is like this - these matters (of this chapter) - there being no difference with regard to him between his life and his death. Since during the time period of his life in this world he was in an image of a dead man in the state of death, so God made him during the state of his being dead just as he was in his state in life - a harmonious recompense!

And one of the attributes of someone with this station in his death: when the observer looks at his face while he is dead, one says about him, 'He is alive.' But when one looks at the pulse probe area of his veins, one says about him, 'He is dead.' So the observer hesitates (and cannot decide), because God has combined in him life and death, during the state and moment of his life and his death.

I saw that with my father, God be kind to him. We almost did not bury him, except with a doubt, because of what he had in his face of an image of the living, and because of what he had with the stillness of his veins and the halted breath of an image of the dead. Before he died, fifteen days earlier, he told me of his death: that he would die on Wednesday, and it was so.

When it was the day of his death and he had been gravely ill with sickness, he sat up without support and said to me, 'My son, today there is the journey and the encounter.' I said to him, 'God has written for you safety in this your journey, and He has blessed you for your encounter.' He was happy with this. He said to me, 'May God give you your deserved good reward from me, my son. Everything I heard from you: you would say it and I would not acknowledge it, and maybe sometimes I would reject some of it; but it is exactly as I am witnessing it.'

Then there appeared on his brow a clear luster, different from the color of his body but not disharmonious. He had a glimmering light by which (my) father was recognized. Then this luster spread from his face until it diffused over his entire body. I kissed him and made final peace with him, and I left from his place, saying to him, 'I am going to the grand mosque until someone comes to me to announce your death.' He said to me, 'Go, and do not let anyone (outside) visit me.' He gathered his wife and daughters. When ẓuhr (midday prayer) came, someone came to announce his death. I went to him, and I found him in a state where the observer doubted about him whether he was alive or dead. And in this state we buried him. He had a tremendous crowd witnessing. Glory to the One who distinguishes one with the supreme compassion of *hu*, whomsoever He wishes.

Therefore, with someone possessing this state, his life and his death are the same. And everything that preceded in this chapter of knowledge, it is knowledge of a possessor of this station - because it is part of learning the breaths, and this is why we cited what we cited.

And God speaks the true, and hu is the guide to the way. *al-aḥzāb 33:4*

وَاللَّهُ يَقُولُ الْحَقَّ وَهُوَ يَهْدِي السَّبِيلَ

Chapter 36

The Jesus-Based

On ma'rifah of the Jesus ones and their Pivots, and their origins

Those who make their truth alive
and heal from the sickness of the veils:

They are Jesus; we are not pinned above us
onto anything causing doubts.

His firmly rooted character provided him
a step-level rising high over the step-levels.

You will recognize him by a wholly apart epithet,
in the pure, clear inspiration and the revealed books.

No one was so provided - except his inheritor -
with this quality, in the bygone periods.

Flowing through existence is his energy ƒ,
in non-Arabs and in the 'Arab.

Ibn al-'Arabī is connecting the creative process of kun spoken as an imperative in the other world to the kun of some of the 'ārifūn in this world (both called himmat) to the animating creative process of Jesus with the clay bird and the dead Lazarus.

By her their souls were re-animated,
and by her the recurring afflictions
were cleared away.

إعلم

Learn, may God assist you, that whereas the Law of Muḥammad ﷺ encompasses the entirety of the preceding Laws, and as there remains no authority in this world except what is confirmed by the Muḥammadī sharī'ah ƒ - so, by her confirmation, the Law is solidly fixed. Then we ourselves worship through her, in the place where Muḥammad ﷺ confirmed her, not in the place where a prophet - singled out for a particular Law in his own time - confirmed her. And this is why Messenger of God ﷺ was given the All-Encompassing Words.

For the relationship between the various prophets and Laws sent to humanity, and the rūḥ muḥammadī, see also the opening pages of Chapter 12.

So when the Muḥammadī (Muḥammad-basis) is put into practice - and the entire world tasked today including human and *jinn* is Muḥammad-based - then there is today no Divine Law in the world except this Muḥammadī Law. It may be that you, a practitioner belonging to this community, may encounter in your practice something that opens you up, in your heart and along your path, and you may verify it for yourself as a prophetic path based on the previous prophets, which includes this sharī'ah; and your path is confirmed, and its end goal accompanies her. When you are opened up with this understanding, you are put in relation to some of this sharī'ah; and one says about someone, 'He is 'Īsawī', or 'Mūsawī', or 'Ibrāhīmī'. (The ī is 'based on' and '-basis'.) This is to verify what distinguishes their 'face by which one is recognized'; and there appears for them some station based on the sum-total of what is under the encompassment of the sharī'ah of Muḥammad ﷺ.

One is distinguished in this relationship or by that lineage from another in order to recognize that one has inherited from Muḥammad ﷺ only what - had Moses or another of the prophets been alive and following him - one would have inherited from him (the earlier prophet). As their Laws came before this sharī'ah, we take the person distinguished to be the 'ārif (recognizing) inheritor, since the inheritance goes from the earlier to the later generation. If this earlier generation did not have a Law confirmed before the confirmation of Muḥammad ﷺ, we would be placing the prophets and the messengers on the same basis in combining (the earlier period with) the time period of the sharī'ah of Muḥammad ﷺ. It is just as we place on an equal basis today Ilyās and Khaḍir - and Jesus, when he comes down - because the moment rules for this basis, as there is no prophethood providing Law after Muḥammad ﷺ.

Since the advent of the prophethood of Muḥammad, all earlier prophets can be considered equal, each having had his ruling moment before the appearance of the Prophet ﷺ. The ruling moment from now until the end of time is that of the Prophet ﷺ, because there will be no further ruling moments, and his All-Encompassing Words include earlier Laws and are the visible manifestation of the invisible source from which they sprang. See also Chapter 12.

No one says about the family of this path, 'He is Muḥammadī,' except about two persons: either the person is singled out by inheriting knowledge from a rule not in a Law before, so one says about him, Muḥammadī (because this is the all-inclusive category); or, a person combines the stations, then leaves from them to no-station (lā maqām), such as Abū Yazīd and people like him. For this one also you say about him, 'Muḥammadī'. Apart from these two persons, everyone else is related to one prophet among the prophets;

and for this (procedure) there comes in a report that 'the 'ulamā' are the inheritors of the prophets' - and it is not said they are the inheritors of a particular prophet. Addressed with this is the 'ulamā' of this community. And it also came with this phrasing of his ﷺ word, 'The 'ulamā' of this community are prophets, compared with the rest of the communities.' And in another narration, 'they are like the prophets of the Banī Isrā'īl'.

The first 'Īsawīyīn were the ḥawārīyūn

The whiteners (launderers) of clothing, based on the trade of the companions of Jesus; also, people 'free from defect'. The concept of ḥawārī as 'companions' is used for the disciples of Jesus and of Muḥammad, peace be upon them both. In Kitāb al-'ayn (8th century), 'the ḥawāriyūn are the ones with Jesus عليه السلام*.*

who followed Jesus, and whoever among them until today reached the Law of Muḥammad ﷺ and believed in him and followed him; and it may happen that he obtained something from this sharī'ah which before had been a Law belonging to Jesus عليه السلام. Thus, he inherited from Jesus عليه السلام what he inherited without veil; then he inherited from Jesus عليه السلام something inside the sharī'ah of Muḥammad ﷺ as an inheriting follower inheriting from a follower (Jesus), not from one who is followed. Between them there is a taste separating them. About this, Messenger of God ﷺ said concerning the example of this person, 'He has double reward'; and, in this way, he has two inheritances and two openings and two different tastings; and in regard to the two, he is affiliated only to this one prophet عليه السلام.

These are the second 'Īsawīyīn, and their roots are a tawḥīd (transcendent unity) stripped of the mode of the image (i.e. no visible image of God), because the coming into being of Jesus عليه السلام was not from a human male but was rather from an image-making (tamaththala) spirit in the image of a man. This is why the case for the image (ṣūrat) predominates in the community of Jesus son of Mary, unlike in the rest of the communities. Thus, they make images as pictures in their churches, and they apply themselves to worshipful devotion by facing them, because the origin of their prophet عليه السلام was from image-making. This truth flows throughout his community until today. And then, when the Law of Muḥammad ﷺ came and he rejected images, and he ﷺ had enveloped a truth of Jesus, and he had enfolded his Law into his own Law, and he ﷺ made Law for us that we should worship God 'as if' we see Him - thus, he brought Him for us into the khayāl (the image-forming dimension), and this is a meaning dimension of 'imagination'.

cf. fa-tamaththala la-hā basharan sawiyyan, 'There imaged before her a well-proportioned man' = Maryam 19:17 - i.e. Gabriel in the nnunication.

That is, the ṣūrat (image, form) in this dimension is the taṣwīr (imagined, mental image, mental picture) in the meaning dimension.

He forbade image-making only in the physical dimension, that there should not appear in this community any sensory form.

Then, with this particular Law, which is 'Worship God as if you see Him', Muḥammad ﷺ did not tell it to us without intermediary; no, in fact it was his statement to Gabriel عليه السلام (i.e. the ṣūrat - image, form - in this dimension is the taṣwīr - imagined, mental image, mental picture - in the meaning dimension), and he is the
Maryam 19:17 one who came as an image-made for Mary as *a well-proportioned man* at the creation of Jesus عليه السلام. So it was as you say in the metonym, 'I am speaking to you - but listen, neighbor.' So we are the intended audience for this statement, and this is why there comes at the end of the ḥadīth, 'That was Gabriel, wanting that you should learn, when you did not ask'; and in another narrative, 'He came to teach the people their religion.' And in another narrative, 'He came to you to teach you your religion.' None of the narratives depart from the fact that it is we who are the intended audience to be taught.

Then you should know that what we have that is not part of the Law of Jesus عليه السلام is his word, 'Even if you do not see *hu*, *hu* sees you.' Thus, this is part of their roots.

Our teacher Abū'l-'Abbās al-'Uraybī, God be kind to him, was 'Īsawī at the end part of his life - and 'Īsawī was my beginning. I mean the end part of our teacher in this path was 'Īsawī. Then, I was transferred to the opening of the solar Mūsawī; then, after this, I was transferred to Hūd عليه السلام; then, after this, I was transferred to the rest of the prophets, peace be upon them; then, after this, I was transferred to Muḥammad ﷺ - and in this way was my situation on this path. God strengthened it for me and did not swerve me off the evened road. God granted me - on account of this configuration, configured during the above transfers which God configured me as, in this path - a face of the True in every thing. Thus, there is not in the universe, according to us, in our view, anything in existence except there is in it for us some eye-witness of a True entity based on whom we exalt *hu* - nor do we cast aside anything from the world of being.

During our time period, today, there is a group of companions of Jesus عليه السلام and Jonah عليه السلام still alive, and they are cut off from the people. As for the people who are from Jonah's people, I saw a footprint of one of theirs by the shore. He was ahead of me a little. I measured with my hand his stride length in the earth (sand), and I found the length of his stride to be three standard spans plus a half and a quarter of my actual hand-span.

The story is told again in Chapter 198, 6:208 (tawḥīd #21), where the length of his pace in the sand is thalāthat ashbār wa thulthāy shibr (three spans, and one-third span). If x is the shibr and y is 'my' shibr, meaning Ibn al-'Arabī's actual hand-span, which we may arbitrarily put at 8 inches, then we can equate the first and second stories.

$31/3\,x = 3x + \frac{3}{4}\,y$

so $1/3\,x = \frac{3}{4}\,y$

$x = 9/4\,y$

$9/4\,y = 2\frac{1}{4}\,y = 18$ inches.

The stride of this person would then be 60 inches, twice or more times a 'normal' stride in the sand.

My friend Abū 'Abd-Allāh bin Khazar al-Ṭanjī reported to me that he met him also (the Jonah person), in a story (he told); and he brought me a statement from him about what was happening in Andalusia in the year AH 585 - it was the year I was still in Andalusia - and what will happen in the year AH 586 with the Franks; and it was as he said - he did not miss an iota.

The prediction may have been about the siege of Silves by the Almohād caliph.

As for the one who is during our time among the companions of Jesus, and it is something told in a ḥadīth of 'Arabshāh bin Muḥammad bin Abī al-Mu'āllā al-'Alawī, al-Nūqī al-Khabawshānī said, ḥaddathanā Muḥammad bin al-Ḥasan bin Sahl al-'Abbāsī al-Ṭūsī, who said, akhbaranā Abū'l-Muḥāsin 'Ālī bin Abī al-Faḍl al-Fārmidhī; akhbaranā Aḥmad ibn al-Ḥusayn bin 'Ālī; ḥaddathanā Abū 'Abd-Allāh al-Ḥāfiẓ; ḥaddathanā Abū 'Amr 'Uthmān bin Aḥmad bin al-Sammāk, imlā' (teaching ḥadīth) in Baghdād; ḥaddathanā Yaḥyā bin Abī Ṭālib; ḥaddathanā 'Abd al-Raḥmān bin Ibrāhīm al-Rāsabī, ḥaddathanā Mālik bin Anas 'an (from) Nāfi' 'an Ibn 'Umar, who said:

"Umar bin al-Khaṭṭāb wrote to Sa'd bin Abī Waqqāṣ while he was in al-Qādasīyah, that Naḍlah bin Mu'āwiyah al-Anṣārī be dispatched to Ḥalwān al-'Irāq, to attack its outskirts. He said, So he dispatched Sa'd Naḍlah with 300 horses, and they went out until they reached Ḥalwān al-'Irāq, and they attacked its outskirts, and they took booty and women. They turned their attention to selling the booty and the women, until the 'aṣr prayer time overtook them, and the Sun had almost set.

'Naḍlah took the booty and women, to guard them, to the foot of a mountain, then stood up to give the call to prayer. He said, Allāhu akbar Allāhu akbar. He said, He was answered from the mountain with the response: You have declared great the Great, O Naḍlah. Then he said, ashhadu an lā ilāha illā'llāh; and he said, It is the word of ikhlāṣ (purely cleared from, e.g. having partners; cf. *qul huwa Allāhu aḥad*), O Naḍlah. He said, I testify that Muḥammad is a messenger of God. He said, He is the religion and he is the one Jesus son of Mary gave good tidings to us of, peace be upon them both, and at the head (end) of his community will come the End Time. Then he said, Come to the Prayer. He said, Blessed is the one who walks to the prayer and is devoted to her. Then he said, Come to the success. He said, One is successful who answers Muḥammad ﷺ, and one is the continuation for his community. He said, Allāhu akbar Allāhu akbar. He said, You have declared great the Great. He said, No god but God. He said, You have made purely clear the ikhlāṣ, O Naḍlah. May God forbid your body from the Fire.

'The narrator said, When he finished with his call to prayer, we got up and said, Who are you, God be kind to you? Are you an angel? Or an associate of the *jinn*? Or one of the creatures of God - and you made us hear your voice? But we see you are an individual. We, we are delegates of God and delegates of Messenger of God ﷺ, and delegates of 'Umar bin al-Khaṭṭāb.

'He said, There broke off the mountain from the top something like a round cloud, white of head and beard, wearing two tattered rags of wool, someone who said, al-salāmu 'alaykum wa raḥmatu Allāhi wa barakātuhu. We answered, And to you peace and God's kindness and His blessing! Who are you, God be kind to you? He replied, I am Zurayb bin Barthamlā, the trustee of the right creature Jesus son of Mary, peace be upon both of them. I live on this mountain. He called me to stay a long time until his descent from the sky, when he will kill the pig, break the cross, and free himself from what the naṣārī (Christians) have wrongly ascribed to him. But what is the Prophet ﷺ doing? We said, He died. So he cried long sobs until his beard changed color from the tears.

'Then he said, So who is in charge of you after him? We said, Abū Bakr. He said, What is he doing? We said, He is dead. He said, So who is in charge of you after him? We said, 'Umar. He said, Since I have lost the chance to meet Muḥammad ﷺ, do greet 'Umar from me with salām. He dictated:

'O 'Umar, close the gap and come closer; the matter has come close, and they are reporting these peculiarities which I am reporting to you, O 'Umar. When peculiarities appear in the community of Muḥammad ﷺ: the fleeing, the fleeing - when the man is content with the man (and has no need of anyone else), and the woman with the woman, and they make relationships without appropriateness; and they are affiliated with others than their supporters, and their elders and their young ones are not treated kindly, and their elders and their young ones are not respected. Ordering for the good is abandoned, nor are they so ordered; and halting the bad is abandoned, nor do they halt from bad. Their knowledgeable ones teach knowledge only so as to acquire dīnārs and dirhams. The rain is in the dry season; the child is angry; the pulpits are extended elaborately, and the copies of the Qur'ān are gilded, and the mosques are highly decorated. Corruption appears and buildings are erected, and they follow egos. They trade the religion for this world, and tears of compassion disappear. They cut off kinship and sell the government. They eat monetary interest, and the authority becomes vainglorious, and the rich are honored. The man comes out of his house and is replaced by someone better than him. The women will ride on saddles.

'He said, Then he disappeared from us. Naḍlah wrote that to Sa'd, and Sa'd wrote to 'Umar, and 'Umar wrote: Come, you and whoever is with you of the Emigrants (who left Makkah for Madīnah) and the Helpers (anṣār, the residents of Madīnah who helped them), so as to descend this mountain; and when you meet him, greet him from me with salām, because Messenger of God ﷺ said, "Some of the trustees of Jesus son of Mary عليه السلام came down from that mountain near 'Irāq." So Sa'd went down with 4,000 of the Emigrants and Helpers until they arrived at the mountain after forty days, calling with the call to prayer during the time of each prayer.'

Al-Rāsibī did not follow after his statement 'from Mālik bin Anas'; and the well-known one in this ḥadīth is Mālik bin al-Azhar, from Nāfi'; and Ibn al-Azhar is not known. Abū 'Abd-Allāh al-Ḥākim said, 'I have not heard mention of this Ibn Al-Azhar anywhere but in this ḥadīth.' The question from the Prophet ﷺ and from Abū Bakr is in the ḥadīth of Ibn Lahī'ah from Ibn al-Azhar. We say, This ḥadīth, even if what is spoken is in his chain (of formal transmission), it is authentic according to people like us by kashf. His statement about decorating the mosques and gilding the copies of the Qur'ān: the two are not anything blameworthy but are rather an indication of the closeness of the Hour and the rottenness of the times - as also the descent of Jesus عليه السلام, and the coming out of the Mahdī, and the rising of the Sun from her west. It is well known that all of these are not in a blameworthy way, rather are indications of something that may be blameworthy or praiseworthy.

This 'Īsawī trustee Ibn Barthamlā is still on that mountain worshiping, living with no one else. With Messenger of God ﷺ having been sent out to propagate the message, do you see that ascetic staying under the rules of Christianity? No, by God, because the sharī'ah of Muḥammad ﷺ is abrogative. He ﷺ said, 'If Moses were alive, he could not help but follow me.' And this one, Jesus, when he comes down he will lead us using only ours - that is, using our Sunnah - and he will not rule us except with our sharī'ah.

This ascetic monk is one of the ones who is 'upon a clarification from his Lord', whom his Lord taught from Him what He requires of him - in regard to the Law of our prophet Muḥammad ﷺ - on the path which he was habituated to, from God's Side. This, for us, is the taste to be verified for oneself, because we take much from the legal principles of Muḥammad ﷺ confirmed in his Law by the superficial scholars; but we may have no knowledge of these principles - so we take them from this path of tasting and verifying, and we find them with the superficial scholars to be just as they (now) are with us. From this path we authenticate the prophetic sayings, and we reject them too, when we are made to learn by God that they are weak in their chains of transmission, not ṣaḥīḥ (authentic) from Messenger of God ﷺ. Even though the Lawgiver confirms the decision of the mujtahid who tries, even if one errs, to understand independently - still, the people of this path do not take anything except by means of what Messenger of God ruled.

This trustee is one of the Primes. His path to sources for deriving knowings is the path of Khaḍir, the companion of Moses عليه السلام; so he is in our Law, even if the path differs that connects to true knowledge - because that does not disprove knowledge. Messenger of God ﷺ said, about one who was given authority without asking, 'God has appointed him to authority, and God sends angels to him to help him' - meaning, protects him from error in what he rules on. Khaḍir said, *I did not do it from my command*. *al-kahf 18:82* And he (Muḥammad) عليه السلام said, 'There are in my community Speakers, and 'Umar is one of them.'

Now, it is established with us that the Prophet ﷺ forbade that monks be killed. They are the ones who separate themselves from the creation and are isolated alone with their Lord; so he said, 'Go past them and do not become concerned.' He brought the phrase synoptically, and he did not command us to call to them (i.e. to invite them to Islām), because of his awareness that they are 'upon a clarification from their Lord'. But propagation was commanded by him, and he commanded us that the one who eye-witnessed propagate the message to the one who was absent. If not for Messenger of God ﷺ being aware that God has entrusted to Himself their education - like His entrusting the education of Khaḍir and others to Himself - he would not have spoken like this, nor would he have confirmed one with an abrogated Law in this millat (cultus). He is true to his call that he was sent to all of the people, entirely, as God said about him. So his message spreads universally, over the whole of creation. A spirit of this knowledge is that everyone who perceives him in his time, and to whom was propagated his call, believes in God only with his Law; and, indeed, we recognize certainly that he ﷺ did not give the address face to face with the entirety of people in his time - this is the only facet which we are mentioning.

So this monk is among the 'Īsawīyīn who are the ones who inherited from Jesus عليه السلام until the time Muḥammad ﷺ was sent; and when Muḥammad ﷺ was sent, this monk worshiped God by his ﷺ Law and was taught from His Side knowledge, by the kindness which comes from Him. What he inherited also was a state of the 'Īsawī from Muḥammad ﷺ, so he stayed 'Īsawī with two Laws. Do you see that this monk had reported about the descent of Jesus عليه السلام and reported that when he came down he would kill the pig and break the cross? Do you see him maintaining the lawfulness of pig flesh? This monk remains 'Īsawī in two Laws, so he has the double reward: a reward for his following his prophet, and a reward for his following Muḥammad ﷺ. He is waiting for Jesus, until he comes down.

These companions saw him with Naḍlah, and they did not ask him about his state with regard to al-islām and al-īmān (religion and faith), nor about what he himself believed in as a belief system - about the Laws - because the Prophet ﷺ did not command them to ask anything like that. So we know certainly that the Prophet ﷺ did not confirm anyone in one's shirk; and he knew that God had creatures whose education is entrusted to the True from His Side, a knowledge that came down to Muḥammad ﷺ as a kind compassion from Him, surpassing - and the surpassing kindness of God is indeed great. If one is someone from whom jizyah is paid, then we would say that the Muḥammadī Law has confirmed him in his religion as long as he provides the jizyah. This is an intricate issue running throughout his universal message: by his appearance, there remains no Law except what is his Law; and one of the things in his Law is the confirmation of them in their Law - as long as they provide the jizyah when they are among the people of the Book. And how many of these creatures does God have on the Earth?

jizyah is the tax paid 'to ratify the compact ensuring them protection' from outside attack The people of the Book have a law and a prophet - for India historically the Laws of Manu and the prophet Noah.

A root of the 'Īsawīyīn, as we have confirmed, is the divesting of tawḥīd from the outward images in the 'Īsawī community and from the images which they have in their churches, because of their being based on the sharī'ah of Muḥammad ﷺ; but the spirit-being which they have is 'Īsawī among the Christians and Mūsawī among the Jews - part of the prayer niche of Muḥammad ﷺ in his word, 'Worship God as if you see Him'; and 'God is in the qiblah of the one praying'; and 'The creature, when praying, is facing its Lord'; and so on - all this is related about God having correlations such as these.

The 'Īsawī of this community do not have miracles of walking on the air, but they have walking on water. The Muḥammadī walks on air by the principle of following-dependency, because the Prophet ﷺ on the night he ascended through the air, while he was carried by Burāq, he said about Jesus عليه السلام, 'If he increased certain-belief, he would have walked on the air'; and there is no doubt that

Jesus عليه السلام was stronger in certain-belief than us - not even close, because he was first in resolve among the messengers; and some of us - we walk on the air, no question.

I have seen many in creation among the walkers on air, during their walking on the air, and I know certainly that we walk on the air. It is based on the principle of truly following our prophet, not from an increased amount in certain-belief compared with the cer-
cf. al-baqarah 2:60 tain-belief of Jesus عليه السلام. 'Each of us knows his watering place.' So we walk based on the principle of following Muḥammad ﷺ from a particular perspective which has this station - it is not from a power of certain-belief, as we said - by which we exceed Jesus عليه السلام. God forbid that we would say that (we exceed him in certain-belief)! - it is just as the community of Jesus walk on the water based on the principle of following him, not based on their certain-belief being equal to the certain-belief of Jesus عليه السلام.

We are with the messengers in tearing the fabric of the conventional, who are distinguished thereby with God. And their likes appear with us by the principle of following - just as we have given an example in the book al-Yaqīn (Certain-belief): the special slaves (mamālīk) who cling to the shoes of their masters, among the commanders, when they enter in on the sultan. Some of the commanders stay outside the door, as they were not permitted to enter. Do you see the slaves entering with their masters? Is their position not more elevated than the commanders who were not permitted to enter? Do they not enter 'based only on the principle of following' their masters? In fact, every person is at his rank; so the commanders are distinguished from other commanders, and the slaves are distinguished from other slaves, within their genus. This is the way we are with the prophets, with what there is of following, with the tearing of the fabric of convention.

Then the Prophet ﷺ did not walk on the air - he was carried on Burāq, a riding horse, and on foliations like someone borne on the sedan; thus, there appears with Burāq and the foliations a form of the station which one is in oneself, in that one is borne oneself. And also there appears a Divine connection, from His word,
ṭā-hā 20:5 *al-Raḥmān, settled on the Throne*, and from His word, *And bearing the*
al-ḥāqqah 69:17 *Throne of your Lord.* Thus, the Throne is borne. This carrying is a miracle by means of the bearers - and a state of ease, and majestic, magnificent, for the ones borne.

We have confirmed for you in other places that the one borne is higher than the non-borne in this station and in similar ones, and that the 'There is no might nor power except by God' is one of the things the bearer is distinguished by. Even if the entirety of the creation is borne, yet this bearing is not given in kashf to every single one - even if the bearing is in different levels: a bearing from being weak; a bearing from a true feature - like the bearing of the weighty ones; and a bearing because of being noble and majestic. The grace of this group is that they are borne outwardly and visibly, just as the matter is in itself inwardly, so as to free them from presumptions - as we have confirmed in its chapter (Chapter 31).

So, the ʿĪsawīyīn have a stirring energy that is effective, and a call accepted, and a word heard. One of the signs of the ʿĪsawīyīn is: if you want to recognize them, then observe every person who has kind compassion toward the world and affectionate concern for the people, whoever it may be, and whatever religion one may have, and whatever naḥlah (religious culture) one shows - and an unreserved approval of them for God's sake. They do not articulate anything that would constrict anyone's chest concerning the creation (people), all of them, with their addressing the creatures of God.

And one of their signs is that they see in everything its best, and there does not flow from their tongues anything but good. In this degree, they share with the first and second generations. The first are like what was reported from Jesus ﷺ, that he saw a pig and said to him, 'Be safe.' He was asked about this, and he said, 'My tongue is used to speaking good.' And as for the second generation, the Prophet ﷺ, even though he commanded people to kill snakes, in a particular facet reported that God loves the snake - even if there is life in killing it.

For example, in a ḥadīth, Ibn ʿUmar said he killed a snake because the Prophet ﷺ said to kill snakes; but it is then clarified that the command is only for two particular snakes that might cause miscarriage, and therefore it applies only to either of two snakes in a house where a pregnant woman lives. ʿĀʾishah's ḥadīth in the Musnad (#22883) has 'and who leaves the two alone is not one of us' (because he risks the well-being of women).

Despite this, he was in the cave in Minā and the sūrah *wa'l-mursalāt* came down; and by al-Mursalāt that cave is known to this day. He entered the blessed cave; then a snake came out, and the Companions rushed to kill her, but he hindered them. Messenger of God ﷺ said, 'God has protected her from your evil, just as He protected you from her evil.' He called it an evil, despite the fact that one is commanded to kill the snake in a specific situation. An example is His word about qaṣāṣ, *The recompense for an evil (injury) is an evil of its like* - thus, he called qaṣāṣ an evil and recommended overlooking injury. *al-shūrā 42:40*

Manuscript B adds, 'even though recompense is set down in the Law. He ﷺ passed a corpse (of a dog), and the Companions said, "What a stench from that corpse!" The Prophet ﷺ said, "But how white are its teeth." The story is usually attributed in classical Muslim ḥadīth scholarship to Jesus.

So he did not set his ﷺ eye on anything but what was best and most beautiful in the corpse. In this way, the friends of God will see in everything observed only what is best and most beautiful there. They are the ones blind to the vices of creation - not to vice, because they are commanded to avoid vice - just as they are deaf to hearing bad; just as they are mute to saying bad things in speech, even if it is permitted in some contexts. In this way, we recognize them. Glory to Him who has chosen them and selected them and guided them to an evened path! *These are the ones God* al-an'ām 6:90 *guided, so follow their guidance.*

This station of Jesus عليه السلام is in Muḥammad ﷺ, because he came before him in time (when 'Adam was between water and clay'), and these states were transmitted to him. He *exalted* said to His Prophet ﷺ, when He cited in the Qur'ān whomever He cited of the prophets - and Jesus is among the entirety of those He cited, peace be upon them - *These are the ones God guided, so fol-* al-an'ām 6:90 *low their guidance.*

Even though the station of the message requires clarifying the good from the bad so that one will learn - just as He said, *To clarify* al-naḥl 16:44 *for the people what came down to them* - then if he clarified the bad for the sake of a person, it was (so commanded) by a revelation from God. It was just as he said about someone, 'What a bad son of the tribe.' And Khaḍir killed the boy, and he said about him that he had 'an ungrateful nature'; and he reported what would have happened if he had left him to do the bad he would do with regard to his par- See al-kahf 18:82. ents; and he said, '*I did not do it from my command.*'

bi'sa 'bnu'l-'ashīrah: from this ḥadīth. A man asked permission to enter in on the Prophet ﷺ, and when he saw this man (outside) he said, 'What a bad brother of the tribe, and what a bad son of the tribe.' But when he sat down, the Prophet ﷺ showed happiness in his face and was affable to him. When the man had left, 'Ā'ishah asked him, 'O Messenger of God, when you saw the man, you said this and that about him; then you showed happiness with your face and were affable to him.' Messenger of God ﷺ said, 'O 'Ā'ishah, when have you seen me acting in an unseemly manner? The worst of the people, before God, in his alighting place on the Day of Arising for Judgment, will be the one the people gave up on and abandoned, protecting themselves from his unseemly badness.'

This is what belongs to the Great in themselves: good speech, and a view only to the beautiful, and attentive listening only to the good. If there arises in them - in a prophet or blessed friend - some moment different from this, then it is from a Divine command; it is not their own speech. We have discussed this for the states of the ʿĪsawīyīn - whatever God has made easy for my tongue.

And God speaks the true,
and Hu is the guide to the way. *al-aḥzāb 33:4*

وَاللَّهُ يَقُولُ الْحَقَّ وَهُوَ يَهْدِي السَّبِيلَ

Chapter 37

Jesus-Based Pivots

On ma'rifah of the Jesus-based Pivots and their mysteries

Jesus-Based Pivots

Chapter 37

فَاعلَمْ

Now learn, may God assist you with a holy spirit, this:

The Pivot is the one whose feet are
firmly set in the matter.
And the Jesus-based who displays
his forward boldness (iqdām):

The Jesus-based is the one who, one Day,
his banner will be raised up, among the
prophets, when called to testify.

All comes from his father (the second sky) as a
fragrance ʃ,
like the musk with her smell, by
revelation his being informed.

He has the life-force and revives whom he wishes
by her -
so he does not die, and his days do not vanish.

If you see him, his signs have come,
he coming forward to bring out to the worlds his rules.

Confronting with language: 'You! You said, for
their sake,
that you are God? It is God who is his teacher!'

His answer: 'What was said was said, so do
overlook it.' And he did not
look at an offense - the offense by which,
drawing it on himself, he was destroyed.

May the God of creation bless him - (the Pivot)
based on a man (Jesus)
who gave and was given, whose
generous honor was given him.

إعلم

Learn, may God assist you with a holy spirit, that I have taught you that among the Pivots, the 'Īsawī (Jesus-based) is the one who combines two inheritances: the spirit-based inheritance in which occurs the passive object; and a Muḥammad-based inheritance - but from the taste of Jesus عليه السلام, always with this. And we have clarified their stations and their passing states. So now we shall mention in this chapter just a small part of their mysteries.

Part of the mysteries are that they - when they want to give one of the states which they have which is under their dominion to someone they see who is ready, recognizing this either through kashf or Divine informing - they touch that person, or embrace him, or kiss him, or give him a robe to wear, or say to him, 'Open your cloak'; and they scoop up for him what they want him to be given. The people present think that they have scooped up some air. They will place it in his cloak to the extent delimited for them, a certain number of scoops. Then they will say to him, 'Gather your cloak, bringing together the edges to your chest' - or, 'Wear it,' for the duration of the state which they wish to gift. Whatever they do, the state suffuses to this charged person, the intended recipient, at that moment - with no delay.

I saw this with one of my teachers: coming to some people, among the general population, he would say to me, 'This person has readiness in him.' So he would approach him. When he touched him or struck him with his chest onto his back, intending to gift him with what he wished to give, that state would flow through at once - and out would come what he (the recipient) had been involved in, and he would become devoted to his Lord.

Someone else who had this state was the Makkan al-Wāsiṭī, buried in Makkah, a student from Ardashīr; when he was taken by the trance state, he would say to one who was present with him, 'Embrace me.' Or the one ready, and present, would endeavor to learn the teacher's state; and when he saw him clad and caught up in this state, he would embrace him (the teacher) - and that state would suffuse throughout this person and he would be clad and caught up in it.

Jarīr bin 'Abd-Allāh al-Bajlī complained to Messenger of God ﷺ that he was not steady on the back of a horse; so he struck him in his chest with his hand, and he never fell off the back of a horse again. And Messenger of God ﷺ (reached over and) prodded a riding animal that was under one of his friends, a slow-paced walker, when he was at the back behind the people; and after he prodded him, his rider could not rein him in, and he raced ahead of all the animals. And Messenger of God ﷺ rode a slow-paced horse of Abū Ṭalḥah's, on the day the enclosure for animals belong-

In the margin, there is the line, 'Jābir bin 'Abd-Allāh'.

ing to Messenger of God ﷺ was attacked, and Messenger of God ﷺ said with regard to that horse which he borrowed to ride out to investigate, 'I found him fast like the ocean' - and he was never not first afterwards.

And Abū Hurayrah complained to Messenger of God ﷺ that he was forgetting what he heard from Messenger of God ﷺ, so he said to him, 'Abā Hurayrah, open your cloak.' So Abū Hurayrah opened his cloak, and Messenger of God ﷺ scooped up a scoop of air, or three scoops, and flicked them into the cloak of Abū Hurayrah; and he said to him, 'Gather together your cloak to your chest.' And he gathered it to his chest, and he never forgot anything he heard after that. This, all of it, is part of this station.

Consider a mystery of this matter: nothing of this arises except by a sensory movement (e.g. embraces, touching), in order to fix the causes which God has set down - so as to understand that the Divine command (the imperative *Be!*) does not get cut off and diminished and that the Divine command in itself is of this definition. The ʿárif recognizes from this, correlations of the Divine names to their objects and what is anchored by them in the being of entities, and that the anchoring necessitates the Divine Presence, Her very own Self. The one who knows, who verifies for oneself, embellishes these Divine commands and Divine notifications, understanding that the wisdom lies in what emerges, and that the commands do not alter - and that the ropes (secondary causes) are not removed, ever. Everyone who presumes that the cause is removed with no cause: he has no knowledge, neither of the process by which they are removed nor of what removes them. The creature is awarded nothing more excellent than knowledge and its practice, and these are the states of the courteous ones of the ʿibād of God *exalted*.

And part of their mysteries also is that they speak with distinct eloquence in articulation, and they know the inimitabilities of the Qurʾān, while none of them know the ʿarabī language, nor has it reached them - nor studying it in the usual manner, such as reading literary books. They do not know that it reached them from this direction; in fact, it is for them a Divine gift in a special manner they recognize in themselves, when they are given the expression of what is wanted of them in their insides - that is, the truths. They are illiterates; even if they can master writing in the manner of etching letters, they are common people. They articulate what is typically external to their capabilities, as they are not Arab. If they are Arab, they are so only in genetic relation, not in ʿarabī language. They recognize the inimitabilities there, and from there they recognize the inimitabilities of the Qurʾān and that this is True Speech.

In the documentary Koran by Heart (2011), the first- and second-place winners of the recitation contest in Cairo were a Tajik boy and a Maldivian girl, respectively. That these two ten-year old children, who did not know Arabic at all, could memorize and recite beautifully the entire Qur'ān was seen by the judges as one of the 'inimitabilities' - or miracles (mu'ājazah, because one is incapable of producing such) - of the Qur'ān.

I was asked in one encounter, 'Do you recognize what the inimitability of the Qur'ān is?' I said, No. He said, 'The fact that it is predicated on truth; therefore, adhere to the True - your speech will be inimitable (and miraculous).' You see, those who give oblique meanings to the Qur'ān: the first thing they lie about is that they did it based on God - but it is not from God. They speak of God what they know not, so no fruit is harvested and no stability is gained - because the false dies off, having no stability. Then they report in their words about matters connected to the sūrah of the Qur'ān which they want to dispute, by matters related to wordings, about what does not happen and what is not. It is false, and falsehood is non-being, and nothingness does not face against being. The Qur'ān is a report predicated on a being-based matter, true in the matter itself; so, inescapably, the antagonist is unable to bring forth anything like it (and so they are incapable, and it is inimitable). So if you adhere to the True in your actions and your statements and your states, you have been distinguished from the people of your time, and from all who do not journey along your path. So then he is incapable who would imagine alighting onto his station without right.

And of their mysteries too is the knowledge of natures, and their composition and their decomposition, and the uses of remedies; they learn this from kashf. Our teacher Abū 'Abd-Allāh al-Ghazzāl, God be kind to him, reported that he was in Almeria as a wayfarer, after a session with his teacher Abū'l-'Abbās bin al-'Arīf - Ibn al-'Arīf was the most literate of his time. And al-Ghazzāl was in the forest on the way to the palace of al-Ṣumādiḥīyah, when he saw the herbage of that meadow, all of them, addressing him about their benefits. And the bush or plant would say to him, 'Take me, because I benefit (remedy) such-and-such, and I repel such-and-such a harmfulness' - until he ran off frightened; and he remained confused about the call of each bush there showing affection to him and approaching him.

He returned to the teacher and informed him about this; and the teacher said to him, 'For this you are serving me? Where were the harm and the benefit with you, when the bushes spoke to you, that they would benefit or harm?' He said, 'My master, I turn' (in repentance for forgiveness). The teacher said to him, 'God has tempted you and tested you, because I have pointed you only to God, not to another (e.g. a bush). Your repentance is true if you return to that place and these bushes who talked to you do not talk to you -

if you are true to your repentance.' So Abū 'Abd-Allāh al-Ghazzāl returned to the place, and he heard nothing of what he had heard. So he bowed down to God in thankfulness, and he returned to the teacher and informed him. The teacher said, 'Praise to God who tested you Himself and did not drive you to anything like you among His beings; you are honored thereby, and He truly honored you.' Consider his stirring energy - God be pleased with him!

If you learn mysteries of Nature and stand with her truths, you will learn the Divine names that God taught Adam عليه السلام - half of them - and it is a strange knowledge. Since God taught them in this path, we see a tremendous matter, and we learn a mystery of God with regard to His creation and how the Divine power flows throughout every thing - so nothing is benefited except by Him, and nothing is harmed except by Him, and nothing speaks except by Him, and nothing moves except by Him.

The people are veiled by the images, and they relate everything to themselves and to things; but God is saying, *O you people, you are the dependents on God* - and His word is true, and informing. And reports like these do not allow inserted variants, so there is no dependence except dependence on God. In this verse, God cites 'everything' as being dependent on God; and in this context, the faqīr (the one who depends) is the one who depends on everything, and nothing depends on him; so one comprehends the causes as they were set down wisely, nothing interpenetrating them. This is a rare tasting; of the ones I have seen, I have not seen anyone who has it, nor has there been transmitted to me a word (about it) - not about ones who came before nor about ones at the last. But I have seen and there was transmitted to me from a group the confirmation of the causes - though not in this context - because what we cite and mean is Divine diffusion throughout the causes; or tajallī of the True behind the veil of the causes, in the entities of the causes; or the diffusion of the causes in the Divine. This is what we did not find having a taste, except for a word of God - and this is the orphan verse in the Qur'ān, her measure unrecognized, since she has no weight; and everything having no weight is confirmed necessarily as being of unknown measure, even if a value is believed for it.

fāṭir 35:15

e.g. The verse al-ṣāff 61:6 is considered an 'orphan verse'.

And part of their mysteries also is the ma'rifah of the two configurations in this world: the Nature-based configuration and the spirit-based configuration - and what the root of the two is; and ma'rifah of the two configurations in the next abode - Nature-based and spirit-based, and what the root of the two is; and ma'rifah of the two configurations: the configuration of this world and the configuration of the next. They are six knowings. One necessarily has their ma'rifah.

And part of their mysteries is that there is no individual among them who has fully completed this station unless one is gifted with 600 Divine faculties, inherited from one's closest ancestor on one's father's side. You do with them in accordance with what you were provided. If you want, you hide them; and if you want, you bring them out. Hiding them is higher. Worship *f* is taken from the faculty which seeks help with her - in fulfilling the right of the Divine, or some matter of her master - to establish a force of her worshiping. Every faculty removed from this context by searching is not what is sought by the Men of God, because they do not presume themselves to have a firm faculty, as God does not seek from them that they seek assistance except in their worship, or that they bring out with them possessions and mastery - as presume a group of the people of the Book, among whom (are those who) take Jesus as a lord. They say, 'Muḥammad seeks from us that we worship him as we Āl-i-'Imrān 3:64 worshiped Jesus'; so God *exalted* brought down, *Say: You people of the Book, come to an equable word between us and you, that we not worship any but God, and not associate partners with Him, and not take some of us as lords apart from God.*

And part of their mysteries too is that they do not multiply in their ascent routes, with regard to their father the second sky, except they turn to face the nearest ancestor; and it may be that some of them end up at the sidrat (Christ's thorn jujube) at the extreme boundary. Her vantage place is where all the actions of the creations end, none passing beyond her. This is where the True receives them. She is their membrane (barzakh) until the Day of Arising for Judgment, the membrane in which each performer of the action dies (and waits for the Resurrection). This amount is enough, of the knowing of the mysteries of this community (jamā'ah).

al-aḥzāb 33:4 *And God speaks the true, and hu is the guide to the way.*

The 20th manuscript ends, followed by the 21st.

All praise belongs to God.
And the blessing of *hu* to Muḥammad
and his towering people
and his Companions,
and his wives,
and the peace of *hu*.

Chapter 38

Beholds but Does Not Obtain

On maʿrifah of the one among the Pivots who is given to see the Muḥammadī station but does not attain it

Between nubuwwat (prophethood) f
and wilāyat (the sacred authority of a
friend of God) there is a difference;
but she has the vantage view more
complete, more magnificent,

The encompassing orbit yielding to her with his
recessed secret;
and in this way is the Higher Pen,
most grand, eloquent.

recessed secret: For the imagery for ya'nū … bi-sirrih, the first includes the 'depression' of the forehead and knees during the prayer, while sirr is the valley or depression, as well as the secret tucked into recesses. There is also another connotation, with sirr inferring male and female sexual organs.

Indeed, nubuwwat and risālat (messengership):
now they have ended, and wilāyat
has the way most upright.

He set up a house for wilāyat, as a courthouse,
in a friend's regard; it has everlasting permanence.

Do not seek a terminus to proceed to for her sake;
upon reaching it, one would be pulled down.

An adjective of everlasting in the friend's dhát
is person-based,
so one is the constant friend; thus,
one's compelling is made the rule.

In him shelter the prophet of hu and the messenger
of hu,
and the upper world, and whoever is more ancient.

ثبت

It is confirmed that Messenger of God ﷺ said, 'Messengership and prophethood have been cut off, so there is no messenger after me and no prophet'; the ḥadīth continues. This ḥadīth is one of the most difficult that the friends have to swallow, with its bitterness, because it is a disconnection of the connection between the human being and one's ʿubūdīyah (slavehood). When the connection is cut off between the human being and one's ʿubūdīyah in its most complete sense, the connection is cut off between the human being and God, because the slave (ʿabd) - according to the measure he departs from his ʿubūdīyah, he diminishes in (affectionate) proximity to his master, because he is competing for his (the master's) names; and the least competition is in the nominal (i.e. less than with adjectives, such as generous or honorable), so there remains with us the name walī (i.e. the inheritor of the messenger). It is one of His names, *exalted beyond*. This name (walī) was pulled from His Messenger and placed onto Him, so he is named the slave (of God, ʿAbd-Allāh) and the messenger; and it is not appropriate for God that He be called 'the messenger'. This name (messenger), then, is one of the distinguished ones of ʿubūdīyah, which does not appropriately belong to the Lord. The reason for the application of this name is the presence of risālat, and risālat has been cut off. So the property of this name (walī) is lifted off by the message being lifted off, in the place of her being correlated to God.

So when Messenger of God ﷺ learned that in his community would be ones who swallow from this kind of cup, and he knew what would occur to them in their selves, such as pain - for this he was kind to them; and he made for them a lineage, so they would be with this the ʿabīd (here, most devoted) of the ʿabīd (slaves, creatures). He said to the Companions, 'So that you, the one who eye-witnessed, would propagate outwards to the one who was absent'. He commanded them with propagation - just as God commanded him with propagation - so as to attach to them names of the messengers who are distinguished by being ʿabīd. He ﷺ said, 'God is kind to the man who hears my words and heeds them, and conveys them as he heard them' - that is, word for word. This is only for the one who propagates the revelation of the Qurʾān or Sunnah with the phrasing it came with. This is only for the transmission of the revelation by the reciter of Qurʾān or a muḥaddith (speaker of the ḥadīth), not for the legal scholar (who transmits the gist, for legal purposes), and not for the one who transmits the ḥadīth according to meaning - that is, not word by word, as Sufyān al-Thawrī and others saw fit, (transmitting) a share but not a large portion. The transmitter of meaning is rather transmitting to us his own understanding of that prophetic ḥadīth; and who transmits to us his understanding - he is rather a messenger himself! But he will not gather on the Day of Arising with one who propagated the revelation exactly as one heard it and conveyed the message exactly as one heard it - who will gather as the reciter and the muḥaddith, who transmitted the phrase itself of the Messenger, gathering in the row of messengers, peace be upon them all.

With the Companions, when they transmit the revelation with its wording, they are messengers of Messenger of God ﷺ, and (then there are) successors of companions of messengers. The matter is like this, generation after generation, until the Day of Arising for Judgment. If we wish, we can say about the propagator to us: he is a messenger of the Messenger of God. And if we wish, we can attach him to us syntactically (as in 'our Messenger'), whoever is propagating from him. It is permissible for us to syncopate the intermediaries, because Messenger of God was reported to by Gabriel عليه السلام - and he is one of the angels, and we do not say about him, 'Messenger of the Messenger Gabriel'; instead, we say about him, 'Messenger of God' (syncopating Messenger Gabriel) - just as God said, *Muḥammad is a messenger of God, and the ones with him*; and *al-fatḥ 48:29* He said, *Muḥammad is not the father of any one of your men, but he is a messenger of God* - despite His statement, *The peaceful spirit descended with him (the Qur'ān) onto your heart*. Despite this, God did not attach him except to Himself (i.e. messenger of God). *al-aḥzāb 33:40* *al-shu'arā' 26:193-94*

This amount remains for them of 'ubūdīyah. It is a great good that God graciously grants them. However much a person omits transmitting reports along with connective chains of transmission - not disrupting the chains - one does not have this station, and does not smell the sweet breeze; one is one of the friends who are competing with the True over the name walī, and one is less in one's 'ubūdīyah commensurate with having this name. This is why the name muḥaddath, with the *d* vocalized with *a*,

> *The muḥaddith narrates ḥadīth, while the muḥaddath is 'A veracious man; into whose mind a thing is put, and who tells it conjecturally and with sagacity; as though he were told a thing, and said it: occurring in a tradition: such as 'Umar' (Lane). As we have seen, 'Among my community are the muḥaddathūn, and 'Umar is one of them.' The combination of the name applied to literal transmission of ḥadīth and the inspired nature of the person's veracious speech is suggestive.*

is more appropriate for one than the name walī - because the station of risālat is not attained by anyone after Messenger of God ﷺ, except to the extent we have explained. It is what the True made remain with us. From here you will recognize the honored station of 'ubūdīyah, and the nobility of the muḥaddithīn who transmit the revelation by narrations literally. This is why it is difficult for us, this locking of the door; and we know that God has banished us from the state of self-chosen 'ubūdīyah, which it is appropriate for us that we have. As for prophethood, we have explained it to you in what came before this, in the chapter on the ma'rifah of the Primes; they are the companions of the composite mounts.

Then He - in the context of banishing us from 'ubūdīyah and her station - said, 'I have divided the prayer between Me and My creature into halves.' Who are we that there should be a dividing between us and Him? He is the Master, the One who does, the One who makes us move, who makes us speak with our words, *You alone do we worship* - and the likes of this which He attaches to us. And we know that our forelocks are in His Hand, during our standing in prayer, our rukū' (bowing), our sujūd (bowing down), and our jalūs (sitting), and our articulating the Qur'ān.

al-fātiḥah 1:5

The creature says, *All praise belongs to God, Cherisher of the worlds.* God says, 'My creature has praised Me,' as an additional honor from Him, because He is the One who made you say this phrase. What is your measure, such that the master would say, 'My creature said, and I said to it'? This is the curtain falling down. It is appropriate for you, the creature, to recognize that God has hidden plots for His creatures; and every single one is fooled by Him to the extent of one's knowledge of one's Lord. So you should take this Divine generosity as a test from God, as something foisted into a good thing; thus, when you pray and recite and say, 'Praise to God,' you say her as a narrative with regard to your being commanded to say her, to make authentic your 'ubūdīyah in your prayer. And you do not wait for the answer, nor do you speak in order to be answered; no, you occupy yourself with what you have been obligated by your Master to do - that is, an action - so that the answer and good fortune will be from the Master, not based on what you said. The speaker is really a creator of the speech, so we become safe from this plot, even if it is an elevated alighting place; but it is an elevated alighting place in regard to someone who is in another place, lower than this alighting place.

al-fātiḥah 1:2

We did not inherit from Messenger of God ﷺ from this station, whose door is shut to one below us, except what we mentioned of grace from the True to the one to whom kashf is given; and one is sustained with knowledge of revelation transmitted with narrations, from a Book and a Sunnah. How panoramic is the station of the people of narrations, among the reciters and muḥaddithīn - may God make us one of the ones distinguished by transmitting exactly, from Qur'ān and Sunnah, because 'the family of the Qur'ān are the family of God and His distinguished ones.' The ḥadīth is like the Qur'ān in being a key text, because he ﷺ *does not speak from (his own) inclination; it is only revelation revealed.* One of the ones who verified for himself this station in meaning is Abū Yazīd al-Basṭāmī; he was given kashf from Him after asking and pleading, the amount of a needle hole. He wanted to put his foot there, but he was burned; and he recognized that he would not obtain a taste - and this is complete worship.

al-najm 53:3-4

Chapter 38

There came to us from him ﷺ a poem, and this happens often for the one who recognizes (as an ʿārif). Thus, there is not in the side of creation, about *hu*, anything but a shadow of *hu*. When God informed me, it was not from a question, rather it was from grace from God. Then He helped me with it, with courtesy fed to me from His Side - and grace, from God to me - so there did not come about with me what came about with Abū Yazīd. In fact, I became aware of this when the matter came, by the ascent to Abū Yazīd's ladder. I knew that the address was a test and a testing matter, not an honoring address - on account of some tests being honoring; so I halted, and waited, and asked for the veil. Then, understood was what I wanted - so the veil came down between me and the station. I was thankful for this. The poem was a test for me from *hu* - the poem which I mentioned: a specially, Divinely chosen one. So I thanked God for being selected by this poem, without seeking by means of thankfulness any increase. I asked for the veil which is part of complete ʿubūdīyah; so slave-based worship suffused throughout me, and her dominion appeared and interposed between me and the level of a master - to God be the praise for this. How much I sought her, and how I was answered! And it is in this way, God willing, I will be in the next world - a pure, purely devoted slave. If the entire world were put under me, I would own of it nothing but its ʿubūdīyah alone - so that the entirety of the world's ʿubūdīyah would arise from me!

See Ibrāhīm 14:7. Thus, Ibn al-ʿArabī did not thank in order to gain increase, which is the promise of this verse.

This belongs to the people, these levels, but what is appropriate to the slave is that one not add to this name another, because God has attached languages of the creation to Himself - because creation is a walī (protected friend) belonging to God, and it sees that God has attached to creation names He *exalted* has applied to Himself. Thus, one hears it, a name He calls Himself by, only with its having the meaning of the passive - not the meaning of the active; so you will smell there a waft of ʿubūdīyah, because the construction faʿīl (e.g. walī: usually passive - the protected friend) may have the meaning of fāʿil (active: the protector).

When the faʿīl is derived from transitive verbs, it has a passive sense, as in qatīl, slain. The active sense (fāʿil, the nomen agentis) indicates 'a very high degree of the quality which their subject possesses' (Wright).

We have said this on account of what we have been told to do: that we should take Him as an agent for what belongs to *hu*, in regard to which we are ones made khalīfah (the one behind whom One acts) - because in this there is a hidden trick, so beware of it. It is enough of a Divine alert for the one protected from tricks, given you are commanded to do so; so obey His command and take Him as an agent, not arrogating possession because God takes charge of (tawallā) you - because He said, *He will take charge of the integrated ones.*

al-aʿrāf 7:196 - the ṣāliḥīn: people of ṣalāḥ, integrity

And the name 'integrated' is one of the special names for 'ubūdīyah; and this is why Muḥammad ﷺ described himself as having integrity (ṣalāḥ); indeed, he would claim as a state only what belongs to the devoted slave ('abīd) who is complete.

Among them is one for whom integrity is attested by the True,
Āl-i-'Imrān 3:39 as good news from God. Thus, He said about His slave John the Baptist عليه السلام, *a prophet, from among the integrated ones*; and He said
Āl-i-'Imrān 3:46 about His prophet Jesus عليه السلام, *He will speak to the people in the cradle, and in maturity, (he who is) from among the integrated ones*; and He said
al-baqarah 2:130 about Abraham عليه السلام, *He is, in the other world, among the integrated ones* - in the other world, on account of three situations which originated from him in this world: his saying about his wife Sārah that
al-ṣāffāt 37:89 she was his sister by family (in order to protect them); his statement *I am weak*, as an excuse (to stay in the temple); and his statement, *No,*
al-anbiyā' 21:63 *in fact their largest one did it*, making a case (and misleadingly implying that the largest idol broke the others).

So with these three (occasions of providing misinformation) he will excuse and recuse himself before the people, when they request him to ask his Lord to open the door of intercession; and this is why he is cited as an integrated one in the other world, as he was not chastised for this (therefore clearing the slate for having so testified in this world). It is just as God said to Muḥammad ﷺ, *so God*
al-fatḥ 48:2 *may forgive you what came before of your sins and what comes after*; and
al-tawbah 9:43 He said, *God overlooks (your fault); why did you give them permission?* - so good news (God overlooks your fault) precedes the reprimand (for giving them permission en masse). But this verse, according to us, is good news only - there is no reprimand in her; in fact, it is a question asked for understanding (not as criticism), for the One who is just and gives the people of knowledge their right.

As for Sulaymān and people like him, peace be upon them, the True reported to us that he said, *And include me, by Your kind com-*
al-naml 27:19 *passion, in Your creatures who are integrated*. Now, even if they are integrated, as the matter truly is, with God, they are between a petitioner for integrity and someone who is attested to as already being integrated - despite its being a 'ubūdīyah-based characteristic (because they are 'your creatures'), not appropriate for God; so what do you think about the name walī, with which God has named Himself, with the meaning of the active (i.e. authorizing)?

So it is appropriate that this name not be attached to the creature; and if the True attaches it to you, that is up to Him. Human beings need to be creatures, and they need what is specially made for them - the names to which the True is never attached in a phrase, in what came down to His Prophet ﷺ. So when God sends down to His slave Muḥammad ﷺ this verse, then it is so the people may be informed by her; it is as if God narrates to His

Prophet ﷺ what he should surely say and put into words. He *exalted* made him a Qur'ān recited; you see, this is part of the special features of the devoted slaves in the matter as it truly is.

He said, *My waliyyā (Protector) is God, who revealed the Book; and He will take charge* (yatawallā, corresponding to the sense of walī as fa'īl, passive: the integrated are passive, and God is taking charge of whatever is being done) *of the integrated ones.* He testified to him having integrity, since the True is the narrator in this verse. Now, if he (whose walī is God) is the enjoiner, then he is one of the testifiers to their having integrity. (Then the verse reads, *and he gives authority to the integrated*). Now, we are being informed here that God takes charge of him, and he is reporting to us that God is taking charge of the integrated ones; thus, he is testifying on his own behalf to being integrated, in the facet which we have cited - and this has been related about no one else; no, something close has been related, in the statement of Jesus ﷺ: *I am a slave of God; He gave me the Book and made me a prophet. He made me blessed wherever I may be, and He enjoined on me ṣalāt and zakāt, as long as I live. He made me good to my mother, and He did not make me overbearing or miserable. Peace be upon me the day I was born, the day I die, and the day I am raised alive.* God is saying, *These messengers: We have preferred some of them above others* - that is, so in this way you are (preferred); and part of His preference is the provision of a station like this one.

al-a'rāf 7:196

Maryam 19:30-33

al-baqarah 2:253

So protect yourself, my friend (walī), when taking on the names of God that are Beautiful, because the 'ulamā' do not disagree about taking them on. And if you are successful in taking them on, do not be hidden in this process from witnessing their effects in you. And you should be in them and with them a stand-in for them, so you will be like a name of 'the messenger' - not sharing with the True in having applied to you one of His names with this same meaning. And adhere firmly to proper protocol and courtesy. *And say: My Lord, increase me in knowledge.*

ṭā-hā 20:114

And God speaks the true, and Hu is the guide to the way. *al-aḥzāb 33:4*

وَاللّٰهُ يَقُولُ الْحَقَّ وَهُوَ يَهْدِي السَّبِيلَ

Chapter 39

Friend Exiled

On ma'rifah of the alighting place to which the friend is set down when the True *exalted* exiles him from His neighborhood

Chapter 39

When the friend steps down, it is only
an ascent and an elevation to the higher.

Indeed, the True has no shackling there;
thus, in the very distance itself is nearness itself.

The state of the chosen (mujtabā) in every state is
higher - to the higher, to the higher.

There is no ruling against you, in any aspect,
and no scarring in you. To the heights!

إعلم

Learn, may God assist you with a spirit from Him, that God says to Iblīs, 'Bow to Adam!' - so the 'Do' comes out. And He said to Adam and Eve, *Do not approach this tree* - so the 'Do not' came out to both of them. The tasking is divided between *Do* and *Do not*. The two of them are subject to the obligation until the contextual situation exits them from the station of tasking - even though it is our position with regard to the two that they actually have a suspended sentence. Designated is obedience to the *Do* and the *Do not*, and this is the first *Do* to come out in the Nature-based world, and the first *Do not*. We have already informed you that the first thought (previously described as intuition) and all first things are Cherisher-based only (as the origin Mist is the 'where' the rabb was before creating the creation; and the next place, the Throne, is settled on by the name al-Raḥmān), and this is why they are believed and not disregarded, ever. Its possessor is certain of it, and its dominion is powerful. As this is a first *Do* and *Do not*, this is why the punishment occurred at the moment of opposition - and it was not delayed.

al-baqarah 2:35

Note that in the first sentence, 'says' is in the incomplete, present simple tense: God says something to Iblīs. In the second sentence, the verb is in the completed (past) tense: God said to Adam and Eve - it is over and done with.

As this was the first Do *and* Do not, *and 'first thoughts' are powerful, the punishment of 'Get ye down' (al-baqarah 2:36) is immediate - whereas other disobediences have their punishments delayed.*

But then, when commands come through intermediaries, there is not the power of the first command. They are commands coming in to us on the tongues of messengers. They are of two kinds. One is secondhand, and this is what is cast by God to His prophet in his self without angelic intermediary and then connected to us as a Divine command; it has passed into the existent-based presence (of the messenger), and there it takes on a state it did not have before. The Divine names are cast onto him in this existent-based presence, and they come to share with him their properties for his determinative ruling. Or, if this command comes down to him with the angel, the Divine command has passed through two presences of existence: Gabriel, or whatever angel it may be, and whatever prophet it may be. Its effect, and consequence, with regard to power is less than the first and the second. This is why being held accountable is not hurried; either there is a delay in going to the next world, or there is forgiveness - and you will not be held to account, ever. God does so as a compassionate kindness for His creatures.

It is as He has specified the Do not for Adam and Eve; and the Do not is not a tasking that is done, because it may include a nothing - and that is, do not do (e.g. there is no sitting with the command to not sit). Part of the truth of the enabled being is that it cannot do anything - because it was told, 'Do not separate from your root (aṣl).'

So, because God says that He does - and that you did not throw, when you threw, but God threw ۞ al-anfāl 8:17 - the enabled being in its state of 'ubūdīyah (utter humility) knows that it really cannot do anything. The mumkin is a possible being only, not the Necessary Being, and therefore must be enabled in order to do anything.

But the positive command (Do) is not like that, because it may include something solid - that you should do. Thus, it is as if one were told, 'Exit from your basic root and do something unusual.' The Do command is much harder on the soul than the Do not, as it calls you to exit from your root. If Iblīs, when he disobeyed and did not bow to Adam, had not said what he said - from arrogance and the excellence he attributed to himself over others - he would not have exited from his 'ubūdīyah to that extent; so the punishment of God occurred. The punishment to Adam and Eve came to pass because they were tasked to exit from their root, and that is the omit (i.e. a negative-command) eating - and that is a positive matter; therefore, God made Iblīs and Adam and Eve share in a single (plural) personal pronoun: 'Get ye down.' And the punishment was stronger on Adam.

The command to Iblīs was 'positive' and would have left him in his root, but he was arrogant and therefore deserving of punishment. The command to Adam and Eve was for them to exit from their root ('omit eating'), which is much more difficult; therefore, Iblīs should be punished more because he could have obeyed without exiting his basic root.

al-baqarah 2:36 But He said to them, *Get ye down*, with the plural pronoun. But going down to the Earth was not actually a punishment for Adam and Eve; rather, it was a punishment for Iblīs, because Adam was made to go down in order to fulfill a promise, in that he had been made a khalīfah in the earth, not in the Garden - after he turned to Him in repentance and was chosen and 'learned words from his Cherisher' by iʿtirāf (recognizing through being informed by the Divine). So he ﷺ learned to recognize, with regard to the word of Iblīs - *I am better than he!* The True made us recognize through the method of iʿtirāf from God and precisely what the felicity is that is iʿtirāf's end result - so we would take it as a path to forgiveness for our opposition to the Divine. He taught us by means of the presumption of Iblīs and his statement that he is better - so we would be wary of such statements when we oppose.

al-baqarah 2:37

al-aʿrāf 7:12

Then Eve was made to go down to sexual reproduction, and Iblīs to temptation; so the going down of Adam and Eve is a going down of honor (karāmat; arḍ makrumah is fertile land - both root *k r m*), and the sinking down of Iblīs is a loss and a punishment and an acquiring of heavy loads. His disobedience did not require there to be an endless wretchedness, because he did not associate partners with God (shirk); rather, he was proud of what God created him from, but written (in his destiny) for him was wretchedness. The abode of wretchedness is especially for the people of shirk (and Iblīs does not engage in shirk - he tempts others to engage in shirk). So God sent him to the Earth in order for him to make a practice of shirk, by whispering in the hearts of the creatures. When they associate partners with God - and while Iblīs declared himself not responsible for them, neither the one doing shirk nor the shirk itself - one does not benefit from his declaring himself not responsible. He is the one who says to you, *Be ungrateful!* (and when you are ungrateful, he says, *I am not responsible for you! I fear God, the Lord of the worlds* ✽ al-ḥashr 59:16) - just as God told us. But still the heavy load recoils on him of every one who engaged in shirk in the world, even though Iblīs declares God to be One (and he is not a mushrik like them) - because 'whoever puts into practice a sunnah that is bad, on him is its heavy load, and the heavy load of any one who practiced it'.

This is the second part of the report which starts, 'Whoever puts into practice a practice (sunnah) that is fine receives its reward and the reward of everyone who practices it, until the day of Arising.' If only three people teach three people, we have a geometric series Σ 330 - which reaches 1,013 in 30 generations. This is the kind of weight Ibn al-ʿArabī is telling us that Iblīs bears.

The Nature-based person, like Iblīs and the offspring of Adam: certainly there is the situation where they make as an image in themselves an exemplar of what they want to issue forth.

See note in Chapter 22, manzil 8.

Then he makes a practice of shirk and whispers temptingly to someone, until one makes an image in himself - an image such that, when it arrives in the self of the mushrik who is associating partners with God, the image of tawḥīd vanishes from him. Thus, when the mushrik makes an image in himself of this image, his tawḥīd departs - which had been in his imagination in himself, necessarily. In fact, the sharīk (putative partner of God) is something imaged ('made a ṣūrat') for him in himself toward the Side of the True, who is imagined ('put in the khayāl') in himself - that is, imagined based on knowledge of His Being. So he cannot abandon it in himself all alone. Iblīs is a mushrik in himself, with no doubt and no question. He certainly guards in himself the continuance of a form of the sharīk so as to extend that image out to the people of shirk with each breath, because he is afraid with regard to them that there would disappear from them a description of shirk - and they would then declare God One, and they would be felicitous and go to the Garden. So Iblīs keeps on guarding the image of the sharīk in himself; and he watches carefully over the image of the sharīk in the hearts of the mushrikīn, who are situated at this moment east and west, south and north. With this image he will throw back the ones who declare God One, in the future, to shirk - someone who is not now a mushrik.

Iblīs does not detach, ever, from shirk; and this is why God makes him wretched, because he is not capable of imagining tawḥīd in even one single breath - due to his being attached to this adjective, and his greediness that the adjective persist in the breathing of the mushrik. If the image of the sharīk were to depart from his breath, the mushrik would not find anyone to renew in himself the shirk - so the shirk would depart him. Iblīs would not then be able to make an image of the sharīk for him - because it would have disappeared from him, this image of the sharīk. He would not even recognize that concerning this mushrik his shirk has disappeared. This indicates that the sharīk is accompanied by Iblīs perpetually. He is the first to associate partners with God and the first to put into practice shirk, and he is the most wretched in all the worlds. This is why he hopes and craves for compassionate kindness in the eye of grace (herself, having no action deserving of or meriting kindness). This is why we say, The punishment with regard to Adam was in fact from his being combined with Iblīs in the plural pronoun, when the True addressed them with 'Get ye down to earth' - with a wording which is appropriate for His majesty. But necessarily there should be in the sentence the adjective which is required by the pronominal phrase, because the phrasal format seeks a particular meaning. This is a process the 'ulamā' do not put their minds to.

Ibn al-'Arabī is telling us that the second person plural imperative combines the parties involved. The sentence glossed would read, 'Go down, you (Iblīs) to punishment and you to reproduction (Eve) and you to being a khalīfah (Adam).'

We have mentioned the issue of Adam as an emulation for the people of God: when they err and sink down out of their station, this stepping down does not make them wretched at all; in fact, their sinking down is like the 'Get ye down' of Adam, because God is not confined by space or defined. As the matter is of this definition, and God is with this description - that is, a lack of constriction - and this is the sinking down of the friend upon slipping, what arises from it - that is, humility and shame and being broken by it - is an ascent itself to the higher reaches of what is there, because one's elevation is based on knowledge and state. One may exceed in knowledge of God over what one did not have and with regard to the state - and it is humility and being broken - over that which one had not had. This is exactly the elevation to a station more panoramic; and when human beings lose this state during their slipping up, and are not sorrowful or humbled or broken and do not fear the station of their Lord, then they are not one of the people of this path. In fact, that one sits with Iblīs; actually, Iblīs is better in his condition than he is (such a person), because he is saying to the one who is following him in ingratitude, *I am not responsible for you! I fear God, the Lord of the worlds.* al-ḥashr 59:16

We in fact speak of the slips of the people of God, when error occurs to them. He *exalted* said, *and they are not obstinate in what they are doing.* And Messenger of God ﷺ said, 'Sorrow is turning' for forgiveness. In fact, the human being who is a friend (walī), when they are in the station they are in, and in a state which they have, taking pleasure in it, their pleasure is in fact in their state - because God is too exalted to be pleased by it; so when you err, and a condition of humility and brokenness is stripped off of you, there certainly disappears the condition which you were taking pleasure in - and that was a state of obedience and harmonious accordance. When it is lost, you imagine that you have 'stepped down' from God Himself. In fact, with this condition, when it disappears from you, you have stepped down, as your condition necessitated an elevation. You are today in the ascent of humility and sorrow and dependence and brokenness, and being informed, and having courtesy with God and shame before Him. So you rise along this ascent. This creature is found at the utmost of this ascent, with a state more panoramic than the one you had. Then, with this, you recognize that you had not actually been stepped down but you had been raised - in a way such that you did not recognize you were in an ascent. Āl-i-ʿImrān 3:135

God hides this from His friends, lest they be emboldened to perform oppositions - just as He hides gradual leading astray from the one God makes wretched. He said, *We will gradually lead them (astray), in a way they will not recognize.* They are as God has said about them: those whose efforts have been wasted in this life of this world *while they think that they are acquiring good by their works.* Similarly, He hides His closeness and His grace in one whom God makes happy al-aʿrāf 7:182 al-kahf 18:104

by what God makes one be occupied with, such as lamenting over one's faults, and His showing them their error, and their looking at them in His account book and being alarmed that the sorrow would provide them ascension with regard to God - because He had not given good news that repentance was accepted; so one verifies the occurrence of the error, judging oneself to be broken and shameful because of what happened - even if God does not hold one to account for that fault. So the gradual leading ensues, for good and bad, and for the felicitous and the wretched.

I met in the city of Fes a man who had great sadness, who was an assistant at the (communal) bread oven. I asked Abū'l-'Abbās al-Ḥaṣṣār - he was one of the greatest of the teachers - about him, because I had seen him sitting with him and being compassionate to him. He told me, 'This man was in a station and he was taken down from it, and he is now in this station.' It was some place of shame and brokenness in a state obligating him to refrain from speaking in the language of creation. 'I do not stop being tender to him with medicine like this and taking away from him a sickness of this failing with a remedy like this. He gave himself over to me. So I did not stop it until that medicine flowed throughout his limbs. It loosened his face and opened up for him in the core of his heart a door to acceptance - and despite this, shame was called for.' In this way it is appropriate that the slips of the greatest be predominantly their descent into the 'permitted things' - nothing else (e.g. not disliked or forbidden things); and on the condition of their being extremely infrequent, the great sins may occur.

Abū Yazīd al-Basṭāmī, God be pleased with him, was asked, 'Does the 'ārif disobey?' He said, '*The command of God is a measure (already) measured out*.' He means that their disobedience with regard to the force of measured-out predestination has become operative in them, not that they have sought to abuse the sacred taboos of God. They, God be praised, when they are friends with regard to God *exalted and majestic*, they are protected from error in this station; so there does not originate from them any disobedience at all that would abuse the taboo of God - like another disobedient one would - because the *faith inscribed in the hearts* prevents this. Among them there is one who disobeys forgetfully; and among them one who opposes while fully present, with a kashf from the Divine, where God has informed one of it - that is, what has been measured out for one before its occurrence, so one is upon insight in one's matter with an explanation from one's Cherisher.

al-aḥzāb 33:38

al-mujādilah 58:22

This state he has corresponds to the good tidings, announced in His word, *So God may forgive you what came before of your sins and what comes after*. Thus, He has informed him about the failings that occurred being a site of being forgiven; therefore, they have no rule

al-fatḥ 48:2

over him, and they have no dominion in him. Indeed, when the time for their appearance came about, he was in the companionable counsel (sohbet) of the name al-ghaffār (the One who covers over sin with forgiveness). Thus, the failings descend onto the creature, and al-ghaffār covers over their property and force. This corresponds to someone who is cast into the fire but does not burn, such as Abraham عليه السلام, when he was in the fire, but it had no force over him, on account of the covering veil that was a preventer (shield). In this way is the slip-up of the ʿārif, the one with a station of kashf concerning predetermination: the one alighting is interposed, and its force is isolated away, so there is no effect on one's station - different from the one who has interposed in there while he is not upon an explanation nor upon insight of what has been measured out for him. This (latter) one needs shame and sorrow and humility, and this one is not like the other one. Here there are Divine mysteries too vast for me to give expression to.

And then, after you have understood their levels in this station, we differentiate for you between the disobedience of the ʿārifin and the disobedience of the common people, such as the superficial scholars and their followers. So learn that it is related about some of them that one said, 'Sit on the bisāṭ (carpet)' - meaning the carpet of worship; and, 'Watch out for inbisāṭ (same root, 'expansiveness')' - that is, adhere to what the feature of worship / provides (e.g. humility) with regard to her (referring to worship) being obligated by means of matters which her master has defined for her - because, if not for these matters, the station of hers would necessitate taking liberties, and showing pride and haughtiness, on account of the station of the one whose creature (slave) you are, and on account of the step-level - just as he was haughty, one day, ʿUtbah al-Ghulām ('the slave'), and was proud. He was asked, 'What is this haughtiness which we see in your character, which was not seen before in you?' He said, 'How should I not be haughty? He woke me up as a master (step-level 'master') of mine, and I woke up a slave (step-level 'slave') of His!'

The state of idlāl (taking liberties, being proud) does not constrain the creatures, even if they are in this world as they are in the next world; only the tasking does. They are occupied with matters of their master until they are finished with them. When there is no more occupation for them, they rise up to the station of idlāl, which is necessitated by ʿubūdīyah; and that can only be in the other abode - because taklīf (tasked to do things in order to be ultimately felicitous) with them is with every breath here in the abode of this world. Each possessor of idlāl in this abode becomes deficient in understanding of God to the extent of his idlāl, and one will not fully reach the degree of another one who never had idlāl. So, many breaths with taklīf accompanying have passed away, during the state of his being idlāl, hidden from what was obligatory on him - that is, taklīf, the taklīf with whose preoccupation the idlāl is lessened. This world is not the place for idlāl.

Do you see ʿAbd al-Qādir al-Jīlī, with his idlāl? When he was present with his impending death, and there remained for him a few breaths in this abode - that much time - he put his face on the earth, and he informed (his entourage) thereby that what he was upon at that moment was the truth which is appropriate for the creature to have in this abode. The reason for this was that he had been, in various moments, someone of idlāl - because of what the True had informed him of, of events that would happen. But Abū Suʿūd bin Shibl, his student, was protected from that idlāl - and he stayed with the obligatory ʿubūdīyah required with each breath, until he died. There is no report that he changed his state upon his death, as the state changed in his teacher ʿAbd al-Qādir.

Someone we consider reliable related (this) to us. He said, 'I heard him saying, "The path of ʿAbd al-Qādir with regard to the paths of the friends was strange, unique; and our path along the path of ʿAbd al-Qādir is strange"' - may God be pleased with all of them, and may we benefit from them! O God, protect us from things making us opposed to You, even if You have predestined them for us. By God, I ask Him that He make us commit them only upon insight, so that by them we will be lifted many degrees!

al-aḥzāb 33:4 *And God speaks the true, and Hu is the guide to the way.*

وَاللَّهُ يَقُولُ الْحَقَّ وَهُوَ يَهْدِي السَّبِيلَ

Chapter 40

Neighboring

On ma'rifah of an alighting place neighboring partial knowledge (of existence sciences), and its arrangement, and its strange wonders, and its Pivots

نَظم

A poem which includes what we are conveying:

A knowing based on existence neighbors
a knowing based on the Divine;
what is provided you is called a true-based kashf.

It is not purely a knowing of the intermediaries
(such as the barzakh and the Jabarūt);
nor is it based on the upper realm (and the
Malakūt); nor the lower one (and the Mulk).

There is a facet in the upper realm, strange, to be
verified for yourself -
and in the lower, a facet with upper-based truths.

The one who perceives it is not purely an angel -
nor is one a jinn, and nor is one a human.

They are rather the entities; when they
cleave together,
a shape appears to you - an existential effusion.

So say about it what you like, and take it in
its root;
you do not see hu - but hu is,
to the entity-eye, visible.

It is not subject to rule, and it is not a ruling judge;
and it is not unseen, and it is not physically sensed.

Its glow is transcendent beyond being enclosed in
directions and dimensions,
so it is not east and it is not west.

mithāl below: the mithāl is one thing facing another thing, such as a face facing a face in the mirror - the one is the likeness of the other. The mithāl is the projected image flush against the screen (the khayāl).

Glory beyond! is the One whose
dhát is hidden from the eye,
a mithāl based on Him flowing from
hu to us as a connecting link!

We see hu when we see, but this entity-eye is not hu;
yet there is a kashf - authentic, imaginal -

Shining brilliant, radiant tajallī to the sight of the eye, in every image.
This is what I meant by my word, 'a mithāl based on Him' (the projected image against a screen).

إعلم

Learn, may God assist you with a holy spirit, that this alighting place is one of perfect completeness: it is a neighborhood contiguous to an alighting place of the jalāl (Majesty) and the jamāl (Beauty); it is one of the most splendidly radiant places, and the visitor alighting there is the most fully completed visitor. Learn that tearing the fabric of the conventional is of three divisions. One of them is a division that refers to what the sight perceives, or one of the faculties, commensurate with what appears to this faculty - something connected to its being perceived conventionally; but it is itself something other than what is perceived by this faculty. It is like His word, *(Moses) said, No, you throw first. Then behold, their ropes and rods - so it seemed to him, based on their magic - began to move.*

This division comes under the capacity of the human. It is of two divisions: One, something that refers to the self-based faculty and something referring to special, peculiar names. When one invokes these names, there appear these images, in the eye of the beholder or in one's hearing, in the imagination. There is nothing further in the matter itself - I mean in the physical realm - of image to be seen or heard. It is the act of the magician. He knows there is no further thing which occurs to the eyes and to the ears.

This the magic where in the audience's mind the magician has made something happen, but the lady was not really sawn in half.

An example of the nafsīyah faculty is the 'mind's eye' in English - when my mind's eye sees a snake, not the staff.

The other division, which is the self-based faculty, is based on her for what she shows the eye - or whichever perceiving sense, whatever it may be - of the matter which appears from the special, peculiar nouns. The difference between the two (divisions) is that the one who does it with the method of names - that is, the magician - knows that there is actually nothing external out there and that, in fact, she has dominion inside the imagination of the audience. The magician sweeps away the sights of the audience, and they see images in their imagination - just as the sleeper sees in his sleep - and there is nothing then which is 'out there'.

With this other division, which belongs to the self-based faculty, among people there is one who knows that there is nothing out there, and among them one who does not know it; so the latter believes that the matter is as he saw it. Abū ʿAbd al-Raḥmān al-Sulamī spoke in his book Maqāmāt al-awliyāʾ (Stations of the Saints), in the chapter on miracles there - God knows better which chapter it is - about ʿUlaym al-Aswad, who was one of the greatest people on the path: that some of the integrated ones were gathered, in a story leading up to ʿUlaym al-Aswad striking a column standing in the mosque, made of marble; and suddenly it was completely gold! A man looking at the column saw gold, and he was amazed indeed. He (al-Aswad) said to him, 'You - the eyes are not altered, but like this you see it, based on your truth with your Lord. This is other than that.' He quit speaking about what appeared to the one who did not understand things through the sighting of the beholder or from first glance: that the column was rock, as it really was - and it was not gold, except in the eye of the beholder. Then, after that, the man saw it again as a rock, as it was the first time.

He *exalted* said, about the staff of Moses 🕊, *And what is this in your right hand, Moses? He said, 'She is my staff.' He said, Throw her, Moses; and he threw her,* from his hand to the earth. *And behold, she was a snake, moving* Moses 🕊 became frightened of it, as happens usually in people - people are frightened of snakes when they advance, because of what God has made with their context, in which the offspring of Adam are harmed by them. Moses did not recognize God's purpose in this; had he known, he would not have been afraid. So God said to him, *Take her and do not fear; We shall return her back to her former condition* - that is, the staff will return to what it was; or, your seeing it as the staff it was will return - the verse is ambiguous. If the pronoun which is in His word, 'We shall return her back to her former condition (sīratahā, attitude, position),' is not 'the staff' at the moment of her being a snake in the sight of Moses, one will not find what the pronoun refers to. It is just as with the human being. When you are accustomed to something - let us say it is someone that you consider good, but then he is bad to you - you say to him, 'Your sīrat (way) to me has changed; you are not he who was good to me.' But it is understood that he is he. So another says to you, 'Do not worry, he will return with regard to you to his former sīrat, being good to you.' But 'he' in his form did not change; he changed only with regard to what he did with you.

God did this previously for Moses 🕊 as a pre-readiness exercise - as it was in His foreknowledge that the magician would bring out before his eyes something like this - so he should be, then, aware

ṭā-hā 20:17,18
ṭā-hā 20:19,20
ṭā-hā 20:20
ṭā-hā 20:21

of it, so that he would not be alarmed or afraid when this happened with them, when they would throw down their ropes and staffs and it would seem to Moses that they were moving. He is saying to him, 'Do not be afraid when you see this happening with them,' in order to strengthen his self-composure.

When there happened with the magicians what happened, which God cited to us in His Book - the arroyo filling up with their ropes and staffs - and Moses saw what he thought were snakes moving, *Moses felt apprehension in himself, a (kind of) fear.* The relation of the fear to him at this moment is not the relation of the former fear to him. The former fear was fear of the snake, so *he turned from the back and did not retrace his steps*, until God told him to. This latter fear, which appeared in him on account of the magic, was fear for the audience, lest they take the magic as a demonstrating proof (as a proving miracle) - in which case the matter would become mixed up among the people. For this, God said to him, *Fear not, because you have the upper hand.* When there appeared to the magicians the display of fear that Moses had concerning what he was seeing, and they did not know why this fear was connected to him - that is, what it was - they knew that Moses did not have anything of the craft of the magicians. The magician is not afraid of what he has made, because of his knowledge that there is no external truth that the thing actually has, and that it is not really like what appears to the eyes of the beholders. So God commanded Moses to throw his staff, and He told him that *she will swallow up what they have made.*

ṭā-hā 20:67

al-naml 27:10

ṭā-hā 20:68

ṭā-hā 20:69

When Moses threw his staff and she became a snake, the magicians all knew - based on what they knew about Moses' fear - that if that were from him, and he really was a magician, he would not be afraid. They saw his staff as a real snake. They knew from this situation that it must be a hidden matter from God, who calls them to faith in Him - and that Moses did not have any skill in magician-craft. So this snake swallowed up everything that was in the arroyo, the ropes and the staffs - that is, the images of snakes there were swallowed up, so the ropes and staffs became as they were. God took their sights away from this, because God was saying, *she will swallow up what they have made* - and they had not made ropes and staffs; rather, they had made in the eyes of the beholders images of snakes, and the images were what were swallowed up by Moses' staff.

So be alert to what I am citing to you, because the commentators of the Qur'ān are distracted from this perception, concerning the reports of God. He did not say, 'swallowed up their ropes and staffs'; so the sign for the magicians was Moses' fear and the taking of the images of the snakes away from the ropes and staffs. They knew that what Moses came with was from God, so they believed in what Moses came with, down to the last of them; and they dropped down in prostration because of this sign; and they said, *We believe in the Lord of the worlds, the Lord of Moses and Aaron* [al-aʿrāf 7:121-22] - as the confusion was lifted. And they, if they halted with 'We believe in the Lord of the worlds', Pharaoh would have said, 'I am the lord of the worlds! I am the one they mean!' Therefore, they added, 'the Lord of Moses and Aaron' - that is, the One to whom Moses and Aaron call us - so the ambiguity would be lifted. Then Pharaoh threatened them with punishment - but they preferred the punishment of this world from Pharaoh over the punishment of the next world (from God, for shirk and taking Pharaoh as a god). The story God tells us here is based on their words.

As for the general population, they relate what Moses came with its being of the same type as what the magicians came with, except he was stronger than them and more skillful in magic - based on the swallowing up which came about with the snake by the staff of Moses عليه السلام; so they say, *This is clear magic!* [al-naml 27:13] There was no sign from Moses for the magicians except his fear and seizing the images of the snakes of ropes and staffs - only this. The example of this is external to the self-based faculty and external to the specially invoked names, on account of the presence of fear which was visible in Moses during the first time. The doing was from God.

When the magicians produced confusion in the eyes of the beholders, the ropes and the staffs beginning to become snakes in their sight, the True desired that something be brought to them in a context they understood - just as He said, *We should certainly have caused them confusion in what they are already confused about*, [al-anʿām 6:9] because God is watching out over the attribution of things (who did what, the Creator or creation). Thus, He made the staff a snake like their staff-snakes, for the general population; and He confused the magicians by His bringing out a display of fear in Moses. They imagined that he was afraid of the snake, but Moses really was unafraid of the snakes - because of what had come before to him about this from God in the first action, when He said to him, *Take her and do not fear.* [ṭā-hā 20:21] He was negated from having fear of her, and He had taught him that it was a sign of His. So his second fear was for the people, lest they be confused by the demonstration and a resulting ambiguity. The magicians presumed that he was afraid of the snakes, so God confused them with his fear just as they had confused the people. This is the utmost of Divine getting-to-the-roots of the attributions in this context - because the magicians, had they known that the fear of Moses was of being overwhelmed by the demonstration, they would not have gone quickly into faith. Thus, the swallowing up was on account of the snake of Moses; and with regard to their snakes, there was no swallowing up and no effect - because they were really just ropes and staffs.

This alighting place which we are citing in this chapter is a vicinity neighboring a knowing of a portion of existent-based knowings; it is this partial knowing, a knowing of the mu'jizāt.

mu'jizāt, based on 'incapacity', are the miracles performed by a prophet to prove his mission, which incapacitate his opponents. The miraculous acts of friends are called honorings (karāmāt).

It is (a prophetic miracle) because it does not come from the self-based faculty nor from the peculiar (magical) names; indeed, had the effecting of Moses ﷺ of a snake from a staff been from his internal energy, or from names (magic words), he would not have 'turned around from the back' and he would not have 'retraced his steps' in fear. So we know that there are therefore matters particular to the Side of the True in His knowledge, (and it is) not known to you from whose hand there appears this image. This alighting place neighbors what comes with the prophets, in that it is not from a ruse; and it is not like the miracles of the prophets, peace be upon them, because the prophets have no knowledge of this. And these bring out this miracle from themselves, with their internal energy or self-based faculty, or truth-telling (pronouncing something and it actually happens) - say as you like - and this is why it is singled out by the name karāmāt (honorings, miracles performed by friends, not prophets); and it is not called miracles, nor is it called magic.

The miracle (mu'jizah) is (ranges from situations) when creation is incapable (mā yaj'izu) of bringing about something like it - either by artful skill or by its not being within human powers - to a situation where there is a lack of self-based faculty and special, peculiar nouns to invoke and (yet) still it comes about by one's hands. And siḥr (magic) brings about a facet of truth - while as it really is, it is not true. The word is derived from the time of saḥr (pre-dawn), and it is the mix of illumination and darkness; it is not night - given what is mixed in of dawn's illumination; and it is not day - with the absence of the rising of the Sun before our sights. In this way it is called siḥr: it is not truly false, but it is an absence - because the eye perceiving some matter does not doubt it. But it is not purely true; so there is an existence in one's eye, because it is not in itself like what the eye sees, or what the observers think about it - that it is day, or night.

The karāmāt of the friends are not of the category of magic, because they have a truth in themselves which exists; nor are they miracles, because they know what they are doing. They are from the power of internal energy (himmat).

himmat is purposeful intention, ambition, and 'a faculty firmly rooted in the soul, seeking high things, and fleeing from base things', and 'aspiration, desire, ambition, enterprise, emprise' (Lane).

As for the statement of 'Ulaym, 'based on your truth by your Lord, you see it as gold' - in fact, the entities had not altered. This is where, when they looked at it, the matter was magnified as gold at the moment of their looking at it. Thus, 'Ulaym said to him (the one who questioned him): 'The knowledge of it (and what it really is) is more panoramic than what you are seeing (i.e. just the 'gold' column). Therefore, be characterized by knowledge, because it is greater - even if the column were truly gold.' Thus, he taught them that the entities do not alter; and this is what is truly correct - that is, the 'stone' does not go back to 'gold', because this core accepts and receives the truth of stone, just as the organic body accepts heat and you say about it, 'It is hot.' So when God wants to clothe this jawhar (basic matter, gem-core) with the visible image of gold, He strips away from it the image of stone and He clothes it now as gold. So the jawhar of the column (or the organic body) which was stone is now gold, just as the hotness of heat may be stripped off the body and it is now clothed in coldness and becomes cold. The hot entity did not alter into cold, but the body, now cold, is itself - unaltered; it is what is now heated. So the entities have not altered.

These are the skeletal configurations which are stabilized - the a'yān thābitah, every entity in creation, including the skeletal letter upon which the vowel is sounded to give it meaning.

It is in this way that 'Ulaym told the story. The jawhar which accepts the image of gold upon being struck (by him) is the same one which accepts the image of stone. The jawhar is the jawhar itself, so the stone does not return to gold nor does the gold return to stone - just as the jawhar of the hayūlā'ī (primordial matter, hyle) accepts the image of water, for example. One says it is water, no doubt. And when one puts water in the pot and boils it over the fire until the steam rises, one knows certainly that the image of the water (liquid) has disappeared from it, and it has now accepted the image of steam (gas). It begins to seek the ascent toward its great element (air) - just as when it was established as an image of water, it sought its great element, but it took the lower (i.e. earth). This is the meaning of the statement of 'Ulaym in this special alighting place of the friends and the internal energy that neighbors the knowing of the miracle: the entities do not alter.

His statement is, 'based on your truth by your Lord' - that is, when you strive for your truth, you find yourself a purely devoted 'abd (slave, creature): incapacitated, a corpse, weak, nothing, no being do you have. The jawhar is like this: as long as no image is dressed upon it, it shows no entity which is an existent in being.

So this creature gets dressed up with the images of the Divine names, and thereby appears its 'ayn (entity) existence. The first name you are clothed with is being; so a found-being (mawjūd, site of being) appears as your self, such that it will accept the entirety of what it is able to accept as a found-being qua found-being. You accept and receive the entirety of what is divested by the True of the Divine names; and you are described, upon this process setting in, by the names the Living, the Powerful, the Knowing, the Desirer, the Hearer, the Seer, the Speaker, the Thankful, the Gentle, the Creator, the Fashioner - and the entirety of names. It is just as this organic body is described by nouns such as stone and gold and silver, brass, water, air; and no body-based truth passes away from any one simultaneously with the presence of these adjectives. In this way, there never passes away from the human being the truth of your being a creature, a human being, despite the presence of these Divine names in you.

This is the meaning of 'based on your truth in your Cherisher' - that is, for the anchored connection of your truth *f* in your Cherisher. Thus, there will be a Divine image appearing in her. In this same way with this organic body *f*, there will be an image appearing in her. And, just as you are multi-variegated in images of Divine names: in this way applied onto you - to the number of each image - is a name other than the next name. In the same way, loosened and applied to this jawhar is a name - based on stone, or gold - belonging to the (new) description, not to its entity.

Clarified in what we have talked about are the three types of tearing the fabric of the conventional: miracles, honorings, and magic - and there is no further tearing the fabric of the conventional than these. There is only - I mean for the honorings - what comes from the internal energetic power. I do not mean by this, in this context, the conventional sense of getting closer to the Divine for this person, because that may be a temptation and trick. I attached the name honoring to it because it is most often so, and very few people indeed are tricked with honoring. This alighting place is a neighboring vicinity - signs for the friends, peace be upon them - and it is 'the partial knowledge of the knowings based on existence'. Magic does not neighbor (this place). The karāmāt of the friends and their tearing of the fabric of the conventional are in fact by following a messenger and flowing along with his sunnah practice *f*. It is as if she is among the signs of that prophet, as by following him the signs appear - for the ones who verify for themselves - in the act of following. So this is why it neighbors the vicinity.

When good 'karma' occurs, spiritually alert people will not assume that it is because they are 'realized beings'.

The Pivots of this manzil are each friend who brings out a tearing of the conventional not from internal energy; so they will be closer toward prophethood than the one who brings out a tearing of the conventional from internal energy.

The prophets are 'abīd (slaves) flush against their root. The Pivots of this manzil are similar. As much as your states come to approximate the states of the prophets, peace be upon them, you will be stronger in 'ubūdīyah; and the demonstrated proof will be yours, and Satan will have no dominion over you - just as He said, *Indeed, over My creatures you have no dominion.* And He said, *He makes walk before him and behind him a guarding band (raṣadan)* (from al-jinn 72:27 - Qurṭūbī describes this as a band of angels who guard the messengers). There is no effect of Satan on them, and it is the same for the one who approaches nigh to them. When I beheld this vision, I recited a qaṣīdah, whose first part is this:

al-hijr 15:42; no dominion: because the slaves (ʿibād) are flush against their root - ʿubūdīyah - just as the prophets are.

The angels descend at night to my heart (qalb) m,
and they orbit him like a circling qulb (bracelet) -

Wary of a casting from the cursed one, if he should see
a descent of knowledge of the unseen, as an entity, coming flush onto my heart.

This is a guarding of God, for a likeness of our equal in measure,
and His protection from error for the ones sent (messengers) - with no doubt.

The qaṣīdah in its fullness is given in the beginning of the 330th chapter of this book.

ʿAbd al-ʿAzīz notes that the poem begins Chapter 160, not Chapter 330.

The arrangement of this chapter is what we cited of the step-levels of the tearing of the conventionals. As for what there is of strange wonders, the human attaches to the spirit-beings in tamaththala,

The angel Gabriel took on the image form of a well-proportioned man for the Annunciation to Mary (Maryam 19:17), and the human person Qaḍīb al-Bān could shift shapes.

and the spirit-beings attach to the human in image, and an image appears from them like the image by which they are made to seem like (tamaththala). He exalted said, *There was 'imaged to seem like' (fa-tamaththala) to her (lahā) a well-proportioned man (basharan sawiyyan)* - called a spirit, like Gabriel being a spirit. The dead are revived just as Gabriel revives. Ibn ʿAbbās said, 'Wherever Gabriel عليه السلام walked on a spot of the Earth, there in that spot was life.' This is why the Sāmirī took a handful from his footprint, when he understood what was happening, which he brought to Moses. He knew that his footstep brought to life whatever he stepped upon, so he grabbed a handful of the footprint of the messenger Gabriel - because Satan knows the step-level of the spirit-beings. The Sāmirī found in himself this power, and he did not know that it was taught (cast into him) by Iblīs - so he said, 'I saw what they saw not, so I took a handful from the footprint of the messenger and threw it onto the calf; *thus did my self suggest to me.*' Iblīs did this from a greed-

Maryam 19:17

ṭā-hā 20:96

ṭā-hā 20:96

iness to mislead, through what he believes about the sharīk associated with God *exalted*.

Then Jesus was conceived from the image of Gabriel in meaning, name, and imaged form - so a human may reach and join the spirit-being, and the spirit-being may reach and join an image of a human in a single alighting. Now this amount is enough for this chapter, because the chapter has become extended. For Mary, for Āsiyah, for the truths of the messengers, peace be upon them, there is here a generous radiating brilliance - because it is a manzil of the perfectly complete (i.e. the perfectly complete human beings who are 'the souls', including Mary and Āsiyah). And whoever reaches here becomes a master over the people of one's genus and comes out as a determiner over someone of the Majesty and the Beauty.

The 'someone of the Majesty and the Beauty' is ṣāḥib al-jalāl wa'l-jamāl, referencing the first prose line of this chapter and also described in Chapter 387: 'they say, one is dhū'l-jalāl' ۞ al-Raḥmān 55:27 - that is, someone of the jalāl which we find in our souls, for Him, wa'l-ikrām ۞ al-Raḥmān 55:27, honoring us. Thus, if you observe with the True eye, God opens for you an eye of understanding: you learn whom you are naming, and whom you are describing, and whom you are categorizing, and who has these categories, and who establishes them, and in which entity they are attributed. As for His word which He describes Himself by, descriptions which are, according to the philosophers, qualities belonging to the creation truly - and they take them to relate to God possibly (instead of essentially) - such as hunger (I was hungry and you fed Me not), thirst (I was thirsty), sickness (I was sick), anger (My kindness outstrips My anger), being well-pleased (I am well-pleased with Islām as your religion), and hating (This arrogant walk is hated by God), and wondering at (Our Cherisher wonders at two men - 'one killed the other, and both are in the Garden!'), and delighting (God is more intensely delighted in the repentance of one of you than the man who lost his camel and would have died with no water - but then found her), and being cheered (except God becomes cheerful toward him as the family of the man who is away becomes cheerful when he returns to them); up to having a foot (al-jabbār places His foot), and a hand (in whose Hand), and an eye ۞ ṭā-hā 20:39, and an arm-span (I approach him an arm-span) - and things such as this which are recorded in the reports coming from God on the tongues of the messengers, and what is recorded of this in the word attributed to God expressed as folios, and as a Qur'ān, and a Torah, and an Injīl, and Zubūr; the matter according to the ones who verify for themselves is that these, all of them, are True, not qualities (adjectives) of creation, and that the creation is described by them only by competing with the True - just as the universe is also described by the entirety of the Most Beautiful Divine Names (which the philosophers agree upon), but the whole are His names - without restriction, absolutely. This is the way of the ones who verify for themselves. Such a person is truthful.'

It is one of the stations of Abū Yazīd al-Basṭāmī and the Primes.

And God speaks the true,
and He is the guide to the way.

al-aḥzāb 33:4

The 21st manuscript ends,
and with its end ends the
3rd book of the Openings Revealed in Makkah,
followed by the 22nd manuscript,
and the 4th book =
God willing!

(Added in the margin is)
'I have read this,
and I am Maḥmūd bin 'Ubayd-Allāh bin Aḥmad al-Zanjānī -
all of this volume from its first to its last -
to its composer,
the shaykh, the imām, the teacher,
Muḥyīddīn,
Shaykh al-Islām,
Abū 'Abd-Allāh
Muḥammad bin 'Alī bin al-'Arabī al-Ṭā'ī -
may God multiply his honor -
during a session on Wednesday,
the 21st of Ramaḍān, AH 636,
in his house in Damascus,
with his record book.
And God bless our master Muḥammad and his family,
the pure ones!'
(Then the testimony of the Shaykh al-akbar, in his hand)
Correct - what he said concerning the recitation to me.
Written by Muḥammad bin 'Alī bin al-'Arabī
al-Ṭā'ī al-Ḥātimī.'

al-Zanjānī: of the people of Zanj, 'the whole of the countries of the Negroes known to the Arabs of the classical period' (Lane)

Glossary

ʿabathan: idly, uselessly - from ʿabitha, 'playing or sporting with that which does not concern him and for which he does not care, and doing that in which is no profit' (Lane).

ʿabd (pl. ʿibād): the creature, the slave (see ʿubūdīyah).

abdāl (sg. badal): the Alternates, who can be male or female. When one leaves, another takes his or her place.

Abū Bakr Shiblī (d. 945): a student of Junayd; renowned for his 'eccentricities'.

Abū'l-Ḥakam bin Barrajān (d. 1141): born in Sevilla; an important Andalusian Ṣūfī and master of religious sciences; associated with Ibn al-ʿArīf (d. 1141), with whom he was summoned to appear before the Almoravid sultan in Marrakesh. See Claude Addas (1993) Quest for the Red Sulphur, 51ff.

Abū Madyan Shuʿayb al-Ghawth: he passed away in 1198 before Ibn al-ʿArabī could visit him in this world, but he became his greatest teacher - they would meet often in the barzakh. In Quest for the Red Sulphur and an article on the Ibn al-ʿArabī Society website, Claude Addas explores their close relationship, expressed by Ibn al-ʿArabī's term for him: the Master of Masters. Born in Cantillana and a central figure in taṣawwuf in the West. He later settled at Béjaïa (Bougie) in the Maghreb and died at Tlemcen, where his tomb is still a site of pilgrimage.

Abū Naṣr Bishr bin al-Ḥārith (d. 841/842): an Iranian Ṣūfī and ascetic. He was known as al-Ḥāfī ('the barefoot').

Abū'l-Qāsim Aḥmad ibn al-Husayn al-Qasī (d. 1151): from Mirtulah (Mertola, in present-day Portugal), author of Khalʿ al-naʿlayn (Removing the Sandals).

Abū Saʿīd al-Kharrāz (d. c. 890-898): said to be the earliest writer on fanāʾ (annihilation, passing away).

Abū Yazīd al-Basṭāmī (d. c. 875): 'Sultan of the Gnostics' (sūlṭān al-ʿárifīn).

Aḥmad bin Ḥanbal (d. 855): born in Baghdad; influential jurist, theologian, and author of the Musnad, a large collection of ḥadīth.

alastu: 'Am I not?' When the children of Adam are removed from his back, they (we) all bask in the radiant brilliance of our Cherisher, who asks us, 'Am I not your Cherisher (Lord)?' All respond, 'Yes! You are' (al-aʿraf 7:172).

arḥamu'r-rāḥimīna: the most mercifully compassionate of the mercifully compassionate; the kindest of the kind. A title especially of the Messenger of God ﷺ, who is invited to intercede on behalf of his community (the entirety of human beings from Adam to the last person born).

ʿárif (pl. ʿárifūn - nominative; ʿárifīn - dative): the one who recognizes the Divine everywhere.

awliyāʾ (sg. walī): the friends of God whose authority (wilāyah) is derived from being close to God.

ʿayn: a letter of the alphabet; also eye, point, dot, source, well, entity.

Badīʿaʾl-Zamān al-Hamadhānī (d. 1008): writer in Arabic and inventor of a new literary genre, the maqāma; see W.J. Prendergast (1915) The Maqāmāt of Badīʿ al-Zamān al-Hamadhānī.

Bahlūl: the name given to Wāhab ibn ʿAmr, a companion of the 7th Shīʿah Imām, Mūsā ibn Jaʿafar al-Kāẓim. Bahlūl lived at the time of Caliph Hārūn al-Rashīd (8th cent.) and supposedly initially feigned insanity, at the imām's suggestion, to escape persecution under the caliph.

al-Barbarī: a teacher who told Ibn al-ʿArabī, 'My son, when you have tasted honey, leave the vinegar!'

barzakh: a bounded null surface; a membrane; an intelligible but non-physical line separating two matters, especially the two seas crashing together, in the Qurʾān - 'between the two a barrier they do not breach' ❋ al-Raḥmān 55:19-20. The spirit (soul) in this world somehow shifts into this realm during sleep and after death. The barzakh is entered during every dream.

basmalah: the term used for the opening bismi'llāhi'r-raḥmāni'r-raḥīm (By the name of God, the Supremely Compassionate, the Gentle) ❋ al-fātiḥah 1:1.

ḍanāʾin: special ones; 'Indeed, God has special ones in His creation He nourishes in His kindness.'

al-Darānī: Ṣūfī sage born c. 757 in the village of Dāriyā in Damascus.

dhát: essence, core; who one is - essential identity.

dhikr: the recitation of Divine names; the gathering for the remembrance of the Divine - the Ṣūfī training of dhikr is to populate the heart with the Divine names.

Glossary

dunyā: the near world, the world closest to one; next is the barzakh, the separating membrane; then the ākhirah, the next (or other) world.

faṣl bal waṣl: this phrase occurs especially in the fiqh passages where it separates each legal case. The first word means an analytic section, in the sense of separating out the trees from the forest in order to understand the whole. The word bal is a conjunction when followed by a single word. The word waṣl is a link and a connector. A gloss is, 'Now we will consider a section; no, it is also a link coming from what preceded it.'

fātiḥah: the mother of the Qur'ān, opening and commencing the Qur'ān.

fatwā: giving an answer to a legal question. The lexicographers say fatwā is connected to the root word fatā (the youth in his prime) because the muftī (jurist) makes a decision about a newly arising issue.

ḥadīth: a saying, typically a saying of the Messenger of God ﷺ; or a ḥadīth qudsī, a statement from God transmitted by the Messenger of God.

Ḥasān bin Thābit (d. 647): one of the Companions; renowned for his poetry in defense of the Prophet.

himmat (pl. himam): internal stirring; the enthusiasm and energy - and charisma - that make things happen.

hu: the third masculine singular pronoun: when referring to God, it is referred to as the huwīyat f. The pronoun is ḍamīr - that which is concealed in the heart, such that when we reference a noun with the ḍamīr, the entirety of the noun is hidden but fully present inside, in the heart. Pronouns conventionally follow their referent, but anna-hu, huwa'lladhī, and many other Qur'ānic phrases break this convention. We are therefore directed to hear and consider that anna-hu is not 'Indeed He' but 'Indeed hu', and huwa'l-ladhī is 'hu is the One who'.

'ibād (sg. 'abd): the creatures of the Creator, the slaves of the Divine (see 'ubūdīyah).

Ibn al-'Arīf (d. 1141): born in Ceuta, north Africa; spent most of his life in Almeria, an important center of taṣawwuf (the Ṣūfī way) in Andalusia; prominent Ṣūfī teacher, along with Ibn Barrajan, in 12th-century al-Andalus. See Claude Addas (1993) Quest for the Red Sulphur, 52-55.

Ibn al-Rūmī (d. 896): a poet born in Baghdad.

idlāl: taking liberties, being proud - especially liberties taken by the lover toward the Beloved.

ijtihād: independent judgment exerted to decide what to do in a legal (religious) situation.

ikhlāṣ: sincerity; delivering God's religion to God without one's own interpretations or alterations.

i'tirāf: recognizing through being informed by the Divine. Related to 'ārif (the one who recognizes), ma'rifah, and ta'arafa (to introduce, to have be recognized; especially in 'I am a treasure, concealed; but I love to be recognized - so I introduce Myself to the creation, and they recognize Me').

Jabarūt: the dream realm, the middle realm of the barzakh, between Mulk (here) and Malakūt (the angelic realm).

jawhar: the gem, the core; the basis upon which variegations and changes take place, with each Divine tajallī.

jizyah: tax; this payment ratifies the contract with the Muslims for protection against outside aggression. 'This is an intricate issue running throughout his universal message: by his appearance, there remains no Law except what is his Law; and one of the things in his Law is the confirmation of them in their Law - as long as they provide the jizyah, when they are among the people of the Book. And how many of these creatures does God have on the Earth?' Historically, the 'people of the Book' was an inclusive category, with the people of India, for example, being considered people of the Book, with their book being the Laws of Manu and their prophet Noah.

al-Juwaynī (d. 1085): Iranian jurist and theologian; his title Imām al-Ḥaramayn means 'leading master of the two holy cities' (Makkah and Madīnah); teacher of Abū Ḥāmid Muḥammad ibn Muḥammad al-Ghazālī.

kāfir: the one who covers up the truth that it is God who provides, and he is therefore an ingrate; antonym of the thankfulness (shukr) and faith (īmān) which give one certainty that the unseen God provides the blessings one is thankful for.

karāmāt (sg. karāmah): what certain honored people are given to perform - bounteous miracles.

kashf: the lightning flash of disclosure; the veil ripped away to reveal what truly is.

Glossary

al-khabīr: the All-Aware, who knows the tested truth of all. But Ibn al-'Arabī also makes the case that khabīr is the 'object of knowing', in Chapter 31.

kun: the imperative Be! from 'Indeed, Our word to a thing, when We desire it, We but say to it Be! and it is' ❋ al-naḥl 16:40.

al-laṭīf: the Subtle, who sees what is unseen.

laylatu'l-qadr: the Night of Power, when the entire Qur'ān was first sent down to the Messenger of God ﷺ.

Malakūt: the angelic realm.

manāzil (sg. manzil; dual manzilayn): the place the visitor alights.

ma'rifah (pl. ma'ārif): recognition; the 'ārif is the person with ma'rifah and 'irfān, recognizing Divinity / wherever She may be.

mawāqi' al-nujūm: see Denis Gril's 'The Journey through the Circles of Inner Being according to Ibn al-'Arabī's Mawāqi' al-nujūm' - www.ibnarabisociety.org/articles/journeyofbeing.html

millat: the religion of Abraham; the particular features of a religion.

al-Muḥāsibī (d. 857): born in Basra and spent most of his life in Baghdad. The moral psychology and rigorous analysis of egoism in his Kitāb al-ri'āya li-ḥuqūq Allāh (The Book on the Observance of the Rights of God) was influential for later Ṣūfīs. See Michael A. Sells (1996) Early Islamic Mysticism, Ch. 5; Gavin Picken (2011) Spiritual Purification in Islam.

Mulk: kingdom, this world; the mulk is the possessions of the Possessor (mālik).

munāfiqūn: from anfāq, the holes the jerboa makes, going in one hole and out another - hence, people who say one thing and mean another.

mushrikūn: the ones who commit shirk, who associate gods with God; they hedge their bets by praying to many gods, and they attribute Divine action to other gods. They say, 'We worshiped them only in order that they would bring us closer to Allāh, nearer' (al-zumar 39:3).

mutawātir: the Qur'ān and a very few ḥadīth are mutawātir, coming to us from an unbroken chain of transmission. The rest is a preponderance of estimations.

nafas: the breath; the nafs is the soul breathed into.

nawāfil (sg. both nāfl and nāflah): the 'supererogatory' practices, the extra good deeds.

al-Niffarī, Muḥammad bin 'Abd al-Jabbār: a 10th century Ṣūfī concerning whom little is known, who died in Egypt and may have been from the area of modern-day Iraq. His transcendent unveilings are translated in A.J. Arberry (1935) The Mawāqif and Mukhāṭabāt of Muhammad ibn 'Abdi 'l-Jabbār al-Niffarī.

nubuwwat: prophethood; being given messages from the Divine. After the Prophet (nabī) Muḥammad ﷺ, nubuwwat ended; but a fraction remains - the true dream given to the faithful.

nuqabā': based on the Zodiac. Chapter 73: 'They are numbered by the Zodiac orbit - twelve watchtowers.' The naqīb (sg.) sees the insides of people, and the niqāb is the slit in the veil.

Qaḍīb al-Bān (d. 1177): from Mosul; a famous companion of one of Ibn al-'Arabī's teachers, 'Alī ibn 'Abd Allāh ibn Jāmi'. He was the teacher of Jāmi', who invested Ibn al-'Arabī with the khirqa of Khadir in his garden in Mosul. See R.W. Austin (2008) Sufis of Andalusia, 157, and Stephen Hirtenstein (1999) The Unlimited Mercifier, 177-78.

qawwāl: the singer of a qawl (saying), singing at the tombs of the awliyā', especially using their own poetry.

quṭb: the pivot around whom beings circulate; the tent-pole holding up the world. When the pole is taken away, the entire world will collapse into itself.

rabb: Cherisher, a Divine name; the One who tends to us, cares for us. The word used to describe a woman stroking her child's head to put the child to sleep is rabbabti.

al-raḥīm: the gentle, compassionate, kind; a name shared by God and creation, especially by the Messenger of God ﷺ, who is ra'uf raḥīm (tenderly compassionate, supremely gentle).

raḥmah: kind mercy, from raḥm (womb).

al-Raḥmān: The Supremely Compassionate One - from raḥm (the womb). This name sits on the cosmic Throne, so the entire universe is tended to and ordered by supreme compassion. Ibn al-'Arabī locates for us the six ṣifāt (Divine attributes) in the word's six letters, with the +1 being the Living - in writing, the dagger alif above all six letters so that life radiates over them all.

Glossary

al-Rāzī, Muhammad bin 'Umar bin al-Khaṭīb (d. 1210) - also known as Fakhr al-Dīn al-Rāzī: Iranian theologian, scholar, and philosopher; author of the Tafsīr al-Kabīr (The Great Commentary).

Sa'dūn: a mystic from Cairo; the teacher and spiritual director of the Egyptian Ṣūfī, Dhūl-Nūn al-Miṣrī (d. c. 860).

salām: peace; in ṣallāllāhu 'alayhi wasallam, sallam is an imperative: bless him with peace and security. The greeting, pronounced as-salāmu 'alaykum, is always addressed to a plurality (the -kum is second person plural), and we are to greet many more beings than just our fellow humans. Ibn al-'Arabī tells us that the response (wa 'alaykum as-salām) always comes, even when we see no one responding. The blessing will be returned to us, from the highest beings if no lower one responds.

ṣalāt: the five daily prayers. And the blessing al-salāt wa's-salām; and the verb yuṣallī in 'hu is the One who yuṣallī (blesses) all of you, as do His angels, to extract you from the darknesses to the Light; and He is to the faithful raḥīma (kind, gentle, merciful)' ❋ al-aḥzāb 33:43.

sami'a Allāhu li-man ḥamidah: from the statement, 'God says upon the tongue of His slave, "God hears the one who praises Him."'

sharī'ah: the way to the water. 'If your Cherisher had so willed, all in the Earth would have believed - all of them, entirely' ❋ Yūnus 10:99. Therefore, to receive the message of sharī'ah is to be blessed with goodness in this life and felicity in the next.

sharīk: the putative associate of God, the idol; on the Day of Judgment, the sharīk will disavow anyone who worshiped it.

shirk: associating gods with God; attributing God's actions to putative gods. The person who does shirk is a mushrik.

sijillāt: the recorded judicial decisions; the scroll of records.

Sufyān al-Thawrī (d. 778): a scholar, jurist, and hadīth compiler; one of the Successors, who learned from the Companions.

sūrah (pl. suwar): an enclosure ('chapter') in the Qur'ān.

tahajjud: rising in the night to pray prayers beyond the obligatory ones.

tajallī (pl. tajalliyāt): the brilliant radiance of Being. God turns to face the entity, and this attention is the radiance of one Divine vision. These brilliances shower every entity every moment, but they are unperceived by most people; and if one tajallī is perceived, the effect could be to eclipse one's intelligence and render one insane (majnūn). The tajalliyāt are unique for each individual, never repeating, and so each individual potentially has a unique vision of the Divine every moment.

taklīf: addressed and obligated; tasked to do things in order to be ultimately felicitous.

tamaththala (fifth form of mithāl): tamaththalat is the feminine verb form and the noun is tamaththul - to 'take on the likeness of'; the image projected on the screen; and Gabriel assuming the form of a 'well-proportioned man' for the Annunciation.

tanzīh: incomparability; transcendence; clear of all imposed qualities.

taqwá: being aware of God, cautious lest one step wrongly and incur rightful Divine wrath. If you have taqwá, God promises to teach you.

tawḥīd: the statement that God is One (waḥīd).

Tirmidhī (d. c. 869): born in Khorasan in the city of Termez (in present-day Uzbekistan); his questions asked in The Seal of the Saints are answered in Chapter 73 of the Futūḥāt.

'ubūdiyah: the state of being a slave. For Ibn al-'Arabī this is the highest and most noble position to be in, and the exemplar of this station is Muḥammad ﷺ, who is called 'by whatever name my Beloved calls me' - hence he is simply 'Abd-Allāh ('the slave of Allāh').

'ulamā': the ones with 'ilm, the ones who know; also the experts and scholars who may lack direct knowledge and knowledge they have verified for themselves. The experts and scholars may be qualified by the term rusūm: the rasm is the trace left when raindrops spatter onto the dry desert - and hence they are 'superficial', because the living and reviving knowledge which is water (rain) has hit them, but instead of absorbing it and becoming soft and moist and alive, the only effect is superficial impressions.

umm: the mother, the matrix.

ummah: the mother community.

walī (pl. awliyā'): the friend of God; his authority (wilāyah) derives from proximity to God (pl. awliyā').

watad (pl. awtād): a peg; each of the Pegs anchors a cardinal direction.

wujūd: being, from wajada ('found'). The stabilized entities are 'lost' in the void; then they hear Be! and they are found, and they become.

yawm: the day; from the longest day of indeterminable periodicity (the aṭlas orbit) to the shortest quantum of time, which is the yawm of 'Each day He is upon a radiant brilliance' ⁕ al-Raḥmān 55:29.

zamān: time period; zaman fard, the quantum of time, the smallest indivisible moment of time.